Yesteryear's Faith Seeking Understanding

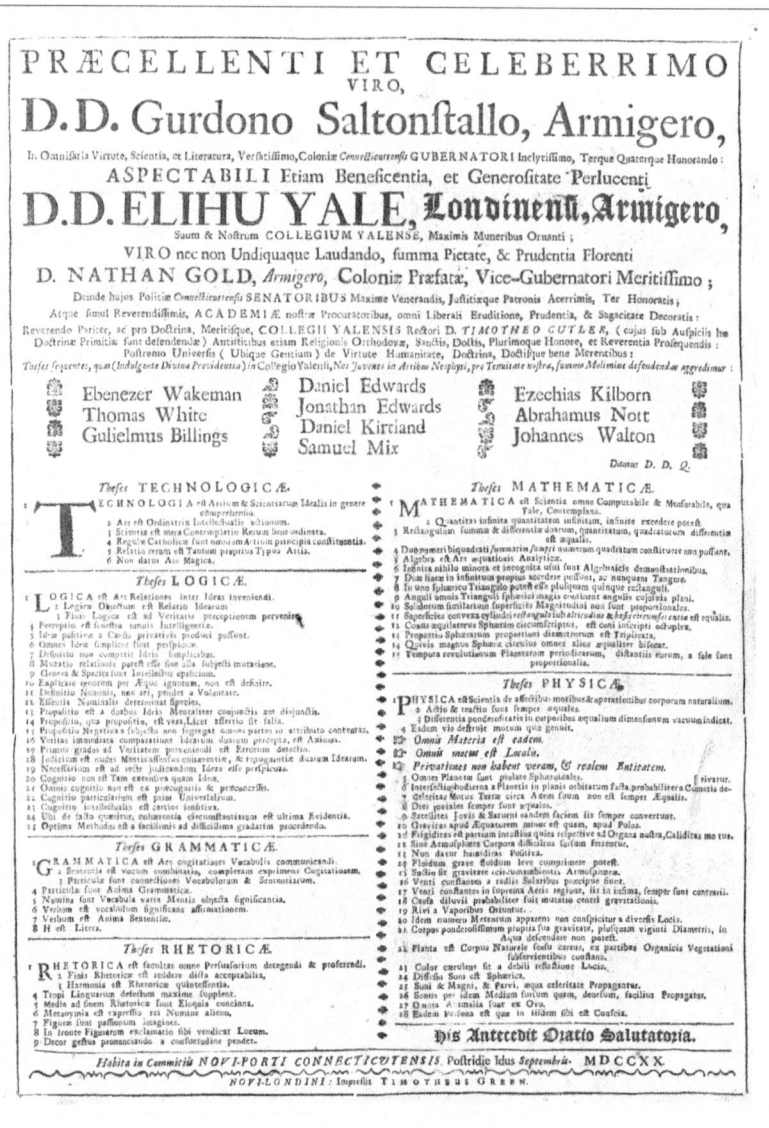

Praecellenti et Celeberrimo Viro, D.D. Gurdono Saltonstallo, Armigero... [
Yale College Commencement broadside,] (New London, Timothy Green, 1720).
Manuscripts and Archives, Beinecke Library, Yale University

Yesteryear's Faith Seeking Understanding

New England Disputations on Providence;
With a Historical-Theological Introduction

Philip John Fisk

Foreword by Gerald R. McDermott

RESOURCE *Publications* · Eugene, Oregon

YESTERYEAR'S FAITH SEEKING UNDERSTANDING
New England Disputations on Providence;
With a Historical-Theological Introduction

Copyright © 2022 Philip John Fisk. All rights reserved. Except for brief quotations in critical publications or reviews, no part of this book may be reproduced in any manner without prior written permission from the publisher. Write: Permissions, Wipf and Stock Publishers, 199 W. 8th Ave., Suite 3, Eugene, OR 97401.

Resource Publications
An Imprint of Wipf and Stock Publishers
199 W. 8th Ave., Suite 3
Eugene, OR 97401

www.wipfandstock.com

PAPERBACK ISBN: 978-1-6667-3405-8
HARDCOVER ISBN: 978-1-6667-2949-8
EBOOK ISBN: 978-1-6667-2951-1

JUNE 22, 2022 4:30 PM

Unless otherwise indicated, Scripture quotations are from the New Revised Standard Version Bible. Copyright© 1989 by the National Council of the Churches of Christ in the United States of America. Used by permission. All rights reserved worldwide.

For Cynthia Joy,
Ashley and David, Zachary and Aubrey, Jonathan and Fabia,
Professors Antonie Vos and Andreas J. Beck, and the students at
the Evangelische Theologische Faculteit Leuven, from whom I have
learned much and engaged in dialogues such as these.

Contents

Foreword by Gerald R. McDermott | ix

Preface | xii

PART I   HISTORICAL AND THEOLOGICAL INTRODUCTION

1. Genre and Practice of Medieval Disputation | 1

2. Logica Moderna and Medieval Scholastic Distinctions | 4

3. Maimonides: A Medieval Jewish Guide to Views on Providence | 23

4. Jewish-Christian Disputations | 32

5. Reformation and Scholasticism | 36

6. Post-Reformation Scholasticism and Providence | 67

PART II   NEW ENGLAND DISPUTATIONS ON PROVIDENCE

1. Immutability | 95

2. Contingency | 106

3. Concurrence | 118

4. Middle Knowledge | 127

5. Contingent Propositions | 141

6. Universal Rules | 153

7. The Essence of Free Choice | 168

8. Necessity and Freedom | 178

9. Moral Necessity and Physical Necessity | 190

10. Providence | 203

Concluding Roundtable with President Edwards | 220

Bibliography | 231

Subject Index | 247

Name Index | 253

Scripture Index | 257

Foreword

When I was in grad school studying historical theology, I read books and heard lectures regularly disparaging "scholasticism." By this term they meant the schools of thinkers who followed the great theologians such as Aquinas, Luther, and Calvin and tried to answer the theological and pastoral questions that these luminaries had raised. The implication of this regular disparagement was that the scholastics were dry, uninteresting, and uncreative.

When I was led to explore some of these scholastics, I was surprised and delighted to discover the opposite. In most cases, the scholastic theologians were answering new questions that scratched where I itched and exploring pastoral problems that I was encountering as a young pastor. They posed—and tried to resolve—questions of logic and consistency that any serious student of theology or Scripture will find when diving beneath the surface of things.

I was eventually led to focus on America's greatest theologian, Jonathan Edwards. One of his great tomes was *Freedom of the Will*, arguably his most difficult philosophical work. In this weighty volume he tried to resolve one of the greatest conundrums of theological history—How can man be free when God is sovereign? If God is ultimately sovereign over everything, as Scripture suggests, that means he is in control of everything that happens in history, including our choices. But if God is in control of our choices, how can they be free, especially if God knew yesterday how we would choose today? Doesn't the latter mean that our choices today were determined by God's foreknowledge yesterday? And if they were determined, how could they be free? Edwards argued in *Freedom of the Will* that our choices are sovereignly determined by God, and yet we still act freely, both in our good choices and our bad choices. In virtue *and* in sin. One would think, then, that God is the author of sin.

Edwards denied that God is the author of sin even though he wrote that God superintends our sin. After all, the Bible denies that God is the author of sin (Jas 1:13). In order to thread this historically-near-impossible needle, Edwards distinguished between moral and natural necessity. By moral necessity he meant that we choose necessarily what we want. Let's say I want an Envy apple. That is my favorite. If I have an Envy apple available, I will *necessarily* choose it over a Red Delicious, which I think has lost its crispness and taste in recent years. I choose according to my strongest desire, and so, all other things being equal, it is *necessary* that I will choose an Envy over a Red Delicious if I have the opportunity.

That's where natural necessity comes in. Ordinarily when I am at the store getting new apples, there is nothing in *nature* preventing me from choosing a Red Delicious. It too is at my supermarket, and costs no more. So Edwards would say I have natural *freedom* to decline an Envy and choose a Red Delicious, but by moral *necessity* (following my strongest desire in the matter of apples) I will choose an Envy.

Edwards's students formed a school of theology called the New Divinity. They were, you might say, his scholastics working out problems he did not get to. Or at least applying his basic principles to a new era, the early American republic. As Calvinists who promoted Edwards's revivalism, they had to explain how their Calvinism could motivate sinners to repent when Calvin taught that the elect were already decided by God and no sinner could change unless God sovereignly chose to act on him. The New Divinity used Edwards's distinction between natural and moral necessity to cut this Gordian knot.

The most eccentric *and* influential New Divinity scholastic theologian was Nathanael Emmons (1745–1840). I say "most influential" because he trained more ministers in his home than any other Edwardsean scholastic—nearly one hundred, many of whom became influential in their own right. This tobacco-chewing thinker is famous for the way he resolved the problem of the human will and God's sovereignty.

In a word, Emmons concluded that God makes human beings sin. He produces both their right and wrong volitions, even the first sin of Adam: "There is but one true and satisfactory answer to be given to the question which has been agitated for ages. *Whence came evil?—and that is, it came from the great First Cause of all things.*" God is "the efficient cause of sin."[1] This was too much for Harriet Beecher Stowe, author of

---

1. McDermott, "Nathanael Emmons," 120.

Uncle Tom's Cabin, who grew up under Emmons's influence and came to reject his god. She and the rest of the Beecher family finally rejected all things Calvinist and Edwardsean because of Emmons's take on God and human choices.

This splendid review of sixteenth- and seventeenth-century Reformed scholastic debates on God and human willing by Philip Fisk shows two things. First, that there were many other ways besides Emmons's to resolve this weighty question of providence—how we can be free if God is sovereign. Second, that we can gain much delight and insight from these creative and thoughtful wrestlings with Scripture and theology.

Fisk's easy-to-follow analyses look at not only Reformed but also Lutheran and Catholic scholastics. And the most important Jewish philosopher in history! Not only obscure thinkers but also well-known figures such as Erasmus, Maimonides, Luther, Melanchthon, and Edwards.

Many of the questions under this scholarly microscope are similar to those being asked today in the church and in the world: Is God's foreknowledge the cause of evil? Does it impose necessity on the will? Can God do other than he does? How can God permit evil? Does that make him the cause of evil? Can the elect be damned?

If serious Christians wrestle with any of these questions, and want to see how previous Christian thinkers have worked out their answers, this book is a wonderful resource for them. It might even inspire Christian thinkers today to come up with responsible ways to think about radical evil and God's providence in this new century.

Preface

Of all kinds of knowledge that we can ever obtain, the knowledge of God, and the knowledge of ourselves, are the most important. As religion is the great business, for which we are created, and on which our happiness depends; and as religion consists in an intercourse between ourselves and our Maker; and so has its foundation in God's nature and ours, and in the relation that God and we stand in to each other; therefore a true knowledge of both must be needful in order to true religion. But the knowledge of ourselves consists chiefly in right apprehensions concerning those two chief faculties of our nature, the *understanding* and *will*. Both are very important: yet the science of the latter must be confessed to be of greatest moment; inasmuch as all virtue and religion have their seat more immediately in the will, consisting more especially in right acts and habits of this faculty. And the grand question about the freedom of the will, is the main point that belongs to the science of the will. Therefore I say, the importance of this subject greatly *demands* the attention of Christians, and especially of divines.

—JONATHAN EDWARDS, PREFACE TO *FREEDOM OF THE WILL*

VOICES ARE SILENCED. Scholastics are vilified. Scholastic distinctions discarded. Yesteryear's *faith seeking understanding* cancelled. And the church today is paying the price. This book turns to the university professors and tutors who brought classical, medieval, Reformation and Renaissance thought to bear on the Harvard, Yale, College of New Jersey, and College of Rhode Island and Providence Plantations curricula in order to answer questions about the doctrine of providence. I consult and translate primary sources and recognize the significance of scholastic method and distinctions in the eighteenth-century New England colleges in their quest to understand God's will and providence. Unfortunately, the practice of scholastic method and understanding of its Latin idiom declined in the colleges as they entered the nineteenth century.

My aim is to let Protestant scholastic approaches to the mystery of divine providence speak for themselves. The Scholastics framed their disputations on providence around two frequently quoted Bible verses: "For in him we live and move and have our being" (Acts 17:28); and "For it is God who is at work in you, enabling you both to will and to work for his good pleasure" (Phil 2:13). Questions arose from the study of these verses, such as, What is the essence of free choice? Is God the author, even actor, of evil? How does God concur with both good and bad human actions? Do we live in a fated world?

I write this book for busy pastors who wish to refresh their knowledge of what the doctors of the church taught on crucial questions related to divine providence. I also have in mind beginning theology students who might not otherwise have the time, resources, or linguistic skills in Latin to consult all the primary sources gathered here together in one book. Senior homeschoolers are also on my mind, since many have begun acquiring reading skills in classical Latin and may wish to acquire a taste for reading scholastic Latin from primary sources and learning about providence as taught by New England university professors. Lastly, fans of Jonathan Edwards will not be disappointed in the prominent role he receives.

In Part One, I provide a guided tour to primary Latin sources in translation of medieval, Reformation, and post-Reformation Scholastic disputations on providence and related questions. Imagine taking a tour of European city centers. Instead of a general guided tour of the city's highlights, I take you into Old World libraries. I pull books off the shelves and examine what the Scholastics had to say about God, providence, freedom, contingency, and necessity.

In Part Two, I showcase eighteenth-century commencement broadside sheet theses and *Quaestiones* of New England colleges: Harvard, Yale, the College of New Jersey, and the first Baptist college in New England, the College of Rhode Island and Providence Plantations. The common overarching theme of the selected theses and *quaestiones* is providence. Latin was the language of the colleges, and therefore I have provided translation into English of the selected bachelor's theses and master's *quaestiones* that were debated by the student respondents, the young scholars and commencers, as they were called. The broadside sheets also gave the name of the presidents who presided over the commencement day exercises and disputations.

Since we know who presided over the commencement day disputations, and who the student respondents were, and since dialectic was the "battlefield of academic disputation," I have cast each chapter in Part Two into narrative form. Though I have had to imagine the narrative, the time, location, and characters are real, as are the texts of writers that I quote. I offer these historical and literary renditions of the commencement day disputations in the belief that these Platonic-like dialogues relieve some of the stress of following scholastic argumentation.

My conclusion is that a proper analysis of the debated scholastic disputations and distinctions in the New England colleges largely supports the classic-Protestant doctrine of providence that claims that reality is contingent, not deterministic or necessitarian. What was at stake was a defense against the charge that some forms of the Protestant doctrine of providence, labeled "Calvinistic," made God the author of sin and evil. This book is as much about overturning modern misconceptions about scholastic method and the function of distinctions in the classic-Protestant tradition as it is about overturning claims that we live in a fatalistic and necessitarian world where God is the author of evil.

While there are other recent monographs that analyze medieval and Protestant scholastic teaching on the doctrine of providence and related issues, this book builds on my research and analysis of Harvard, Yale, and the College of New Jersey commencement broadsides and the Protestant scholastic tradition. Without a knowledge of medieval and Post-Reformation scholastic method and terminology, it is near impossible to understand the scholastic theses and *quaestiones* studied at the New England colleges. This point was driven home to me when years ago I asked a seasoned classics scholar to help me translate some broadside theses and *Quaestiones*. He told me that he had no clue what they were about. If the reader would like to pursue the subject matter of medieval and Protestant Scholastics, and New England theology, I would recommend these mostly recent monographs: Beck, *Gisbertus Voetius*; Craig, *The Problem of Divine Foreknowledge and Future Contingents*; Fisk, *Jonathan Edwards's Turn*; Gerhard, *On Creation and Angels*; McClymond and McDermott, *Theology of Jonathan Edwards*; McGraw, *Reformed Scholasticism*; Molina, *On Divine Foreknowledge*; Muller, *Dictionary of Latin and Greek Theological Terms* and *Divine Will and Human Choice* and *Post-Reformation Reformed Dogmatics*; Neele, *Before Edwards*; Sturdy, *Freedom from Fatalism*; Sweeney, *Nathaniel Taylor, New Haven Theology, and the Legacy of Jonathan Edwards*; Sweeney and Crisp, *After Jonathan Edwards*; Van Asselt et al, *Reformed Thought on Freedom*; Van Asselt and Dekker, *Reformation and Scholasticism*; Van Asselt and Gootjes, *Introduction to Reformed Scholasticism*.

Part I

Historical and Theological Introduction

1. Genre and Practice of Medieval Disputation

THE CULTURE OF PUBLIC commencement day disputations had its origins in the medieval culture of disputation. Lanfranc's and Anselm's legacy was their development and use of dialectic. The composition of the dialogue between Anselm (1033–1109) and his interlocutor Boso famously exemplified the demonstrative purpose and method of this rational art. Novikoff points out that this is but one of seven of Anselm's literary works, all of which took the form of dialogue.[1] For himself, Anselm modeled his internal disputations and meditations on Augustine's practice.[2] Novikoff and Ann Collins have demonstrated how Lanfranc's glosses on St. Paul's letters in the New Testament showed his interest in a method of drawing out the dialogue that he imagined Paul had with his opponents. This hermeneutic led to a classroom style of disputation.[3] The university classroom culture of reciting disputations was further developed in the post-Reformation era of confessionalization, which in turn shaped the New England curricula and commencement day debate exercises. This will be looked at in more detail below.

---

1. Novikoff, *The Medieval Culture of Disputation*, 42.
2. Novikoff, *The Medieval Culture of Disputation*, 42.
3. Novikoff, *The Medieval Culture of Disputation*, 39. On this matter he refers to the work of Ann Collins on Lanfranc's manuscripts and glosses in Collins, *Teacher in Faith and Virtue*.

From an interdisciplinary approach to scholastic method, Novikoff identified five stages of development of a culture of medieval disputation.[4] First, it was Anselm who successfully "pioneered" and demonstrated the power of both reason and dialectic in Christian faith seeking understanding.

Second, scholars in northern France and Italy began to organize themselves better and better, and with the rise of universities in the latter part of the twelfth century they played their part in passing on the knowledge and practice of oral and literary renditions of disputation.

But not all were enthusiastic about scholastic method and disputation. Novikoff notes that although important figures such as "Rupert of Deutz, Bernard of Clairvaux, and William of St. Thierry" looked unfavorably upon this method of the study of Scripture; nevertheless, these same critics practiced the literary art of polemical dialectic.[5]

Third, translations originating in Sicily, Constantinople, and Toledo of the works of Aristotle into Latin and mediated to scholars in the schools in the middle of the twelfth century served as a catalyst to launch the use of new models of dialectical argumentation. He names, for instance, the *Ars disserendi* (1132) of Adam of Balsham, who taught in Paris and was an opponent of Abelard. Abelard's student, John of Salisbury (ca. 1115–1180), gave qualified "endorsement of scholastic disputation" in *The Metalogicon*, which is not without critique of those who abuse Aristotle's advice on the advantage of disputants "taking cognizance of several opinions on a topic." John writes, "In what a pernicious manner logic is sometimes taught." He chides his contemporaries who "show off their knowledge" by citing and analyzing far too many opinions, giving instruction in an unintelligible manner, as if "every letter of the alphabet is pregnant with the secrets of Minerva," rather than privileging "simplicity, brevity," and "profundity," which properly belong to introductory studies.[6]

Fourth, Novikoff identifies how the Dominicans institutionalized the art of debate and disputation in their preaching program and how the university integrated disputation into its curriculum. "Both institutions sent their graduates off into the world," taking scholastic method with them. The art of disputing *quaestiones* in the schools as well as opening the

---

4. Novikoff, *The Medieval Culture of Disputation*, 225.

5. Novikoff, *The Medieval Culture of Disputation*, 226.

6. Novikoff, *The Medieval Culture of Disputation*, 226; see too Klima et al., *Medieval Philosophy*, 7–12, 63. Also Schoedinger, *Readings in Medieval Philosophy*, 539–40.

art to the public for other questions, the *quodlibetal quaestiones*, further developed the medieval culture of disputation. This then led to a culture of literary renditions of disputation. The Dominican Thomas Aquinas's *Summa theologiae* famously exemplifies "the arguments pro and contra" and "preserves the essential structure of the classroom debate."[7]

Fifth, and Novikoff stresses the essential nature of this point, was the public performance of disputation, which welcomed both learned scholars and the unlearned to listen, observe, and thereby allow the audience to draw their own conclusions on a subject. A unique contribution of Novikoff's study is his observation of how the scholastic art of disputation grew beyond the schools and permeated society in ways often unnoted by historians of scholasticism. For instance, at Note Dame, the emergence of liturgical "polyphony" and "the art of counterpoint, motets, and musical debate poems (jeux-partis)" paralleled the rise of scholasticism.[8] "Harmony, in simple terms, is counterpoint slowed down; counterpoint, like disputatio, is a cultural expression of dialectic and rhetoric," writes Novikoff.[9] These liturgical innovations formulated "arguments pro and contra," and engaged in "dialectic and irony," so much so that "by the end of the thirteenth century the motet (like the quodlibetal) deployed these tactics in virtuoso fashion."[10]

Concerning Novikoff's third point, however, scholars have suggested that the institutions of disputation were already developing prior to the rediscovery and fuller assimilation of Aristotle. Moreover, scholars have recognized that the question and answer method in Aristotle's *Analytics* and *Topics* differs from the art and method of disputation that sets forth arguments in dialectic.[11]

---

7. Novikoff, *The Medieval Culture of Disputation*, 227.

8. Novikoff, *The Medieval Culture of Disputation*, 6, 146–47.

9. A *motet* is "simply defined as a piece of music in several parts with words (from the old French, *mot*)." Novikoff traces its use and development back to Philip the Chancellor of Notre Dame, who was "head of the University of Paris from 1218 until his death in 1236," in Novikoff, *The Medieval Culture of Disputation*, 148.

10. Novikoff, *The Medieval Culture of Disputation*, 149.

11. Kretzman, Kenny, and Pinborg, *The Cambridge History of Later Medieval Philosophy*, 25.

2. Logica Moderna and Medieval Scholastic Distinctions

The twelfth and thirteenth centuries introduced a creative era of biblical scholarship in the cathedral schools and later in the universities. It may sound strange to speak of "modern logic" the origins of which date back to the twelfth century. But for those theologians teaching in the schools at that time, De Rijk remarks that it meant new developments in logic that could not simply be traced back to Aristotle's theory of logic.[12] *Logica moderna* was quite simply a fruitful illustration of faith and renewal. The significance for this study of establishing the starting point of *logica moderna*, propositional analysis, modal logic, and scholastic distinctions in general is to demonstrate the continuity between these innovations in propositional logic, their use in the medieval and post-Reformation lecture halls of Europe, and those of the New England schools of the seventeenth and eighteenth centuries. Some of the technical features of examples given here from the twelfth and thirteenth centuries will reappear in certain dialogues as used by theologians in the curricula of the New England schools.

Early on in his education, Peter Abelard (1079–1142) quarreled with his teachers and later earned an appointment as master lecturer and debater at Notre Dame, Paris (ca. 1116). It is likely the case that his *Dialectica* (ca. 1116–18) was drawn from his lecture material. Abelard said, "Dialectic offers to Faith valid weapons to defend itself against the sophisms of the heretics."[13] One such weapon was the interpretation of a modal proposition. Abelard pondered the temporal nature of an indeterminate modal proposition. For instance, Abelard started with the proposition, "It is necessary that Socrates is running, while he is running." He could interpret it in the sense of a hypothetically time-indexed determinate event, in which case it was categorically true. But he also considered the change in interpretation if one added a modal feature. If we restate the above proposition, we have, "Socrates is running and that it is necessary that he is running." Now suppose we add the modal operator "It is possible" to either the subject or the predicate. Abelard evaluated the proposition "It is possible that Socrates is running, while he is sitting"

---

12. De Rijk, *Logica Modernorum Volume 1*, 14–15.
13. Abelard, *Dialectica*, xciii.

as false. Clearly, Socrates cannot both be running and sitting at the same time.[14]

Likewise, Abelard knew that it was false to hold "Standing, he sits" (*stans, sedet*). But if one were to disconnect the action of running from sitting, as in the divided sense of composition, *per divisionem*, the interpretation then would be that "It is possible that Socrates be running, though he is sitting." This interpretation in the divided sense of the proposition assumes a different time of actualization of running or sitting. The possibility operator also applies to an indeterminate action at an alternative time, not both actions simultaneously. Likewise, Abelard could hold as valid, "While Socrates is sitting, it is possible for him to stand."[15] These compositions in the divided sense of interpretation were applied in a diachronic sense, not synchronic.[16]

Abelard referred to these distinctions *per compositionem* and *per divisionem* in sentence exposition as interpretations according to *de sensu simplicis* and *de rebus exponitur*.[17] In the former, the possibility operator applies to the proposition as a whole; that is, it qualifies both predicates. Abelard gave the following example. "It is possible that a man is dead" (*possibile est hominem mortuum esse*). But if by "man" is understood "a living being" (*hominem vivente*), then no, the *expositio de sensu simplicis* is false since the predicates mutually exclude each other. In other words, according to Abelard, *dead* and *man* cannot simultaneously inhere in the one subject. However, if the composition is *expositio de rebus*, then it can come about that the subject die. In this sense, it is true, "*possibile est hominem esse mortuum, idest id quod est homo, potest mortuum fieri*."[18] In other words, a man who is alive today can (*potest*) be dead. But the

---

14. "*Necesse est Socratem currere, dum currit*" is equivalent to "Socrates currit et necesse est eum currere." But "possibile est Socratem currere, dum sedet," is equivalent to "Socrates sedet et possibile est eum currere"; in Abelard, *Dialectica*, lxv–lxvi.

15. Abelard, *Dialectica*, 487.15; Knuuttila, *Reforging the Great Chain of Being*, 179; De Rijk, *Logica Modernorum Volume 1*, 57, notes that Abelard refers to Aristotle's distinction between the *sensus per divisionem* and the *sensus compositionem* (Aristotle, *Soph. Elench.* 165b 26; 166a 23–38).

16. Abelard, *Dialectica*, lxvi–lxvii, 487. On this topic, see Knuuttila, "Modal Logic," in *The Cambridge History of Later Medieval Philosophy*, 342–57, in particular, see 347–48; also Knuuttila, *Reforging the Great Chain of Being*, 178–87; see too Vos, *The Philosophy of John Duns Scotus*, 224–26.

17. Abelard, *Dialectica*, 197.1–3.

18. Abelard, *Dialectica*, 196.29–197.4; on this topic see Knuuttila, *Reforging the Great Chain of Being*, 179–80.

divided sense is not yet linked to an alternate possibility at that same moment of time, as it will be in Scotus's thirteenth-century *Lectura* 1 39. Even so, Knuuttila remarks that in both cases above, "the application of a modal distinction presupposes the possibility of transferring the focus of attention from a temporally qualified case to a treatment in which time is indifferent."[19] For Abelard, the sense of *de rebus* was indifferent to time. What Abelard avoided with this atemporal solution was the apparent determinism that if God knows a time-indexed proposition to be true, then it must necessarily be true.[20] This supposed what later, with Gisbertus Voetius, will be called a neutral proposition, namely, that God knows a proposition yet without having assigned it a time-indexed truth value by an act of his will. The above distinction would become important in later scholastic dialectic and will be referred to below as the *divided* and the *composite* or *compound* sense in the chapter dialogues of this book.

Before proceeding to Peter Lombard's approach to the dilemma of reconciling divine foreknowledge with human free choice, the theological background to Lombard that arguably set the terms of the debate cannot fail to mention how Augustine approached Cicero's dilemma of divine foreknowledge and human free choice. In the year 415, Augustine (354–430) finished chapter 5 of the *City of God*. He said that in Cicero's book *On Divination*, "he assumes that the admission of foreknowledge entails the acceptance of fate as a logical necessity." But for Augustine, "whatever may be the twists and turns of philosophical dispute and debate (*disputationes philosophorum*)," he recognized and confessed God's "supreme power and foreknowledge." Augustine said that he was "not afraid that what we do by an act of will may not be a voluntary act, because God, with his infallible prescience, knew that we should do it. This was the fear that led Cicero to oppose foreknowledge and the Stoics to deny that everything happens by necessity, although they maintained that everything happens according to fate."[21] According to Augustine, the dilemma for Cicero was, "If we choose foreknowledge, free will is annihilated; if we choose free will, prescience is abolished." Cicero, thus, chose free will, said Augustine. For Cicero reasoned, "if there is prescience of

---

19. Knuuttila, *Reforging the Great Chain of Being*, 180. See Knuuttila's comments on the divided sense linked to *potentia* by the thirteenth-century Dominican logician Lambert of Auxerre, who wrote *Logica* (*Summa Lamberti*), mid-thirteenth century, 192.

20. Knuuttila, *Reforging the Great Chain of Being*, 180.

21. Augustine, *City of God*, 190. Latin from Augustine, *De Civitate Dei*, 203.

the future, the logical consequences entailed lead to the conclusion that nothing depends on our free will."[22] Augustine argued that we can foresee that which we are about to do, but we act nonetheless freely. He asserted both foreknowledge and free will. "God knows all things before they happen and that we do by our free will everything that we feel and know would not happen without our volition."[23]

There is a sense in which Augustine approved of using the word "fate," if one understood it as a derivation from the word "*fari*" (speak). Both in the *City of God* and *The Spirit and the Letter* (412) he referred to the Bible passage, "God has spoken once," which he understood to mean that "he has spoken immovably, that is, unalterably."[24] God knows all that will happen just as he knows "what he himself is going to do." Augustine reasoned that it did not follow that because there is "a fixed order of all causes" in God's foreknowledge free choice was denied us. Rather, "our wills themselves are in the order of causes."[25]

Indeed, said Augustine, "our wills are ours and it is our wills that affect all that we do by willing, and which would not have happened if we had not willed."[26] In *The Spirit and the Letter*, Augustine made a crucial distinction between our being naturally endowed with *liberum arbitrium*, on the formal level of speaking, and gifted with *voluntas*, on the material level. *Voluntas* is derived from *velle* and has to do with the disposition of the will to materially achieve what we will, a power lost in the fall.[27] According to Augustine, "the power of achievement comes from God."[28] He wrote that "willing is one thing, ability another; willing does not necessarily imply ability, nor ability willing."[29] He posed the question, "Is the will by which we believe also the gift of God, or is it exerted by the freedom of choice which is implanted in us by nature?" He answered that God endowed human beings with "freedom of choice" in "the way of nature." Before the fall, this faculty was a "neutral power." After the fall, it was God's call that gave rise to someone eliciting an act

22. Augustine, *City of God*, 191.
23. Augustine, *City of God*, 192.
24. Augustine, *City of God*, 192; see also Augustine, *Augustine: Later Works*, 242.
25. Augustine, *City of God*, 192.
26. Augustine, *City of God*, 195.
27. See Augustine, *Augustine: Later Works*, 237, 242.
28. Augustine, *City of God*, 195.
29. Augustine, *Augustine: Later Works*, 237.

of faith in God. Augustine's classic argument was, "What do you have that you have not received?" (1 Cor 4:7).[30] The classical ethic of praiseworthiness and blameworthiness was fully reconcilable, said Augustine, with the teaching of God's foreknowledge of human action in response to warnings, exhortations, and the like since God himself does not cause the moral nature of human action. What God does is gift and empower humans with the ability to achieve the good in response to exhortations. Likewise, "prayers are effectual in obtaining all that God foreknew that he would grant in answer to them."[31]

Is God's Foreknowledge the Cause of Evil?

The twelfth century also saw a creative literary form develop in biblical scholarship. Instead of glosses and a running commentary on Scripture, such as Anselm of Laon's (ca. 1050–1117) compilation of *Glossa ordinaria*, alongside the study of Scripture there developed the theological casebook.[32] The prime example of the casebook was *The Sentences* of Peter Lombard (1100–1160).[33] The pattern he established was to introduce a *quaestio* or problem. Then he established authorities, namely, Scripture, *glossa ordinaria*, and church fathers, such as Ambrose, Augustine, Boethius, Cyril of Alexandria, Pope Gregory I, Hilary, Jerome, John Chrysostom, John of Damascus, and Origen. He proposed how to reconcile their opinions, if needed. Then, any anomalies were addressed, as well as objections. One problem that he posed was "Whether knowledge or foreknowledge is the cause of things, or things are the cause of foreknowledge?" in *The Sentences* I 38.1.[34] In the course of the discussion, he argued that it is impossible for things which God foreknows will come about to fail to come about. He drew on the authority of Augustine in *The Trinity* 15.22 where Augustine wrote a gloss on Matt 6:8: "For your Father knows what you need before you ask him." Lombard explained that

---

30. Augustine, *Augustine: Later Works*, 241–42.
31. Augustine, *City of God*, 195.
32. Smith, *The Glossa Ordinaria*.
33. Unless otherwise indicated, the English quotes are taken from Lombard, *The Mystery of the Trinity*. The Latin text upon which Silano based his translation is Lombard, *Sententiae*. On Lombard in the context of the intellectual debates of the day, see Colish, *Peter Lombard*.
34. Lombard, *Sentences*, 213 (I 38.1).

God did not know these things from some point in time (*ex aliquo tempore*), but he knew beforehand without any beginning (*sine initio*) all things that would pass in time and, among these, he even knows that which we will seek from him, when we will seek it, and whose requests and as to which things he will grant or not grant. He does not know all his creatures, both spiritual and corporeal, because they are, but they are because he knows them. For he was not ignorant of what he would create. It was because he knew that he created, and not because he had created that he knew. And he does not know things that have been created any differently from those that are yet to be created. For nothing was added to his wisdom from them, but with all these things existing when and as they ought, his wisdom remained as it was.[35]

But what then of foreknown evil? Is God the cause and thus author of evil? Suffice it say at this point that Lombard denied this conclusion. But neither is evil the cause of God's foreknowledge. God's foreknowledge does not depend upon the future actions, whether good or evil, of human beings. The created is not the cause of the uncreated.

On the problem of God's knowledge of evil, Lombard's argument made use of a distinction between God's knowledge (*notitia*) of what he himself does not cause, on the one hand, and God's knowledge of his good pleasure (*beneplacito*), on the other. God's foreknowledge of human infidelity therefore drives no one to commit sin. God knows and owns by the knowledge of his good pleasure the good to be done. However, he does not know as his own the evil to be done.[36]

In *The Sentences* I 38.2, Lombard replied to the objection that what had been said, namely, "that a thing can happen otherwise than God foreknew," implied that "God's foreknowledge is fallible." Consider the ambiguity of the following argument: God foreknows that someone will read a book. But it is possible (*sed potest esse*) that he does not read. Therefore it can be otherwise than God foreknew, therefore God's foreknowledge can fail. Lombard argued that while the conclusion is false, one can read the premises in another way. Here is the proposition: "Something can happen otherwise than God foreknew" (*aliter potest fieri, quam Deus praescivit*). Lombard replied by making use of a distinction between a reading in the *conjunctive* or compound sense and a reading in the *disjunctive* or divided

---

35. Lombard, *Sentences*, 213 (I 38.1); Latin: Lombard, *Sententiae*, 276 (I 38.1). Cf. Augustine, *The Trinity*, 414.

36. Lombard, *Sentences*, 215 (I 38.1); Latin: Lombard, *Sententiae*, 278 (I 38.1).

sense. If one read the proposition in the conjunctive sense, Lombard said it was a contradiction. That is, both parts cannot be true at the same time. In other words, it cannot simultaneously be the case that God foreknows I will read this book and that I not read this book. However, Lombard said that when the proposition was read in the disjunctive or divided sense, it was to be understood as possible. He determined, "For a thing can happen otherwise than it does, and yet God foreknew that it would happen in this way." Alternatively, the conjunctive sense is true and the disjunctive sense false when it says that "it is impossible for a thing not to happen which God foreknew, or as God foreknew it."[37] In the seventeenth century, the Presbyterian pastor Stephen Charnock (1628–80) made a true statement similar to that read above in the divided sense, perhaps with Lombard's *Sentences* I 38 in mind. He said, "Man hath a power to do otherwise than that which God foreknows he will do."[38] That is, while it is possible for human beings to do otherwise than they actually do as to their power, God knows both what they actually do in time and what they could have done.

Can the Elect Be Damned?

In *Sentences* I 40, Lombard again made use of the distinction between the conjunctive and the disjunctive senses. The problem he addressed was "Whether any of the predestined may [*possit*] be damned or any of the reprobated be saved?"[39] It seems as if this could not be possible. Either one is elect or not. One objection raised against denying the possibility, which amounted to an affirmation of the possibility posed, was the opinion that the number of the elect can (*posse*) be increased or diminished. Lombard, however, replied that in reality, "both cannot be true at the same time" (*quia non potest utrumque simul esse*).[40] Taken in the conjunctive sense, the proposition "one predestined cannot be damned," would mean that both parts are true in reality at the same time, which is a contradiction. However, taken in the disjunctive or divided sense of sentence composition, the proposition holds true, since it is possible that an elect one be damned. In the divided sense, the elect one is not both

---

37. Lombard, *Sentences*, 216 (I 38.2); Latin: Lombard, *Sententiae*, 279 (I 38.2).
38. Charnock, *Existence and Attributes of God*, 1:450.
39. Lombard, *Sentences*, 221 (I 40); Latin: Lombard, *Sententiae*, 284 (I 40).
40. Lombard, *Sentences*, 221 (I 40); Latin: Lombard, *Sententiae*, 285 (I 40).

elect and non-elect at the same time. Lombard concluded, "For he could have been not predestined, and so he would be damned."[41] Furthermore, as to whether what is said and done by God in eternity can be said or done otherwise, or be unsaid or undone, Lombard said that that was impossible given "the nature of an existent thing." When dealing with possibility or impossibility in reference to the power of God, Lombard said that "predestination, foreknowledge, power is one thing in God" (*quia praedestinatio, praescientia, potentia unum in Deo est*).[42] Here, in addition to the distinction between a conjunctive and a disjunctive sense, Lombard raised the related issue of the simultaneity of potencies. The relation between the divided sense and the "simultaneity of potencies" (*simultas potentiae*)—as opposed to the contradiction of coupling the composite sense with the "potency of simultaneity" (*potentia simultatis*)—would become developed and used by later scholastics, including Reformed scholastics in the seventeenth century. But here Lombard made the point that there is but one potency or power in God exercised in relation to the elect. For Lombard argued against the potency of simultaneity when he said that "it cannot be true simultaneously that he is predestined and he is not predestined."[43] However, to the point of the objection that if one was predestined from eternity, "it cannot now be true that he is not predestined," the proposition can be understood "conjunctively and disjunctively." Conjunctively understood, Lombard agreed that the two parts—from eternity and now—cannot both be true. But disjunctively understood, in the divided sense, Lombard agreed that it can be true; "But yet it could be true from eternity that he was not predestined, and he could have been not predestined from eternity" (*sed tamen potuit esse ab aeterno quod non esset praedestinatus, et potuit ab aeterno non esse praedestinatus*). From eternity past, God *could* (*potuit*) not predestine him, and some concede that "even now" God *can* (*potest*), in the sense of it is possible, "not have predestined him" (*et modo potest Deus eum non praedestinasse ab aeterno*).[44]

When Thomas Aquinas (1225-74) commented on Lombard's *Sentences* I 40 on the problem "Whether any of the predestined can be damned?" like Lombard he made use of a distinction between the

41. Lombard, *Sentences*, 221 (I 40); Latin: "*Potuit enim non esse praedestinatus, et ita damnaretur*," Lombard, *Sententiae*, 285 (I 40).

42. Lombard, *Sentences*, 222 (I 40); Latin: Lombard, *Sententiae*, 286 (I 40).

43. Lombard, *Sentences*, 222 (I 40); Latin: Lombard, *Sententiae*, 285 (I 40).

44. Lombard, *Sentences*, 222 (I 40); Latin: Lombard, *Sententiae*, 285-86 (I 40).

composite sense and the divided sense. Aquinas posed the problem "Whether predestination is certain?" in the *Summa Theologica*.[45] For instance, one objection supposed that Peter had sinned and died. Would that mean that God's will for Peter was thwarted? That he was not one of the elect? Aquinas subsumed predestination under God's providence. As such, "predestination most certainly and infallibly takes effect; yet it does not impose any necessity." The order of providence is infallible, but does not rule out contingency. Like Lombard, Aquinas said that in the "composite sense," it is illogical to say that "God is able not to predestinate one whom he has predestinated." However, here Aquinas did not use the term "divided sense," but a related term. He said, "absolutely speaking, God can predestinate or not."[46] When Aquinas used the term "absolutely," he considered God's power and will apart from God's ordained power and will, that is, in a free and unrestricted sense. In *Summa Contra Gentiles*, Aquinas was more explicit on this distinction and used the term "divided sense." He said that the statements by some that "'God cannot do the contrary of what he has designed to do' are to be understood compositely." But that when they are "understood in a divided sense," such statements "are false, because they then refer to God's power and will absolutely."[47]

Peter of Spain (ca. 1205–77), who became Pope John XXI, made an important point about how one is to understand the different levels of

---

45. Aquinas, *Summa Theologica*, 130 (I q.23, a.6).

46. Aquinas, *Summa Theologica*, 130 (I q.23, a.6, ad obj.3).

47. Aquinas, *Summa Contra Gentiles*, II 25.24. In I 67.10 of *Summa Contra Gentiles*, Aquinas also made a distinction between the composite and divided senses. On the conditional proposition, "If Socrates is seen sitting, he is sitting," if one reads the proposition as Socrates "must necessarily be sitting, it is clear that the proposition is true" if understood "compositely." However, it is false if understood "dividedly."

Cf. In *The Consolation of Philosophy*, Boethius wrote that when God sees things presently that proceed from free will, there is a distinction to be made between things that are "necessary by the condition of the divine knowledge," on the one hand, and things that are "considered by themselves" which things "lose not absolute freedom of their own nature," on the other, in Boethius, *The Theological Tractates and The Consolation of Philosophy*, book 5, prosa 6. Chaucer's translation of Boethius's *Consolation of Philosophy*, in either the late 1370s or early 1380s, shows that the last terms in the phrase "But certes yif thilke thingis ben considered by himself, thei ben absolut of necessite," meant to be "free of necessity," *Boece*, book V, prosa 6.203, in Chaucer, *The Riverside Chaucer*, 468. See *Boece*, in Chaucer, *Riverside Chaucer*, 462, where "absolut and unbounden" meant "free and unrestricted," in the context of the sentence, "I suppose that ther be prescience, but that it ne putteth no necessite to thingis; thanne trowe [suppose or think] I that thilke selve fredom of wil schal duellen al hool and absolut and unbounden" (lines 51–55).

meaning of the term "necessity." Peter stated, "Something necessary is a being [or state of affairs] that cannot be otherwise." It is one thing to say, in mathematics, "Every number is either even or odd." And in geometry, "Every triangle has three sides equal to two right ones." But in modal propositions, the placement of the adverb "necessarily" makes a difference in the notion of "necessity." Peter gave an example of a necessity of mode, "Socrates necessarily is running." He said that the proposition itself is contingent. This is because there is nothing about Socrates such that he must be running. If there were, then the placement of the adverb would change to read, "Socrates is running, necessarily." But in the case above, whether Socrates runs or not is a contingent matter.[48]

Likewise, "contingency" can be understood in different ways. "One type of contingent is what is called contingent as regards either of two outcomes (*contingens ad utrumlibet*)." The state of affairs "can both be the case and not be the case," in relation to motion and "operations of the will."[49] A contingent such as this is in itself indifferent and indetermined. But given a cause, it is more determined to one object of choice than another. There is another kind of contingent that is opposite to what is necessary. It is called "a contingent naturally bound to occur (*contingens natum*)," such as that men's hair turns grey as they age. This is more likely to be than not to be. A third type of contingent is that which rarely occurs. It is "less related to being than to non-being." Peter refers to Aristotle's example of news which is similar to the case of the news today. There is more bad news than good news.[50]

The composition of a proposition that makes claims about a state of affairs, about reality, whether it is open or closed, depends upon the placement of the adverb "necessarily." Primarily speaking, the term "necessary" modifies either the subject or the predicate of a proposition. Thus, "A married person has a spouse." Necessarily, this is the case of a married person. The sense of "married" inheres in the predicate. But it is the secondary placement that is crucial to understand. There is nothing necessary about being married. Peter of Spain stated that the entire

---

48. John XXI, *Syncategoreumata*, 283–85.

49. The expression "freedom *ad utrumlibet*" will be encountered in chapter 10 in a dialogue with Jonathan Edwards, who rejected the implications of the term as late as the mid-eighteenth century.

50. John XXI, *Syncategoreumata*, 285–87.

composition itself is a relative matter. The relative necessity belonging to a composition will reappear in dialogues below.[51]

John Duns Scotus (1266–1308) commented on Lombard's *Sentences* and addressed the problem that Lombard had posed. In *Lectura I 40*, Scotus asked "Whether an elect can be damned?" (*Utrum praedestinatus posset damnari?*).[52] Like Lombard, he took up the objection that what is past cannot be changed and is necessary. Thus, it would appear that the elect cannot be damned. However, Scotus argued that predestination, in the sense of election, "is an act of will," that is, "a pre-ordination of the divine will."[53] To elect (*praedestinare*) is to ordain someone to grace. Scotus made a distinction between God's power to elicit an act and the actual eliciting of an act of the divine will in relation to an object of volition. Like Lombard, he also made a distinction between the composite sense and the divided sense (*compositionem et divisionem*).[54] In the composite sense, the modal operator "can" is applied to both parts of the proposition, "Whether the elect can be damned?" The proposition, thus, is false. Understood from eternity, the elect one cannot be both elect and damned. However, in the divided sense, the modal operator "can" is applied to only one part of the proposition, namely, the subject in question, the elect one. On the question of whether the past is necessary and how "now" is to be related to "eternity," questions which both Lombard and Scotus took up, Scotus brought into his reply the notion of the "eternal now" (*nunc aeternitatis*). From the perspective of eternity, there are not past, present, and future acts of the divine will, nor of the human will. Furthermore, to be elect by God from eternity does not deny God the power to do otherwise than he does. "With the same volition by which he wills to elect a person, he can will to condemn that person for the same moment of eternity" (*pro eodem instanti aeternitatis*).[55] In other words, if God wills to elect someone, which is to be understood as in eternity, that is, apart from time, he retains the power in relation to that object, and thus it is possible that he not will to elect that person.

---

51. John XXI, *Syncategoreumata*, 287–89.
52. Scotus, *Divine Love*, 132–33.
53. Scotus, *Divine Love*, 133.
54. Scotus, *Divine Love*, 135.
55. Scotus, *Divine Love*, 134–35.

Can God Do Other Than He Does?

In *Sentences* I 43, Lombard entertained the problem posed by some who had said that "God is not able to do other than what he does."[56] First, they reason that God cannot but do "what is good and just to do." For if he did not do so, he would fail to do the good he must do. Second, they argue that God's justice requires that God do so. Indeed, Lombard saw that this kind of reasoning actually restricted God's power. To the first, Lombard replied that God can (*potest*) "do many things which are neither good nor just" for no other reason than that he is not omnivolent. That is, there are many possible good and just things that simply are not and will not be. Furthermore, there are things that will not be well done simply because God will not do all that he could do. "They neither are nor will be, nor are they or will they be well done, because they shall never be done."[57] To the second, Lombard argued that the meaning of the word "require" was ambiguous. It simply was not true that God "cannot do anything other what his justice requires." For if that were the case, then the "favor" the Lord granted Lot, that he flee to a nearby little city in Genesis 19:22—"Hurry, escape there, for I can do nothing until you arrive there"—would have been meaningless if in fact God could not have, had he so willed, overthrown that city. But, indeed, it was true if they understood by these words that God cannot "do anything other than what, if it were done, would be consistent with his justice."[58] Which was the case with Lot.

Furthermore, the statement that God's "will is most equitable" and thus God cannot do other than he does, and that there are very good reasons why God does what he does and leaves other things undone, Lombard held to be true. Nevertheless, he added that God "can, in accordance with the same reason, leave undone the things which he does and do what he leaves undone."[59] Here Lombard spoke, as in other places, of God's power to do otherwise than he in fact does. Indeed, Lombard affirmed that God is not omnivolent. That is, God can or "is able to do more things than he wills, because more things are subject to his power

---

56. Lombard, *Sentences*, 233 (I 43); Latin: Lombard, *Sententiae*, 298 (I 43).

57. Lombard, *Sentences*, 234 (I 43); Latin: Lombard, *Sententiae*, 299 (I 43).

58. Lombard, *Sentences*, 234 (I 43); Latin: Lombard, *Sententiae*, 299 (I 43). In the second reply, Lombard cited Augustine's *Contra Gaudentium*. Augustine had said concerning Lot (Gen 19:21–22) that without a doubt God was able to do through his power what he did not do through his justice.

59. Lombard, *Sentences*, 235–36 (I 43); Latin: Lombard, *Sententiae*, 300 (I 43).

than to his will. And so let us profess that God can do many things which he does not will, and can leave undone many things which he does."[60]

In *Lectura I 39*, Scotus argued that as concerns the proposition "This is to be done," God understands the proposition whether something was to be done or left undone as a neutral proposition. It is not something primarily true, such that it must be done. The reason is that God's intellect does not suggest or guide the will. There is no last dictate of the practical understanding as is spoken of in human beings. For who could imagine God not willing what his intellect presents to the will as something to be done? One must not pit God's will against his intellect.[61]

Is God the Author of Evil?

In *Sentences* I 46, Lombard posed the problem "Whether evil things are done by God's will or against his will?"[62] Ultimately, the problem comes down to distinguishing between whether God merely allows that evil take place, or whether God wills that evil take place, or whether God wills to allow that evil occur. Lombard denied that God wills evil to be or be done, for that would make God the "author of evils. But he is not the author of evils."[63]

Some argued, said Lombard, that nothing happens without God willing it to be. Evil happens; therefore, God wills that it happen. If God had willed that evil not be done, yet it is done, then evil has resisted God's will, God is powerless to defeat it, all of which is unacceptable. In addition, it was argued that there must be some good that comes out of evil, otherwise God would not have allowed it to be done.

But Lombard challenged the idea of God merely allowing evil to be or to be done. He began by saying that "God neither wills evil things to be done, nor wills them not to be done or is unwilling that they be done, but only that he does not will them to be done."[64] How then does Lombard both guard the sovereignty of God's will and exonerate God

---

60. Lombard, *Sentences*, 237 (I 43); Latin: Lombard, *Sententiae*, 302 (I 43).

61. Scotus, *Contingency and Freedom*, Lectura I 39, 106, 162. I cover this in detail in chapter 2.

62. Lombard, *Sentences*, 248 (I 46); Latin: Lombard, *Sententiae*, 314 (I 46).

63. Lombard, *Sentences*, 250 (I 46); Latin: "Non est autem auctor malorum," in Lombard, *Sententiae*, 316 (I 46).

64. Lombard, *Sentences*, 249 (I 46); Latin: Lombard, *Sententiae*, 316 (I 46).

from being the author of evil? Lombard overcame the problem by setting forth a two-step approach to God's willing. He knew that if he had agreed that God wills evil to be or be done, it would make God the author of evil. But God is not the author of evil. He then entertained the solution that God is the "permitter of evils."[65] He gleaned the solution of God's "permissive" will from what might appear to us today to be a peculiar reading of John 1:3: "All things are made through him, and without him is made nothing." Since evil is the absence of good and thus nothing, then sin (nothing) was made "without his will." But is God's "will" absent from Lombard's final formula? No, not at all. The next step for Lombard with respect to evil things being done was to distinguish between "God willing [*volente*], unwilling [*nolente*], and not willing [*non volente*]." Evil is not done by God willing or unwilling, but by God not willing. It appears at first that God's will is removed from the formula and that he chose the formula of mere permission. But Lombard intended to remove evil from being the direct object of God's willing. At the end of his explanation, Lombard concluded that it is for good that God allows evil. But God does not merely allow evil to be done. "He allows it entirely willingly, not willing evil things, but willing to allow that they be done" (*sed volens sinere ut ipsa fiant*).[66] Willing, not just allowing, then, is the second step in the formula, namely, that God wills to allow that evil be done.

Chronologically, Aquinas would be next up for discussion. But since Scotus's approach was very similar to Lombard's, indeed it was an adaptation of Lombard's solution, and Aquinas's approach quite different, I first consider Scotus, then Aquinas.

Scotus posed the problem whether "Divine permission is an act of will?" in *Ordinatio* I 47.[67] In addition to Lombard's considerations of willing, unwilling, not willing, and willing to permit, Scotus entertained another solution to the problem of reconciling God's sovereign will with the existence of evil without making God the author of evil. Scotus started with the human will, then moved to discuss the divine will. Human beings have "a twofold act of will," namely, "willing" (*velle*) and "willing it not be the case that" (*nolle*). He considered both as belonging to the line of "positive" acts of the will. And if the will specified the same object, suppose a person who is the object of one's love or withholding of love, then

---

65. Lombard, *Sentences*, 250 (I 46); Latin: Lombard, *Sententiae*, 316 (I 46).
66. Lombard, *Sentences*, 250 (I 46); Latin: Lombard, *Sententiae*, 316 (I 46).
67. Scotus, *Divine Love*, 178–79.

Scotus said that they were "contrary acts," such as, "to love or to hate" (*amare et odire*).[68] One can will that one love or will that one not love or withhold love. The positive line of acts of the will was to be distinguished from the negative line of acts of the will, namely, not willing (*non-velle*) and not willing it not be the case (*non-nolle*). There were thus four possible formulations of volition. Scotus held that this model applied to the divine will as well. Along the positive line, there was (1) "An effective volition," and (2) "A restrained volition." Along the negative line, there was (3) "An effective nolition," and (4) "A restrained nolition."[69] Positively, the first case realizes that which the will wills. In the second, that which the will wills is not realized, since the will willed that it not be realized. Negatively, the third object is effectively nilled. In the fourth case, that which is not willed is realized. For instance, either God or a human agent does not not will that evil happen. For example, I do not will to prevent a crime.

It ought to be clear that the fourth formulation granted a line of permission. In other words, I will not to will to prevent a crime. I will to permit evil. Like Lombard, Scotus concluded that God wills to permit that evil be done. Scotus adapted Lombard's notion of "willing to allow" and formulated a new theory of permission, a "second-order volition," that is, the will not to will an act of the will to permit evil. The answer, thus, to the problem posed in the beginning is, yes, divine permission is an act of will, a second-order act. The act of the will itself becomes an object of volition.[70]

Aquinas's approach to the question of whether God is the author of evil had some things in common with Lombard, but was fundamentally quite different. In keeping with this introduction's genre of the disputation, the following exposition gives attention to one of Aquinas's works, *De malo*, in which he handled disputed questions on evil. He began by asking "Whether evil was an entity?"[71] It seemed as if this were the case, since the prophet Isaiah wrote that God created evil (Isa 45:6–7). After listing twenty reasons why it seemed that evil was an entity, he turned to contrary opinions, as was the custom, citing Augustine, who said "in the *City of God* that evil is not a nature, but that the lack of good took on this

---

68. Scotus, *Divine Love*, 179.
69. Scotus, *Divine Love*, 185–86.
70. Scotus, *Divine Love*, 188.
71. Aquinas, *On Evil*, 55.

ascription." And like Lombard, he cited John 1:3, "'All things were made by him.' But the word did not cause evil, as Augustine says. Therefore, evil is not an entity." Moreover, "John 1:3 adds: 'Without him was made nothing,' that is, sin, 'since sin is nothing, and human beings become nothing when they sin,' as a gloss says."[72]

Aquinas then turned to his own answer to the question and said that evil is twofold. On the one hand, evil is a subject; on the other, evil itself is a "privation of a particular good, not an entity."[73] Death deprives one of life, blindness of sight. When Aquinas turned to the question of "the causes of sin," he directly asked, "Does God cause sin?"[74] He gave three opinions to the contrary. First, Augustine said in effect that although God is the author of life, he does not corrupt human beings, who are made in his image. "Therefore, God is not the author of sin." Second, he cited Fulgentius (ca. 467–533) who said, "God is not the author of what he punishes." Third, "God causes only what he loves. God loves everything that exists, 'and you [God] hated nothing that you have made'" (Wis 11:24). Since God hates sin, he did not cause it or author it.[75]

In many ways, Aquinas said, sin is missing the mark, not attaining the intended end. This is due to "a deficiency in the causal source." He gave the example of a student who wrote a poor essay composition due to deficient writing skills. But God has no deficiencies. God's will never fails to attain its end. Therefore he cannot be the cause or author of sin. For Aquinas, "good" is an achievement term. But human beings turn their sights and wills away from the supreme good and end, God himself.[76]

There was an axiom that said that "in things necessary, the deficient cause must be reduced to the efficient cause."[77] But Aquinas challenged the implication. He offered the example of a lame animal; let's say, a horse. The horse has the power to cause his legs to move. But suppose the horse limps. If one traces the cause back to the prior cause, it seems as if the horse has deficient will power, and is to blame. But the limp comes from a deficient leg bone. Perhaps a curved or injured leg. Therefore, the horse's "locomotive power" is not the cause of limping. "Therefore," said

---

72. Aquinas, *On Evil*, 57.
73. Aquinas, *On Evil*, 57.
74. Aquinas, *On Evil*, 141.
75. Aquinas, *On Evil*, 143.
76. Aquinas, *On Evil*, 143–44.
77. Aquinas, *Summa Theologica*, 254 (I q.49 a.2). "*Causa deficiens, in rebus necessariis, ad causam per se efficientem reducenda est.*"

Aquinas, "free choice, as it defects from God, causes sin. And so God, although he causes free choice, need not cause sin."[78] Aquinas considered when Jesus told Judas, "What you do, do quickly" (John 13:27), and asked if Jesus commanded Judas to sin or permitted Judas to sin? Aquinas took the side of permission. He reasoned according to Aristotle that there is a distinction to be made between the power to act, on the one hand, and to act, on the other. The implication Aquinas drew was that although God "causes a power in human beings to be able to act, God is not responsible for the human act itself."[79]

Aquinas then posed the question, "Do acts of sin come from God?" After all, human beings cannot act independently of God. "In him we live and move and have our being" (Acts 17:28). But Aquinas declined to think so since acts of sin are not entities and as such cannot come from God. Furthermore, "Acts of sin are acts of free choice, which we call free because the will moves its very self to act."[80] In other words, the will is master of its own acts and therefore responsible for them. Therefore God is not the author of acts of sin. Although God is the "first source of the movement of everything," he moves secondary causes, like the soul and will of human beings, in such a way that they move themselves. Those who are "properly disposed" to receive God's impulses will produce "good acts." These good acts may be traced back to God. However, if human beings use their power of free choice to turn away from God, then "disordered acts that are acts of sin result."[81] These disordered and deformed acts of will are not to be traced back to God. God is therefore situated asymmetrically behind good acts and bad acts.

Aquinas adds to his argument a distinction between the different species of acts of the will. The "deformity of sin" results not from the natural powers to act, but rather from the "species of acts as moral, as caused by free choice."[82] There is thus a distinction between a natural influx or movement of God upon the soul enabling it to elicit an act of will, on the one hand, and the moral character of an act of will, on the other. It should be said that the human "intellect and will necessarily tend toward what

---

78. Aquinas, *On Evil*, 144.

79. Aquinas, *On Evil*, 146.

80. Aquinas, *On Evil*, 147–48. "I concede that every will is in control or master of its own act," Scotus, *Will and Morality*, 155.

81. Aquinas, *On Evil*, 148.

82. Aquinas, *On Evil*, 148.

HISTORICAL AND THEOLOGICAL INTRODUCTION 21

nature has ordained as their object."[83] The intellect necessarily assents to the first principles known naturally, such as that two parallel lines will never cross one another, or that a body feels pain when wounded. "The will likewise naturally and necessarily wills happiness, nor can anyone will unhappiness."[84] These first principles naturally move the soul of a human being. One would think that God as the supreme good would be linked to the human desire for happiness, but unfortunately "the necessity of this connection is not fully evident to human beings in this life," since they do not behold the beatific vision in this life.[85] Aquinas concluded from this that the human will was naturally inclined from within and therefore the efficient cause of a voluntary act toward what the intellect and will thought was the soul's own happiness, but in fact was sin, belonged to the will of the master of its own act.

On the question of whether Aquinas believed that God is the author of evil, editor Brian Davies echoes what has been said above. He places responsibility for evil at the feet of human action or inaction: "God can be said to cause sin only insofar as he is the creative source of human activity, an activity which often fails or falls short with respect to goodness."[86] But all failure is ascribed to a deficient human free choice, just as a limping horse is ascribed to an injured or deformed leg.

Davies reminds the reader that one ought not approach Aquinas's work *On Evil* in the modern-day sense of approaching "the problem of evil." Aquinas was not operating with the Enlightenment understanding that there is a sufficient reason for why things are the way they are and not otherwise. In other words, Aquinas did not attempt to wed a theory of divine permission to the principle of sufficient reason. Aquinas made no attempt to show that "the evil we encounter is something permitted by God for a morally sufficient reason."[87] The end did not morally justify the (sometimes evil) means. Nor did Aquinas's worldview entertain the modern view of God granting human beings independent freedom, allowing the concomitant and consequent evil, in order to achieve a greater good.[88]

---

83. Aquinas, *On Evil*, 151.
84. Aquinas, *On Evil*, 151.
85. Aquinas, *On Evil*, 152.
86. Aquinas, *On Evil*, 42.
87. Aquinas, *On Evil*, 50.
88. Aquinas, *On Evil*, 52.

Davies sums up Aquinas's view on God and evil by pointing out that although God is the creative source of all human activity in the world, he cannot be the author of evil, since evil is no real created thing. Evil is a result of some kind of failure which, though, God can turn around to good. "Moral evil occurs as free, rational agents turn from what is actually good in order to pursue other goals. As with all evil, its 'reality' is that of failure. And it is not something creatively made by God."[89]

Late Medieval Scholasticism

The Flemish scholar Peter De Rivo or Peter Van Der Beken (ca. 1420–1500), professor of philosophy and rhetoric at the University of Leuven, was born near Aalst, Belgium. Famously, he was involved in a serious quarrel on whether Christ's forecasting of Saint Peter's denials denied Peter's freedom of choice. The quarrel spread to the theological faculties of Paris and Cologne.[90] The literary rendition of Peter De Rivo's quarrel on future contingents, disputed in Leuven in 1465, serves as an example of the use made of scholastic distinctions, such as the necessity of the consequence, and the compound and divided sense of a proposition! He argued that there was contingency in things and that Saint Peter had the power not to deny Christ, even after Christ told him he would deny him.[91]

The question considered was, "Was it in Peter's power to deny Christ after Christ had said to him, 'Thou wilt deny me thrice?'" De Rivo knew that the question concerned whether when God determines things he wills them necessarily or contingently. He named three apparent objections. First, the logical objection understands determination to mean that what God wills to come about comes about necessarily, not contingently. Second, the physical objection understands "physical" in terms of the natural disposition of "heavenly bodies" or Peter's natural inclination in the sense that God's will imposes necessity upon the heavenly bodies as well as Peter's disposition, with the fated result that Peter is denied the power to act otherwise than he does. Things, then, do not occur contingently. Third, the metaphysical objection holds that if God

---

89. Aquinas, *On Evil*, 52–54.

90. Masolini et al., "Petrus de Rivo (ca. 1420-1499): Portrait(s) of a Louvain Master."

91. De Rivo, "A Quodlibetal Question On Future Contingents"; Baudry, *La Querelle Des Futurs Contingents*, 70–78.

foreknows future things, and he does, then he knows them necessarily, not contingently. For no thing that is future is contingent; neither can future contingents be known. In sum, the objections hold that God cannot possibly will anything contingently, and therefore his knowledge of what he wills is necessary.[92]

Peter De Rivo's answer was that whatever God determines to come about he determines contingently. And thus God's knowledge of future contingents also is contingent. The sequence of events that comes about happens contingently. In the case of Peter, before he denies Christ three times, at each moment he retains the power to act otherwise than he does. "Before the occurrence of a thing in being it is in the power of the cause to bring it or not bring it into being." Thereafter, its occurrence is "unimpedible." Thus, until a proposition occurs, it remains contingent, since it has of yet no time-indexed truth value. Prior to God determining whether a proposition is true or false, it is a neutral proposition.[93] At the "moment" God determines by his will what will take place in time, He appoints the truth value and time indexation of the hitherto neutral proposition of the future contingent.

Furthermore, Peter De Rivo holds that all things, past, present, and future are present to God.[94] To the argument that "Everything foreknown will come about of necessity," Peter De Rivo says that some would argue that the premise is false in the divided sense, but true in the compounded sense. But he says the application of this distinction will not do since *foreknown* is an inseparable feature of the thing said to be foreknown. This begs the question, since the question is whether the thing is knowable, which it is not if it is still a neutral proposition.

3. Maimonides: A Medieval Jewish Guide to Views on Providence

Having briefly touched on the Christian views of Augustine, Abelard, Lombard, Aquinas, and Scotus on the problem of evil and God's providence, I turn to a famous Jewish rabbi and philosopher, Moses Maimonides (1135–1204), whose writings, *Moreh Nebuchim* (*The Guide*

---

92. De Rivo, "A Quodlibetal Question On Future Contingents," 254.

93. Baudry, *La Querelle Des Futurs Contingents*, 13, 17, 138; De Rivo, "A Quodlibetal Question on Future Contingents" 254.

94. De Rivo, "A Quodlibetal Question on Future Contingents," 257.

for the Peplexed) and *Mishneh Torah* (*A Codex: A Copy of the Law*), had a major influence on medieval Torah studies, and whose historical, philosophical, and spiritual legacy was insured by his transmission of Aristotle's philosophy to Christian theologians such as Albertus Magnus and Thomas Aquinas.[95] In *The Guide for the Perplexed*, he laid down the proposition that "all evils are negations." The negation of life is death. To deprive someone of life is death and thus evil, since death is that person's non-existence. "Illness, poverty, and ignorance are evils for man." They are all "privations of properties." Evil, thus, is a relative term. All "so-called evils are evils only in relation to a certain thing." For instance, health is a relative term and "denotes a certain equilibrium." When equilibrium is disturbed, relatively speaking, health is absent. "The absence of that relation" results in illness.[96]

Given these propositions, Maimonides said that God cannot be the one who "directly creates evil." Nor is it possible that God directly intend "to produce evil." God only "produces existence," all of which is good. On the contrary, "evils are of a negative character, and cannot be acted upon."[97] According to Maimonides, when Isaiah said, "'I form the light and create [*bore*] darkness: I make peace, and create [*bore*] evil' [Isa 45:7], for darkness and evil are non-existing things," the prophet did not say, "I make ['*oseh*] darkness, I make ['*oseh*] evil, because darkness and evil are not things in positive existence to which the verb 'to make' would apply." The prophet used the verb *bara*, "he created," because in Hebrew this verb is applied to non-existing things. *Bara*, thus, is the verb used in Genesis 1:1.[98]

Maimonides described four different theories of divine providence, in addition to Moses' view and his own. Thus, six in all. In the order he gave them, the first theory was that of Epicurus, which Maimonides summarized as follows: "There is no providence at all for anything in the

---

95. The English translation is from Maimonides, *The Guide for the Perplexed*. For a text-critical edition, see Maimonides, *Le Guide Des Égarés*. For Latin, see Maimonides, *Doctor Perplexorum*. For biography, see Heschel, *Maimonides*. See Levinson, whose notes on Deuteronomy tell of the approach of the Greek Septuagint which was to translate *Mishneh Torah* as *deuteronomion*, "Second Law." But "the Hebrew phrase *Mishneh Torah* is found in Deuteronomy's Law of the King, where it more properly means 'a copy of the law' (see 17.18n)," in Coogan, *The New Oxford Annotated Bible New Revised Standard Version with the Apocrypha*, 247.

96. Maimonides, *Guide for the Perplexed*, 449.

97. Maimonides, *Guide for the Perplexed*, 449.

98. Maimonides, *Guide for the Perplexed*, 448.

Universe." The universe owes its provenance "to accident and chance." There is no Ruler of the universe. Aristotle, said Maimonides, had "proved the absurdity of the theory" that there is no God who rules and governs the universe.[99]

The second theory was that of Aristotle. The upper part of the universe "owes its existence to Providence." God rules and governs it. The lower or sublunary part of the universe owes its existence to "chance."[100] When a leaf or stone falls, when a hurricane destroys trees and knocks down power lines, when gale force winds sink a ship and "the good and noble people" die, Aristotle attributed these movements to chance.[101] Maimonides said that Aristotle's views were associated with "his theory of the Eternity of the Universe, and with his opinion that everything different from the existing order of things in Nature is impossible." He showed that for Aristotle, "the Universe was inseparable from God; He is the cause, and the Universe the effect." For his part, Maimonides said, "We, however, hold that all things in the Universe are the result of design, and not merely of necessity."[102]

The third theory of providence, according to Maimonides, reversed the second. Nothing in the Universe is due to chance. No class of beings, no individual beings. "Everything is the result of will, intention, and rule." The Ruler of providence knows everything that is under his control. "The Mohammedan Ashariyah adhere to this theory, notwithstanding evident absurdities implied in it." A leaf does not fall, nor does a ship go down, but by God's divine decree and his timing. "It is not in the power of man to do a certain thing or to leave it undone." There is no possibility that things occur otherwise than they do. But at what cost? Maimonides said that the logical consequence is that "precepts are perfectly useless," since those who receive those commands cannot freely act upon them. Thus, commands, injunctions, and promises are rendered meaningless, without freedom. Of what use then for God "to send prophets, to command, to forbid, to promise, and to threaten," when people have "no power over their own actions?"[103] Here the Islamic sect of the Asha'ariyah would

---

99. Maimonides, *Guide for the Perplexed*, 473.

100. Maimonides, *Guide for the Perplexed*, 473.

101. Maimonides, *Guide for the Perplexed*, 474–75.

102. Maimonides, *Guide for the Perplexed*, 475. Cf. Maimonides's comments on Aristotle's theory of the motion of the spheres caused by natural laws and Aristotle's theory of the "Eternity of the Universe," 310–17, 318–20, 321–23.

103. Maimonides, *Guide for the Perplexed*, 475.

seemingly approve the ancient proverb, a proverb which God rejected, due to its fatalism, namely, "The parents have eaten sour grapes, and the children's teeth are set on edge" (Ezek 18:2).[104] The supporters of this theory said "It is the will of God" when a person is born blind or leprous.[105] If I were to take Augustine's maxim in the *Confessions*, this theory would twist it to say, "Command whatever you will,"—without God giving what he commands—by empowering the individual with grace to be able to comply.[106]

The fourth theory taught that "man has free will."[107] This theory makes sense when one considers divine commands and prohibitions, rewards and punishments. God acts wisely, justly, and "he does not inflict the good." This is the theory of the Islamic sect of the Mu'tazila, known as "the separatists." Contrary to the Asha'ariyah, they taught that "humans act according to the power which has been created in them."[108] But this power was from God, and thus humans do not have "absolute free will." Unlike Aristotle's theory, divine "providence extends over all things." When a leaf falls from a tree, God takes note of it. However, Maimonides saw "contradictions and absurdities" in this theory. For instance, birth defects were attributed to God's wisdom for those so born. Moreover, they held that it was not for us to question why God reasons that it was best that way. When pious persons are slaughtered, they have a greater reward in heaven. This applies to slaughtered animals as well.[109]

Maimonides had his own ideas as to why people followed these four theories. As for Aristotle, "the nature of things" guided him. In the third theory, "the Asha'ariyah refused to ascribe to God ignorance about anything."[110] In the fourth theory, "the Mu'tazilites refused to assume that God does what is wrong and unjust." But they contradicted themselves, holding that God knows everything and yet humans have free will.

---

104. Maimonides, *Guide for the Perplexed*, 191, 214. Maimonides says that the Mohammedan sect of the Asha'ariyah ascribed human action not to human power, but to God. For instance, the act of writing involved four acts, all of which God himself set in motion. I will to write, I have the power to write, I move my hand, the pen moves, and so I write.

105. Maimonides, *Guide for the Perplexed*, 476.
106. Augustine, *The Confessions*, 204.
107. Maimonides, *Guide for the Perplexed*, 476.
108. Maimonides, *Guide for the Perplexed*, 191, 215.
109. Maimonides, *Guide for the Perplexed*, 476.
110. Maimonides, *Guide for the Perplexed*, 476.

Maimonides had his own theory. But before explaining it, he turned to the fifth theory, that of Moses in the law and in the prophetical books.[111]

The fifth theory was "generally accepted by our sages," wrote Maimonides. It taught that "man's perfectly free will is one of the fundamental principles of the Law of our Teacher Moses." What did the theory teach? And why did Maimonides propose his own theory? The theory taught that a human being "does what is in his power to do, by his nature, his choice, and his will." But human action is not due to God having endowed humans with "any faculty created for the purpose." Even "irrational animals" move spontaneously by their own free will. It is God's eternal will "that all living beings should move freely." And what of a human being? God's will was that he or she "should have power to act according to his will or choice within the limits of his capacity." Crucially, "wrong cannot be ascribed to God in any way whatever." Whether evils or blessings, whether upon individuals or a community, God distributes and metes out his justice in strict fashion. The problem with human beings is that they cannot comprehend God's justice.[112]

Maimonides then summed up the theories. Everything among humans happens by chance (Aristotle), by God's will (the Ashariyah), by divine wisdom (Mu'tazilites), according to human merits ("our opinion," that is, the opinion of the Jewish law).[113] But what was Maimonides's opinion?

Maimonides said that his theory was not based on "demonstrative proof," but on his "conception of the spirit of the Divine Law, and the Prophets." He held that divine providence, both good and evil fortunes, extend only to individual human beings in "the sublunary portion of the universe," but not to individual members of other species, in agreement with Aristotle on the latter point. Thus, for Maimonides, that means that when a leaf falls to the ground, or a bug is squashed, these are not the result of divine providence, nor divine decree, nor "the will of God in that moment." These are "due entirely to chance, as taught by Aristotle."[114] Human beings benefit from the influence of the connection between "divine providence" and "divine intellect" upon them, endowing them with a rational intellect. "Divine Providence examines all their deeds in

---

111. Maimonides, *Guide for the Perplexed*, 476–77.
112. Maimonides, *Guide for the Perplexed*, 477.
113. Maimonides, *Guide for the Perplexed*, 477.
114. Maimonides, *Guide for the Perplexed*, 479.

order to reward or punish them."[115] A ship and cargo may go down in a storm, the roof of a house may cave in and harm those inside, as in the case of Job's family, all by chance. However, in Maimonides's view, "it is not due to chance" that the ship's crew boarded on such and such a day, nor is it by chance that a family chooses to stay inside during a storm. Those people's choices are "due to the will of God."[116] Again, the problem is that we human beings have difficulty understanding God's ways, which are higher than ours. Indeed we cannot understand them. But Maimonides reached this conclusion about distinguishing people from things, he said, by studying the prophets of the Hebrew Bible, where he saw that "Providence" was always "in relation to human beings."[117] One need look no further than the patriarchs Abraham, Isaac, and Jacob "for proof that Divine Providence extends to every man individually."[118] And one need look no further than the prophet Habakkuk for evidence that other species and living beings fall under providence only as described by Aristotle, above. Habakkuk mourned the collapse of the distinction between classes of living beings when he "perceived the victories of Nebuchadnezzar, the multitudes slain," saying, "O God, it is as if men were abandoned, neglected, and unprotected like fish and like worms of the earth." Men were no different than fish, than "crawling things that have no ruler over them" (Hab 1:14–15).[119] The prophet, however, said, "Hold on, I will not accept the abandonment of God's providence." No, the people who suffered such things "deserved all that befell them." It is for this reason that Habakkuk said, "'O Lord, Thou hast ordained them for judgment'" (Hab 1:12).[120] Any benefit of God's providence given to an *entire* species of animal, such as food and subsistence, differs from that given to *individuals* within a species.[121]

In concluding this chapter, Maimonides desired that the student thoroughly understand his theory. He ascribes no ignorance to God of anything, nor any weakness. "Divine Providence is related and closely connected with the intellect." God acts upon living beings in proportion

---

115. Maimonides, *Guide for the Perplexed*, 479.
116. Maimonides, *Guide for the Perplexed*, 479.
117. Maimonides, *Guide for the Perplexed*, 479.
118. Maimonides, *Guide for the Perplexed*, 480.
119. Maimonides, *Guide for the Perplexed*, 480.
120. Maimonides, *Guide for the Perplexed*, 480.
121. Maimonides, *Guide for the Perplexed*, 481.

to their intellectual capacity. Indeed, "Providence can only proceed from an intelligent being, from a being that is itself the most perfect Intellect." The other theories "either exaggerate Divine Providence or detract from it." To exaggerate is to confuse and deny reason. To deny that providence extends to individual human beings is to implicate God in absurdities. The latter "disturbs all social order, removes and destroys all the moral and intellectual virtues of man."[122]

Maimonides was not satisfied with leaving his theory as stated. He followed up with additional exposition in the next chapter. With Aristotle's theory in the *Nicomachean Ethics* in the background, Maimonides expounded upon the idea of God's divine influx upon the individual intellect, an idea that Christian scholastics will explore in the future. "The greater the share is which a person has obtained of this Divine influence, on account of both his physical predisposition and his training, the greater must also be the effect of Divine Providence upon him." Why is this the case? "The action of Divine Providence is proportional to the endowment of intellect." Thus, not all human beings are equal in this regard. "The greater the human perfection a person has attained, the greater the benefit he derives from Divine Providence."[123]

The above proposition plays a key role in explaining Maimonides's understanding of divine providence and why bad things happen to certain people. When one person escapes the deadly effects of a virus, and another perishes, the difference is not owed to one's physical condition, but rather to one's "degree of perfection." Some are nearer to God than others, and are therefore better protected. This he premised upon the biblical passage, "He will keep the feet of his saints, and the wicked shall be silent in darkness; for by strength shall no man prevail" (1 Sam 2:9). Philosophically reasoned, Maimonides proposed "that every person has his individual share of Divine Providence in proportion to his perfection." Again, he reasoned, thus, that the divine influx extended to individual human beings, not merely to a species, as the philosophers taught. This is because a species, as such, does not exist. "Only individual beings have real existence," and share in "Divine Providence" and in the "Divine Intellect."[124]

---

122. Maimonides, *Guide for the Perplexed*, 481–82.

123. Maimonides, *Guide for the Perplexed*, 483. Aristotle, *Nichomachean*, in *Basic Works*, 1108 (1179a23–33).

124. Maimonides, *Guide for the Perplexed*, 484–85.

How did Maimonides explain the different views on providence in the book of Job? Which opinion did Maimonides share? He said that the Book of Job itself appeared to take the position of Aristotle. Eliphaz took the position of strict justice, that Job deserved his fate. This was also the opinion of Scripture, said Maimonides. Bildad defended the position of reward and compensation for the truly innocent. Maimonides said that this opinion was widespread. It was also the opinion of the Mu'tazilah, discussed above. Zofar held that everything was the result of God's will. But who can fathom God's wisdom? This was the opinion of the Asha'riyah, discussed above.[125] The younger Elihu announced a new idea. Elihu held that the intercession of a heavenly being, an angel, can secure deliverance. Not always. But it was possible.[126] Maimonides concluded that God's ways were not our ways. His providence and intentions differed from ours. The principal lesson of the book of Job, he said, was to live by faith. Whatever befell us, if we lived by faith, we could bear our fate. In fact, "our fate will increase our love of God." Indeed, "'The pious do everything out of love, and rejoice in their own afflictions.'"[127] In sum, Maimonides believed that the object of God's will was what was possible, and what his wisdom decrees be done. "When God desires [wills] to produce the best work, no obstacle or hindrance intervenes between Him and that work." Creation itself, thus, was not by the mere will of God, but the wisdom of God, which we are unable to comprehend."[128] Profoundly articulated, Maimonides concluded that the one main obstacle that kept human beings from understanding the grand question, "What is my place in the Universe, and why do bad things happen to me?" is the "erroneous idea that man has of himself." Namely, "he believes that the whole world exists only for his sake." Secondly, and this proposition arguably led Maimonides down a path of necessitarianism, he said that human beings were "ignorant both about the nature of the sublunary world, and about the Creator's intention to give existence to all beings whose existence is possible, because existence is undoubtedly good."[129] Thus, everything that is in the state of possibility will in the end be realized.

---

125. Maimonides, *Guide for the Perplexed*, 502–03.

126. Maimonides, *Guide for the Perplexed*, 503–04.

127. Maimonides, *Guide for the Perplexed*, 505–06. The last quote cited by Maimonides is from the Babylonian Talmud, Tractate *Shabbat*, 88b.

128. Maimonides, *Guide for the Perplexed*, 514.

129. Maimonides, *Guide for the Perplexed*, 515.

While reading through Maimonides's *Guide for the Perplexed*, one observes how he interprets and adapts the teachings of Aristotle to what he considered to be the biblical doctrine of providence and its related issues of act, design, and will. Likewise, in the chapter dialogues below, a similar method and approach to Aristotle will be observed in the post-Reformation scholastic theologians. However, they have the advantage of building upon all the teaching and scholastic distinctions that have thus far been introduced. Maimonides's adaptation of Aristotle's theory of how God moves the Universe and how he moves upon human beings will be further developed by Christian scholastics in their theory of divine concurrence of the wills. Contrary to Aristotle's theory, as Maimonides conceived it, Protestant scholastics will devise different theories on how human beings act in ways that guard their free choice yet demonstrate their dependence upon God and his sovereign providential dealings with humans. Besides the doctrine of providence, there were other Aristotelian doctrines that Maimonides and the later scholastics took up and adapted in their theodicies and explanations of the divine-human concurrence of wills. For instance, the propositions that God is pure act, that there are "no moments of non-action, or of potentiality in any respect,"[130] that "everything produced comes into existence from non-existence," that things transition from "potentiality to reality,"[131] "that God's knowledge of future [and possible events] events does not change their character,"[132] that God's knowledge does not increase,[133] that "everything that passes over from a state of potentiality to that of actuality, is caused to do so by some external agent,"[134] "that God's knowledge of one or two eventualities does not determine it, however certain that knowledge may be,"[135] that "His knowledge and His essence are one and the same thing,"[136] that creation is *ex nihilo*, and has by God's "design and will come into existence."[137]

---

130. Maimonides, *Guide for the Perplexed*, 321.
131. Maimonides, *Guide for the Perplexed*, 302.
132. Maimonides, *Guide for the Perplexed*, 491.
133. Maimonides, *Guide for the Perplexed*, 490.
134. Maimonides, *Guide for the Perplexed*, 250.
135. Maimonides, *Guide for the Perplexed*, 491.
136. Maimonides, *Guide for the Perplexed*, 490.
137. Maimonides, *Guide for the Perplexed*, 323.

4. Jewish-Christian Disputations

The inclusion of medieval Jewish-Christian disputations in this introduction is admittedly an excursus. However, it serves the purpose of drawing attention to the broad interest in and public nature of disputations. This public interest helped shape what has been described as the culture of disputation in the universities. Moreover, the difference in approaches to these disputations by the Jews and the Christians reveals that the latter were accused of using scholastic syllogisms in debate and Greek philosophy when it came to defending, for instance, the impassability of God. The Christian approach can be contrasted with the Jewish debaters' reliance on the skill of interpretation of the Hebrew Bible and the Talmud.

There were three major medieval disputations. The Paris disputation of 1240, the Barcelona disputation of 1263, and the Tortosa disputation of 1413–14. Given the limitations of the present study, I will only introduce the Paris disputation. Furthermore, these disputations were not about the question of whether God is the author of evil, for both Jew and Christian would have defended God against such a charge. The themes of the three debates centered on whether Jesus was the Messiah and whether there were anti-Christian, even blasphemous, passages in the final redaction of the Talmud. In a very real sense, the Talmud was on trial, especially in Paris. What threat did the Talmud pose to Christians? The threat was that the authority of the Talmud to interpret Scripture was analogous to the authority of the church to interpret Scripture. Ironically, by offering critique upon the authority of the Talmud Christians were undermining the authority of the church to interpret Scripture. Maccoby has pointed out that the Christian argument, therefore, was that the Talmud, in its final redacted form, "had no right to exist."[138]

Any historical introduction to the development of a culture of disputation ought not neglect the Jewish-Christian debates, since they left us literary works and renditions that reveal the substance and climate of historical debates. The Rabbi Yehudah Halevi (1075–1141) wrote a literary rendition, *The Chozari*, otherwise known as *Kuzari*, of dialogues "loosely based" on earlier supposed historical dialogues between the ninth-century King Bulan of the Chazars of Central Asia and a Jewish scholar whom the king had appointed to teach him about the Jewish faith. Rabbi Chanan Morrison recently wrote that there was indeed a conversion of

---

138. Maccoby, *Judaism on Trial*, 19, 20.

the Chazar royals to Judaism in the eighth century.[139] Yehuda Halevi completed *The Chozari* in the year 1140 or 1141. The original subtitle was, *A Book of Argument and Demonstration in Aid of the Despised Faith*.

As to the chosen form of the book, the poet-philosopher Yehuda Halevi would have been well aware of the poetic dialogues and cycles of speeches in the book of Job. Yehuda Halevi likely chose a similar ancient form for his book and divided the cycles of speeches into five parts. In the prose prologue, he introduced the cycle of speeches that would took place. In part 1, the speeches begin with the request of the king for a philosopher to tell him how to properly worship God. Unfortunately, with a mix of Aristotelian and Neoplatonic teachings—the eternity of the world, its emanation from God, a chain of causes and beings, the unknowability of God and his inability to personally know individuals, union with the Active Intellect—the sage confused and disturbed the soul of the king even more.[140] Midway through part 1, the king invited a Christian as well as a Muslim into the debate. But the Christian had only one brief speech, whereas the Muslim had three brief speeches. Thereafter, the king invited a Jewish scholar to speak. The rabbi was loath to begin with logical premises, preferring rather to tell of God's covenant faithfulness to the patriarchs and self-revelation to his chosen people. Notably, the Christian and the Muslim gave no more speeches in the rest of the book.

The climate of the Jewish-Christian debates could be hostile. In his account of the June 25–27, 1240, public trial in Paris, Chaim Potok reminds us that in such an "enchanted land" and time as it was, "where a goose was a symbol of magic and a pig could be tried for murder, a book too could be brought to trial."[141] The book, of course, was the Talmud. Chaucer would later refer to "the cursed Jews" in his works "The Prioress's Tale," written sometime around the year 1387, and in "The Parson's Tale," the exact date of which is unknown.[142]

Let us consider the basis of the Paris disputation and then take a closer look at the Christian lines of attack on the Talmud—or rather on

---

139. Rabbi Morrison notes that what triggered Halevi to write the book were discussions "between the author and a Karaite philosopher in 1130," according to a letter by Yehuda Halevi found in "the Cairo Genizah," in Halevi, *The Kuzari*, preface.

140. A philosopher in Andalusia, Spain, whose teachings were similar to the philosopher in *The Chozari*, was Solomon Ibn Gabirol (ca. 1021–ca. 1058), according to Marenbon, *Medieval Philosophy*, 178–80.

141. Potok, *Wanderings*, 417.

142. Chaucer, *The Riverside Chaucer*, 209–12, 307.

"the whole library of books" that comprised the Talmud—the alleged "blasphemies" against the Christian faith as well as Christians themselves, the "unedifying material in the Talmud," and "obscene passages."[143] There was a certain Nicholas Donin, who was a former Talmudist from La Rochelle turned Christian. He appealed to Pope Gregory IX to have copies of the Talmud confiscated until a public disputation, or trial as the case would be, could take place and a determination of the affair be made. Donin charged that the Talmud itself was keeping Jews from accepting Jesus the Messiah.[144] In 1239, the pope sent a letter "to all the kings of Christendom, though the King of France, the pious Louis IX, was the only one who acted on it."[145] The pope wrote that there was no punishment to match the severity of the crime. The charge was that the Talmud had replaced the law of Moses. They alleged, wrote the pope, that the there was another Law given orally to Moses, a "Teaching" which later "Sages" and "Scribes" wrote down, called "Talmud." Given the unspeakable things recorded in the Talmud, the pope urged his "Royal Serenity" to confiscate the Jewish books "on the first Saturday of the Lent to come," while they are in synagogue, on his authority. "Our dear sons, the Dominican and Franciscan Friars," he wrote, would hold the books in their custody.[146]

But what unspeakable things led to substituting the mere suppression of the Talmud with hard censorship? What led to the burning of the Talmud two years after the Paris disputation? "On Friday, June 6, 1242, twenty-four wagonloads of Jewish books were publicly burned."[147] Graetz reports that the debate mainly proceeded upon two points, namely, whether the Talmud blasphemed and insulted the Deity and Jesus.[148] Maccoby describes how Donin alleged attacks in the Talmud on Jesus and Mary. In one passage, Jesus "was executed on Passover eve by stoning on a charge of seducing Israel to idolatry." In another, Jesus is "immersed in boiling excrement" in hell.[149] But was the Talmud reporting

143. Maccoby, *Judaism on Trial*, 20, 26, 34, 36.
144. Graetz, *History of the Jews*, 3.1416.
145. Maccoby, *Judaism on Trial*, 21.
146. Maccoby, *Judaism on Trial*, 21–22.
147. Potok, *Wanderings*, 417.
148. Graetz, *History of the Jews*, 3.1419.
149. Maccoby, *Judaism on Trial*, 26 (Babylonian Talmud, Tractate *Sanhedrin* 43a; Babylonian Talmud, Tractate *Gittin* 56b. Cited by Maccoby as b Sanh., 43a; b Gitt, 56b).

this about the first-century Christian Jesus the Messiah, or another Jesus? In another passage, Mary (Miriam, "the hairdresser"), whose husband was "Pappos ben Judah," allegedly had a lover whose name was "Pandira." Mary was thus "an adulteress" according to the Talmud. And Jesus, the son of Pandira, "was hanged in Lydda on the eve of Passover."[150] But was this Mariam the hairdresser Mary the mother of Jesus the Messiah, whose husband was Joseph?

As to blasphemies against God in the Talmud, the charge was that God was disrespected by anthropomorphic passages describing the passibility of God, God as feeling sorry, grieving, or even repenting of mistakes he had made with respect to his treatment of human beings.[151] Of significance to the historical and theological introduction to the rest of the book is indeed the influence of Greek philosophy in the development of the Christian doctrine of the impassibility of God. The Thirty-Nine Articles of the Church of England (1571) and the Westminster Confession of Faith (1647), for instance, both enshrined in their articles the teaching that God is "without body, parts, or passions (*impassibilis*). Westminster immediately adds that God is immutable (*immutabilis*)."[152] These and teachings akin to these will play an important role in the chapter dialogues below when theologians wish to make scholastic distinctions in order to explain how they exonerate God from the charge that he is implicated in the evil actions of human beings.

As to method, prior to the debate itself, Donin had formulated thirty-five articles, drawn from the Talmud, and charged the Talmud with "allegedly anti-Christian remarks," as well as blasphemy.[153] Transcripts of the charges were sent out ahead of the debate to church leaders in England, France, Castile, Aragon, and Portugal. But only in France were the Jews compelled to turn over their copies of the Talmud, three months before the debate.[154]

Donin debated four Jewish leaders who defended the Talmud. The debate was conducted in Latin and presided over by the archbishop of Sens, the bishop of Senlis, the king's chaplain, and the chancellor of the recently established University of Paris. Notably, according to Maccoby,

150. Maccoby, *Judaism on Trial*, 26, 156–57 (Babylonian Talmud, Tractate *Sanhedrin* 67a. Cited by Maccoby as b Sanh., 67a).
151. Maccoby, *Judaism on Trial*, 34.
152. Schaff, *Evangelical Protestant Creeds*, 486–87; 606.
153. Maccoby, *Judaism on Trial*, 25.
154. Graetz, *History of the Jews*, 3.1418.

the King of France did not preside at the Paris disputation. Graetz reports that "the wise queen-mother Blanche" of Castile was not only present, but likely headed up the trial.[155] Both nobles and churchmen were present.

The principal speaker for the Jews was the renowned Talmudist Rabbi Yechiel ben Joseph of Paris, who responded to the charges over the course of two days.[156] Appeal was made to Jerome and the early church fathers. He asserted that the Talmud's derogatory remarks about Jesus were about another Jesus, not Jesus of Nazareth. The commission determined that the Talmud was to be burned.

Novikoff gives us three concluding thoughts that I wish to convey as I bring this section to a close. First, although there was continuity of form with ancient debates, the culture of scholastic method and practice in the universities, in the education of Dominican preachers and of poets, introduced new forums for debate beyond the schools, in private audiences, and in the public square.[157] Second, there was a pedagogical function wedded to winning public opinion.[158] The public nature of the debates offered the opportunity to score exegetical points on biblical and hermeneutical issues in the presence of a wide and varied audience who could decide for themselves who had the upper hand in the debate to establish one's truth claims. The literary renditions of such debates, both real and fictional, further served the purpose of solidifying a base of opinion. Third, long before the drama surrounding the public disputation in June and July 1519 at Leipzig between the Dominican Johannes Eck (1486–1543) and Andreas Bodenstein Karlstadt (1480–1541), which was presided over by Duke George of Saxony—a public forum which served as a model for other cities to initiate reforms—the medieval art of disputation and debate served as theater not only before a public audience but also kings and queens.[159]

5. Reformation and Scholasticism

Infallibly, when I ask my students, "Who wrote *The Bondage of the Will*, 1525?" they answer, "Luther." But what most do not know is that Calvin

---

155. Graetz, *History of the Jews*, 1418.
156. Maccoby, *Judaism on Trial*, 21.
157. Novikoff, *The Medieval Culture of Disputation*, 218.
158. Novikoff, *The Medieval Culture of Disputation*, 219.
159. Novikoff, *The Medieval Culture of Disputation*, 220.

also wrote a book called *The Bondage and Liberation of the Will*, the first edition of which was published in Geneva in 1543.[160] Luther was writing in response to Erasmus of Rotterdam's *Diatribe Concerning Free Choice* (1524). Erasmus had been reacting to Luther's *Assertio* (1520).[161] Likewise, Calvin was writing in response to the Dutch Roman Catholic Albert Pighius's *Ten Books on Human Free Choice and Divine Grace* (1542), which Pighius wrote in reply to two chapters in Calvin's second edition of the *Institutes* (1539).[162] Chapters 2 and 8 of the *Institutes* concerned human free choice, and predestination and providence, respectively.

Erasmus of Rotterdam on Free Choice

Erasmus began his *Diatribe* with the claim that both Scripture and the church fathers opposed Luther. As a reaction to Luther's *Assertio*, Erasmus intended to offer a mediating view on free choice. He defined free choice (*liberum arbitrium*) from the book of Sirach (Ecclesiasticus) in terms of both before and after the fall. "It was he who created humankind in the beginning, and left them in the power of their own free choice. If you choose, you can keep the commandments, and to act faithfully is a matter of your own choice" (Sir 15:14–15). Erasmus noted that "by free choice in this place we mean a power of the human will by which a man can apply himself to the things which lead to eternal salvation, or turn away from them."[163] In the state of innocence at creation, Adam's will was, according to Erasmus, "so upright and free that, apart from new grace, he could continue in innocence but, apart from the help of new grace, he could not attain the happiness of eternal life which the Lord Jesus promised to his followers."[164]

But at the moment of the fall into sin, Eve's will and intellect was corrupted, and Adam's will and intellect were corrupted by his "immoderate love" for Eve. And although the human "mind" or "intellect"

---

160. Calvin, *The Bondage and Liberation of the Will*. For the best Latin edition, see Calvin, *Defensio sanae et orthodoxae doctrinae de servitute et liberatione humani arbitrii* (Pagination from the 1996 English edition).

161. Luther and Erasmus, *Luther and Erasmus*, 13; Luther, *Assertio*.

162. Pighius, *De Libero Hominis Arbitrio et Divina Gratia*.

163. "*Vim humanae voluntatis, qua se possit homo applicare ad ea quae perducant ad aeternam salutem, aut ad iisdem avertere*," in Luther and Erasmus, *Luther and Erasmus*, 47.

164. Luther and Erasmus, *Luther and Erasmus*, 48.

was "obscured by sin," it was "not altogether extinguished."[165] As for "the will by which we choose or refuse," it was thus "so far depraved that by its natural powers it could not amend its ways, but once its liberty had been lost, it was compelled to serve that sin to which it had once for all consented."[166] Erasmus appealed to the orthodox fathers who said that "it was possible for man, with the help of divine grace, which always accompanies human effort, to continue in the right, yet not without a tendency to sin, owing to the vestiges of original sin, this tendency has passed to all."[167]

What did Erasmus conclude from the above points about the fall? He believed that there was, nevertheless, a "native light implanted in all humans."[168] He therefore proposed three kinds of laws. First, there was "the law of nature" (Rom 1:19, 20). The will was ready to will the good, but powerless to attain it and salvation.[169] Second, there was "the law of works," that is, commands and threats (Gen 2:16, 17). Even so, he concluded that "We cannot perform them without grace."[170] Third, there was "the law of faith." Grace comes in and makes the impossible possible and agreeable to us. For instance, with grace, we can "love our enemies," faith can "cure reason," and love can "bear the weak will along."[171]

The law of faith, Erasmus continued, applied to Adam and Eve, whom he said represented the Jewish people. "If the will had not been free, sin could not have been imputed." Indeed, Sirach 15:15, 16 applied not only to Adam and Eve, but also in a certain sense to all posterity. Free choice is "lame," more inclined to evil than good, yet not completely. But human beings have become accustomed to crime. "The enormity of crimes have become second nature to us, clouding judgment, overwhelming freedom of the will." Thus it seems as if free choice and free will are completely lost, but they are not.[172]

Erasmus then asked about the state of unregenerated people after the fall. He gave three opinions. First, Pelagius taught that once forgiven

---

165. Luther and Erasmus, *Luther and Erasmus*, 48.
166. Luther and Erasmus, *Luther and Erasmus*, 48–49.
167. Luther and Erasmus, *Luther and Erasmus*, 49.
168. Luther and Erasmus, *Luther and Erasmus*, 49.
169. Luther and Erasmus, *Luther and Erasmus*, 49.
170. Luther and Erasmus, *Luther and Erasmus*, 49–50.
171. Luther and Erasmus, *Luther and Erasmus*, 50.
172. Luther and Erasmus, *Luther and Erasmus*, 50–51.

and changed by grace, there was no need for new grace. The human will could attain salvation. Yet, admittedly, the power of the soul was a gift from God.[173] Second, Augustine taught that a human being could not change his or her life by his or her "own powers." The free gift of God must move him or her "to desire" eternal life. This gift Augustine called "operative grace." In addition to this, when free choice and grace work along with the gift of love by the Spirit, Augustine called it "cooperative grace."[174] Third, John Duns Scotus taught that by one's "own natural powers" and the power of free choice a human being could perform "morally good works" that "congruously" merit and thus make the effort acceptable in God's eyes.[175] The much debated proposal in Luther's *Romans Commentary* was whether in any state before or after the fall, one could love God above all else (*super omnia*) "by one's own natural powers (*naturaliter*)."[176] I shall return to the issue of "natural powers" below when I discuss Luther's reply to Erasmus.

Erasmus then sketches three kinds of grace. First, there is "common grace," which is "implanted by nature, vitiated by sin, but not extinguished." Second, there is "peculiar grace," which means that "God in his mercy arouses the sinner, who is wholly without merit to repent, yet without infusing that supreme grace which abolishes sin and makes him pleasing to God."[177] This second "operative grace" or "stimulating grace" assists the sinner, who in turn "behaves like a candidate for the highest grace." This second grace "is not denied to anyone." Human beings can put their powers of free choice "at the disposal" of God's will. God "invites but does not constrain." They can "apply their wills to grace, or turn away from it." Third, there is "cooperating grace" that makes the will effective. The third grace is a "completing grace that carries things to a conclusion." In sum, "the first arouses, the second promotes, the third completes."[178]

Some people attribute all to grace and almost nothing to free choice. Erasmus finds this hard view "probable enough," but still lacking. The "harder" opinion says that "free choice is of no avail save to sin." Try as they may, humans can only sin. "Grace alone accomplishes good works in

---

173. Luther and Erasmus, *Luther and Erasmus*, 51.
174. Luther and Erasmus, *Luther and Erasmus*, 52.
175. Luther and Erasmus, *Luther and Erasmus*, 51.
176. Luther and Erasmus, *Luther and Erasmus*, 51–52.
177. Luther and Erasmus, *Luther and Erasmus*, 52.
178. Luther and Erasmus, *Luther and Erasmus*, 53.

us, not by or with free choice but in free choice."[179] In this view, humans are clay in the Potter's hand. Erasmus says that in this opinion, by avoiding one mistake, namely, merit, one makes matters worse. The "hardest" view says that "free choice is an empty name," a fiction. But this view attributes all human action to God and implies that God works "evil as well as good in us." In this view, all things happen "by sheer necessity." Erasmus concludes that his "dispute" will be with "the two last positions."[180]

Does God's Foreknowledge Impose Necessity on Our Will?

Erasmus explains that human "prescience is not the cause of things which happen." We foreknow things because they are going to happen. "Eclipses of the sun do not happen because Astrologers predict them." It is the other way around. But God's will and the determination of God's will is more difficult to explain, Erasmus admits. "For God to will and foreknow are the same thing." Even so, Erasmus sees no way to escape the conclusion that "God wills what he foreknows as future, and that which he does not hinder, though it is in his power to do so."[181] In the first half of the proposal, Erasmus seems to prioritize foreseen human action above the divine will. Indeed, the difficulty for Erasmus is the implication that foreseen human action determines God's will as much as God himself. Perhaps he envisions a kind of coordination and concurrence of divine and human wills. The second half of Erasmus's proposal seems to accept a permissive willing on God's part. "That which God does not hinder," he permits. But does Erasmus uncouple God's will from this permission? From the language, there appears to be a distinction between the power to will and willing itself. God has the power to hinder evil or apostasy, but he does not exercise his will to do so. Thus, God allows it. If applied to evil deeds (Judas's falling away, for instance), then Erasmus appears to hold that although it is in his power to do so, God does not hinder these things.

A stronger conception would be to say that God *wills* to allow these things, as we saw above with Peter Lombard. At times Erasmus seems to agree that God wills everything and at other times he appears to favor the notion of what God *intends* to do. Thus, to be fair to Erasmus, he

---

179. Luther and Erasmus, *Luther and Erasmus*, 53.
180. Luther and Erasmus, *Luther and Erasmus*, 54.
181. Luther and Erasmus, *Luther and Erasmus*, 66.

probably means that in all situations, good or bad, God's will does not violate nor exclude human freedom. Erasmus then questions the proposition that "the will of God, since it is the principal cause of all things that take place, seems to impose necessity on our will." He points out that not even Paul resolves the question of the apparent imposition of God's will. Paul "rebukes the impious complainer" in Romans 9:20. Now with an emphasis on the divine will, Erasmus points out that "God willed Pharaoh to perish miserably . . . Yet he was not forced by the will of God to be obstinately wicked."[182] Erasmus explains such obstinacy by adding that God wills according to foreseen obstinate behavior and inclination to sin. In this explanation, Erasmus once again makes known that his position on whether God's will unduly imposes necessity on our will is that it does not. This is because God wills according to what he sees is already in the human heart. Thus, once again, foreseen human action appears to determine God's will.

The scholastics made distinctions and applied linguistic tools in order to remove the implication of the imposition of an absolute necessity on the human will and at the same time to save both God's sovereignty and human free choice. To protect his understanding of God's will from attack, Erasmus made the classic distinction between God's "hidden will," on the one hand, and God's "ordained will" or "will signified," that is, God's revealed will, on the other. The former, "none can resist." The latter "men often resist." An example of the former is the crucifixion of Jesus the Messiah. Of the latter, Erasmus gave the instance of Jerusalem resisting gathering together, from Jesus' famous words, "Jerusalem, Jerusalem, How often have I desired to gather your children together . . . But you were not willing!" (Matt 23:37).[183]

In order to support his position that "not all necessity excludes free will," Erasmus reminds the reader that "God the Father necessarily begets the Son, and yet begets him freely and willingly."[184] This rule applies to "human affairs" as well. "God foreknew that Judas would betray the Lord." But God's "infallible" foreknowledge did not impose necessity on Judas. Though God's will was "immutable," Judas was "free to change his intention." And if he had changed his intention, God would have known that, too.

---

182. Luther and Erasmus, *Luther and Erasmus*, 67.
183. Luther and Erasmus, *Luther and Erasmus*, 68.
184. Luther and Erasmus, *Luther and Erasmus*, 68.

How did Erasmus escape the charge that had Judas changed his mind, it would appear that God's infallible foreknowledge had failed, and God's immutable will had been thwarted? Erasmus answered that had Judas changed his mind, this would have been God's intention all along. To explain further, Erasmus, somewhat reluctantly, drew on the classic scholastic distinction between two kinds of necessity, the "necessity of consequence" (*necessitas consequentiae*) and the "necessity of the consequent" (*necessitas consequentis*).[185] According to the former, Necessarily, if God wills that Judas betray him, Judas will betray him, as a consequence of God's will. Given the wording of the whole proposition, Judas's betrayal was implied in the "if-then" proposition. But Judas's act of betrayal is only a mere implicative and inferential act of necessity. That is, there was nothing necessary about the act of betrayal itself such that it had to happen, unconditionally, and thus God had to decree it as such.

The notions of infallibility and immutability only apply to the "if-then" proposition as a whole, not exclusively to the second part, which is called the apodosis. As Erasmus put it, in the case of the necessity of consequence, scholastics "deny that it follows that Judas therefore betrayed necessarily, since this wicked business originated in a perverse will."[186] Note that the placement of the necessity operator, the adverb "necessarily," was placed at the end of the proposition. That would represent the case of the necessity of the consequent, an absolute necessity, such that Judas betrays Jesus necessarily, apart from any conditions, apart from consideration of the proposition as a whole.

In part 2, we shall see many instances of post-Reformation scholastic argumentation using these scholastic distinctions and others. But for Erasmus, he quickly passes over this twofold necessity and summarizes his position as one of divine concurrence with all human action. Any "malice of action" comes from the human will. Even so, Erasmus even entertained the thought of some who taught that in some cases "God can be said in some sense to cause a malice of will in us, letting it go where it wills, without recalling it by his grace."[187]

---

185. Luther and Erasmus, *Luther and Erasmus*, 68.
186. Luther and Erasmus, *Luther and Erasmus*, 68.
187. Luther and Erasmus, *Luther and Erasmus*, 69.

Erasmus's Mediating View

To sum up Erasmus's position, although the human will is not powerless, it cannot attain the good without grace. To use his example, a sailor safely sails a ship into port out of a storm, and rightly says, "God saved the ship and crew, not I."[188] He then asked how one is to interpret Paul, "For God is at work in us, both to will and to work for his good pleasure" (Phil 2:13). Was Paul referring to our good pleasure or God's good pleasure? Ambrose, said Erasmus, rightly interpreted it to mean that God works in us for our good pleasure. Thus, our good will "cooperates" with the action of God's grace.[189] Erasmus also asks, "What is merit without free choice?" Of course, he argues, we owe our power of free choice to God. What do we have that we have not received? "Yet God himself imputes this to our merit, that we do not turn our soul away from his grace, and that we apply our natural powers to simple obedience."[190]

Erasmus concludes that the advantage of his "mediating view" is that it "attributes entirely to grace the first impulse which stirs the soul," yet allows room for human choice that has not "withdrawn itself from the grace of God." He sees three stages in this affair, "beginning, progress, and end." The first and last stages are all of grace. But in the middle there must be room for human achievement and therefore a concurrence of divine and human willing.[191]

To illustrate this, Erasmus gave two parables at the end of his epilogue. The sound human eye sees nothing in the dark. A blind man sees nothing in the light. After the fall, the eye's sight is vitiated by sin. If now I see, I cannot boast. Yet, I see, thanks to my Creator, thanks to a physician. And when exercising prudence, I avert my eyes from evil when necessary. Is there not merit in this? Likewise, a young child who cannot yet walk on his own can be helped by his father to walk, to take an apple from a tree, and to eat it. The child cannot boast, yet he has done something. The child relies on the Father to lift him. The child does not resist, but accommodates the Father's gracious assistance. God works this way with us.[192]

---

188. Luther and Erasmus, *Luther and Erasmus*, 79.
189. Luther and Erasmus, *Luther and Erasmus*, 81.
190. Luther and Erasmus, *Luther and Erasmus*, 84.
191. Luther and Erasmus, *Luther and Erasmus*, 90.
192. Luther and Erasmus, *Luther and Erasmus*, 91.

Martin Luther on Free Choice

In his review of Erasmus's preface, Luther summed up the issue of free choice in terms of the two halves of the Christian *summa*. The first half deals with "knowledge of oneself and the knowledge and glory of God." The second half deals with "knowing whether God foreknows anything contingently, and whether we do everything of necessity."[193] Notably, John Calvin would begin his *Institutes* with the Christian *summa*, writing, "Nearly all the wisdom we possess, that is to say, true and sound wisdom, consists of two parts: the knowledge of God and ourselves."[194] So too would Jonathan Edwards write in the preface to his *Freedom of the Will* (1754), "Of all kinds of knowledge that we can ever obtain, the knowledge of God, and the knowledge of ourselves, are the most important."[195]

Concerning the second half of the *summa*, Luther answered, "God foreknows nothing contingently, but that he foresees and purposes and does all things by his immutable, eternal, and infallible will. Here is a thunderbolt by which free choice is completely prostrated and shattered."[196] Luther's starting point was that God is immutably just, good, and merciful, by nature. And this he extends to God's other attributes, his knowledge, wisdom, and will. For Luther, God's "will is eternal and unchanging, because that is its nature."[197] That is, God is necessarily who he is by nature. Therefore the goodness he wills towards his works *ad extra* also is necessary. In other words, the attributes of God are necessary and so are God's works that he wills *ad extra*. Notably, we shall see below that this also is the starting point of Calvin in his debate with Pighius. For Luther, "it follows irrefutably that everything we do, everything that happens, even if it seems to us to happen mutably and contingently, happens in fact nonetheless necessarily and immutably, if you have regard to the will of God."[198] Luther alerts the reader to the misuse of the Latin term "contingently" when applied to God's acts. For to speak of God acting contingently would wrongly imply that God's will itself is contingent and mutable. But nothing can hinder God's will. Therefore, it is not contingent and mutable.

193. Luther and Erasmus, *Luther and Erasmus*, 117.
194. Calvin, *Institutes*, 1:35 (1.1.1).
195. Edwards, *Freedom of the Will*, 133.
196. Luther and Erasmus, *Luther and Erasmus*, 118.
197. Luther and Erasmus, *Luther and Erasmus*, 119.
198. Luther and Erasmus, *Luther and Erasmus*, 119.

Luther also raised concerns about how people understand the term "necessarily." It implies that God and humans act "under compulsion." But both the "divine and human will" act from "sheer pleasure or desire, as with true freedom." God is not compelled to be good. Ironically, Luther cannot think otherwise than that the fundamental meaning of necessity must be that things cannot be otherwise than they are. For he adds, "And yet the will of God is immutable and infallible, and it governs our mutable will, as Boethius sings: 'Remaining fixed, Thou makest all things move.'"[199]

Luther takes up the two kinds of necessity of which Erasmus spoke, "the necessity of consequence" and "the necessity of the consequent." He dismissively summarizes what the Sophists (by which he means scholastics) have to say, namely, "that everything happens necessarily, though by the necessity of consequence and not by the necessity of the consequent." According to Luther, by necessity of consequence the scholastics mean, "If God wills anything, it is necessary for that thing to come to pass, but it is not necessary that the thing which comes to pass should exist; for God alone exists necessarily, and it is possible for everything else not to exist if God so wills." Thus, according to Luther, the opinion of the scholastics is that "an action of God is necessary if he wills it, but that the thing done is not itself necessary."[200] In this Luther sees no more than a distinction between God who alone exists necessarily, on the one hand, and that whatever is done, is not self-existent, on the other. But this is obvious, he thinks. For Luther, the scholastic distinction amounts to no more than this: "All things are indeed brought about necessarily, but when they have thus been brought about, they are not God himself."[201]

For Luther, the necessity of consequence is a figment of the scholastics' imagination. Take Judas, for instance, he says. Given God's foreknowledge, Judas had no power in him to do otherwise than he did.[202] Whether Judas betrayed Jesus or not, "whichever God has foreknown will necessarily come about." By refusing to see any meaningful distinction between the necessity of consequence and the necessity of the consequent, Luther thought he was protecting God from the accusation that he might otherwise be mistaken. And he thought that the scholastics

---

199. Luther and Erasmus, *Luther and Erasmus*, 120.
200. Luther and Erasmus, *Luther and Erasmus*, 120.
201. Luther and Erasmus, *Luther and Erasmus*, 121.
202. Luther and Erasmus, *Luther and Erasmus*, 240.

wrongly consoled themselves with the belief that Judas could have acted differently. Thus, for Luther, Judas betrayed Jesus, and necessarily so, given God's foreknowledge of what Judas would do. As we have seen, Luther's teaching that equated God's knowledge with God's will teaching did not allow for God to know of any other possibility than that Judas would betray Jesus.[203]

In sum, Luther's doctrine of God is knowledge-based. That is, God's knowledge of what will happen in this world implies that what will happen will happen without distinction between whether it happens with absolute necessity or hypothetical necessity. Luther collapses the distinction between the kinds of necessity discussed above. For him, God's knowledge does not comprise all things that God can possibly do but does not will to do. God is thus all-willing (omnivolent).

Melanchthon and Calvin on Necessity of Consequence

At this point, a brief excursus on where Melanchthon and Calvin stood on the distinction between necessity of consequence and the necessity of the consequent will be instructive. Notably, Philip Melanchthon (1497–1560) changed his mind about the contingency of things between the 1521 edition of the *Loci Communes* and the 1535 edition. In 1521, he denied contingency.

> The fact that the idea concerning predestination commonly seems rather harsh we owe to that godless theology of the Sophists which has so impressed on us the contingency of things and the freedom of our will (*voluntas*) that our tender little ears revolt at the truth of Scripture.[204]

But in 1535, Melanchthon sang a different tune about the contingency of things. He said that "contingency is to be defended lest we make God to be the author or cause of sin."[205] He affirmed the distinction between "the necessity of the consequent" and "necessity of consequence." The former is an "absolute necessity" such that "it is necessary that God exists, that God is good, and just." The latter is not. For instance, he went

---

203. Luther and Erasmus, *Luther and Erasmus*, 248.

204. Melanchthon, *Melanchthon and Bucer*, 26.

205. "*Ideo defendenda est contingentia, ne Deum faciamus autorem seu causam peccatia,*" in Melanchthon, *Loci Communes* (1535), 73. For a fuller treatment, see Vos, "Philip Melanchthon on Freedom and Will."

on to explain that "it was fitting that Jerusalem be destroyed," not that there was something "in its nature" that made it necessary. That Jerusalem be destroyed was a consequence of God's decree. "After the decree it was an immutable" fact that it would be destroyed. But did Melanchthon stipulate that these immutable facts were contingent? In 1535, indeed he did. He continued, "These things are contingent by nature." But did Melanchthon believe that the immutability of God's decree could be reconciled with human freedom of the will? Indeed he did. He continued, "for neither do these consequences remove or violate freedom of the will."[206]

In the 1546 edition of his *Loci Communes*, Melanchthon wrote more extensively about the necessity of consequence. "These are propositions which by nature can be otherwise than they are, but which nevertheless come about of necessity, either on account of preceding causes or because they are determined."[207] For instance, he wrote that "Pharaoh's pursuit of the Israelites was not necessary in and of itself, but, in fact, was contingent. That the opposite come about was not impossible." What came about, he said, was an instance of "necessity of consequence."[208]

John Calvin also distinguished between different kinds of necessity. For instance, he affirmed that the prophecy (John 19:36) that the bones of Christ would not be broken was a relative necessity (*necessitas secundum quid*) in relation to the prophecy, not an absolute necessity.[209]

In his review of Erasmus's definition of free choice, Luther reminds the reader that "free choice properly belongs to no one but God alone." Although "some measure" of free choice belongs to human beings, "strictly speaking," when people hear the term "free choice" they understand "that which can do and does, in relation to God, whatever it

206. "*Caeterum illa distinctio necessaria est. Necessitas alia est consequentis seu absoluta, qualis est haec, necesse est Deum esse, Deum esse bonum, justus. Alia est consequentiae, ut oportet everti Hierosolymam. Haec non sunt natura sua necessaria, sed fiunt immutabilia postquam decreta sunt . . . Haec sunt natura contingentia. Neque enim haec consequentia libertatem voluntatis tollit*," in Melanchthon, *Loci Communes* (1535), 73.

207. "*Sed alia est necessitas consequentiae, quae est earum rerum, aut propositionum quae possent se natura sua aliter habere, sed fiunt necessariae, vel propter praecedentes causas, vel quia determinatae sunt*," in Melanchthon, *Loci Communes* (1546), 82.

208. "*Sic fit necessaria, Pharao persequetur Israëllitas. haec non est sua natura necessaria, sed revera contingens. Ac fieri oppositisitum, non esset impossibile: sed quia sic evenit, dicitur necessaria, necessitate consequentiae*," in Melanchthon, *Loci Communes* (1546), 82.

209. Calvin, *Eternal Predestination of God*, 170. See too Calvin, *Institutes*, 210 (1.16.9). For a fuller discussion, see Fisk, *Edwards's Turn*, 327-29.

pleases, uninhibited by any law or any sovereign authority." But human beings "live under the absolute sovereignty of God"; they therefore do not have free choice in this sense.[210] "On the authority of Erasmus," writes Luther, "free choice is a power of the will that is able of itself to will and unwill the word and work of God, by which it is led to those things which exceed both its grasp and its perception. But if it can will and unwill, it can also love and hate, and thus it can also in some small degree do the works of the law and believe the gospel." But if the human will has such powers, "what is left to grace and the Holy Spirit?" asks Luther. Erasmus, thus, "attributes divinity to free choice." But these powers belong to God alone.[211]

Luther mocked Erasmus by asking whether free choice can "move itself by its own power" and apply itself to things eternal. What a "truly novel" and unprecedented idea. Luther replied that "far more tolerable" was Peter Lombard, who taught that "free choice is the capacity for discerning and then also choosing the good if grace is present, but evil if grace is absent." Against Erasmus, Luther said that Augustine and Lombard taught that "free choice by its own power alone can do nothing but fall." Indeed, said Luther, Augustine had said that free choice was "enslaved."[212]

Luther and Scotus on Loving God above All Else by One's Own Powers

In the introduction to his chapter on "The Dignity of Man," Paul Oskar Kristeller noted the complexities of defining Renaissance thought about perennial issues concerning human beings in the years from 1350–1600. There is at least, he said, one "core truth" in the view that "Renaissance thought was more 'human' and more secular, although not necessarily less religious, than medieval thought." Both Renaissance and Reformation thinkers concerned themselves with "the problems of free will, fate, and predestination," problems which were "intimately connected with the concept of man."[213] Kristeller noted that the "Oration" composed in 1486 by Pico della Mirandola (1463–94), but published posthumously, spoke

210. Luther and Erasmus, *Luther and Erasmus*, 170.
211. Luther and Erasmus, *Luther and Erasmus*, 173.
212. Luther and Erasmus, *Luther and Erasmus*, 174.
213. Kristeller, *Renaissance Thought*, 167–68.

of the gifts with which the Creator endowed man. His nature was neither "celestial nor earthly, neither mortal nor immortal. On the contrary, he may become all of this through his own will," that is, naturally. Human nature had "the germs of every sort of life." He possessed "all possibilities within himself."[214] Even so, Kristeller pointed out that by saying this, Pico did not deny the need for teaching on grace and predestination. Notably, the state in question of the first human being was one of initial creation, before the fall.[215]

Heiko Oberman noted that in the view of those scholars who followed Kristeller, they preferred to include the later Middle Ages in "Renaissance" studies. Their view sought "to overcome the misconception of a programmatic opposition between scholasticism and Renaissance humanism." Oberman noted "the connections" and "rivalries" between "Renaissance humanism and nominalism."[216] In *The Harvest of Medieval Theology*, Oberman examined the teaching of the nominalist Gabriel Biel (ca. 1420–95), who came in for critique by Luther in his *Romans Commentary* on the issue of whether one can love God above all else by one's natural powers. His study examined Biel's teaching on the term *ex puribus naturalibus* and the question "What are man's intellectual and moral powers in this state of 'pure' nature?" The answer was that in the pure created condition, thus before the fall, the intellect innately knows the difference between good and evil and "the will is able to conform to this judgment and elicit a morally good act." The will does "what it is able to do" thereby readying itself to receive grace.[217] Even after the fall, "the liberty of the will to choose freely between good and evil" was not diminished. Only the "ease with which good acts are elicited" was diminished. Grace merely facilitated the acts of the will.[218] For Biel, human beings did not elicit acts alone, but always with God's general concurrence. In this way one must nuance what Biel was saying about human beings who elicited acts with their own natural powers. The "general influence of God," as opposed to a specific, or as later Reformed theologians would say, a "previous concurrence," implied for Biel that much room was given to human beings to act "more completely" under *their own powers*, as

214. Kristeller, *Renaissance Thought*, 174.
215. Kristeller, *Renaissance Thought*, 175.
216. Oberman, *Harvest of Medieval Theology*, vii.
217. Oberman, *Harvest of Medieval Theology*, 48.
218. Oberman, *Harvest of Medieval Theology*, 49.

opposed to those who acted with the help of divine grace.[219] For Luther, with his predilection for building up a biblical theology, Paul made it clear that his teaching, "I can will what is right, but I cannot do it" (Rom 7:18), in no way implied that anyone could elicit an act of the will and accomplish it.[220]

Before turning to Luther and Scotus and their different contexts (medieval and Renaissance) and thus different understanding of the words "nature," "natural," and "naturally," and the meaning of "by one's own powers," it will be helpful to conduct a brief word study. Lewis and Short stated that the classical meaning of *natura* speaks "of character, nature, natural disposition, inclination, bent, temper, character."[221] In his *Studies in Words*, C. S. Lewis conducted an extensive study of the word "nature." He noted that if Julius Caesar asked what the land of the Belgians was like, he was asking about the land's *natura*.[222] Likewise, "Cicero's title *De Natura Deorum* could be translated 'What the gods are like.'" And Horace spoke of "*humana natura*." A species had a nature, but so too an individual. "Cicero said that '*omnis natura* strives to preserve itself.'" Indeed, the idea of one's *natura* gets at its "'innate' character."[223]

Lewis noted that the Greek word *phusis* could also perform like the word *natura* and mean "character or 'description.'"[224] Aristotle defined *phusis* "as that which has in itself a principle of change."[225] With this understanding of *phusis* and *natura* came the Christian medieval understanding of laws that were immutable, yet dependent upon God, and God who was immutable and self-existent, God who is the Creator.[226] With this meaning we come closer to the medieval understanding of *natura*. Lewis noted the difference between nature and grace, that human nature was "man as he is of himself," which was to be contrasted with "man as he can become by moral effort" and with "man as he can become refashioned by divine grace." In John Bunyan's *Pilgrim's Progress*, Christiana

---

219. Oberman, *Harvest of Medieval Theology*, 50.
220. Luther, *Lectures on Romans*, xlix. See too l, li on Luther's attacks on Biel.
221. Lewis and Short, "Natura."
222. Lewis, *Studies in Words*, 24.
223. Lewis, *Studies in Words*, 25.
224. Lewis, *Studies in Words*, 34.
225. Lewis, *Studies in Words*, 39. Latin text: Aristotle, *Metaphysics*, in *Basic Works*, 861 (1064a30).
226. Lewis, *Studies in Words*, 39.

said, "The loss of my husband came into my mind, at which I was heartily grieved; but all that was but *natural affection*."²²⁷

In his *Lexicon Theologicum*, Johannes Altenstaig (ca. 1460–1525) noted that there were different ways to understand *natura* in medieval times. Citing Saint Bonaventure (1221–74), who in turn cited Peter Lombard, he noted that one kind of *natura* was "something that is naturally; for instance, a property that exists naturally."²²⁸ Altenstaig noted that Bonaventure referred to Lombard's *Sentences* and the example of the soul which "naturally has intellect and ingenuity and will."²²⁹ Another kind of *natura* referred to all things that "exist naturally" with God as their author, all good things, that is. And yet another kind referred to "all things which do not deprive a nature of the good."²³⁰

In their glossary for the treatise of Scotus on *God and Creatures*, Felix Alluntis and Allan Wolter noted that to act "naturally" was to act according to one's nature. The terms "natural, naturally" meant "whatever is in accord with the nature or essence of a thing." These terms speak of an agent acting "without deliberation and in a manner determined by the nature of the agent." Crucially, even though an agent essentially acts freely, *naturaliter* is such that "a measure of natural determinism accompanies the rational self-determination on the part of the will."²³¹ Here we see that the notion of freedom in terms of rational self-determinism is logically compatible with being *naturally* determined. This is because for Scotus the will elicits an act freely. Nevertheless, "the will is rational in that it has an inborn inclination to act in accord with right reason."²³²

Notably, the inclination to act differs from eliciting an act. How then are we to understand the inclination of the will? Following Anselm, Scotus made a distinction between "affection for justice" (*affectio justitiae*) and "affection for the advantageous" (*affectio commodi*). This distinction will help us better understand what Scotus meant by one's power to love God above all else. It also will help us better understand the medieval as

---

227. Lewis, *Studies in Words*, 53. Emphasis mine.

228. "*Uno modo natura dicitur res quae naturaliter est, vel proprietas quae naturaliter inest*," in Altenstaig, *Lexicon Theologicum*, 205.

229. Lombard, *On Creation*, 187. Latin source for Bonaventure citing Lombard's *Sentences*: Altenstaig, *Lexicon Theologicum*, 205.

230. Lombard, *On Creation*, 188. Latin source: Altenstaig, *Lexicon Theologicum*, 205.

231. Scotus, *God and Creatures*, 522–23.

232. Scotus, *God and Creatures*, 523–24.

opposed to the Renaissance humanist meaning of the term "natural." God endowed human beings with a will that has a twofold disposition. There is in the will as it were an *affection for justice* that is not only acquired but is an "innate justice." It implies a "congenital liberty" given in creation whereby one wills the good for what it is, not for oneself. *Affection for the advantageous* is oriented towards oneself: what is good for me.[233]

Scotus argued that "to love something for its own sake" is a more giving act and "a freer act than is desiring that object for oneself." This kind of act properly belongs to the will. There is a sense here in which the will is "the seat of innate justice."[234] Scotus nuanced different meanings of a so-called "natural will." In one sense, the *natural will* is not a will, nor is a "natural volition" a true volition.[235] In another sense, the *natural will* is the will in its "natural state," without the added "gifts of grace." In still another sense, the *natural will* is that which acts according to its natural inclination or disposition to seek "its own advantage." In this sense, "the will is free insofar as it lies in its power to elicit an act opposed to his inclination." Without this power to will the opposite of that to which it is naturally inclined, the will is not truly free. "I concede that every will is in control or master of its own act," concluded Scotus. He then nuances what he means by the inclination of a *natural will* as such, which in fact he says is not a genuine will, nor a "potency." The inclination is passive; its potency has a "tendency towards its proper perfection," not an "inclination to act." Formally speaking, therefore, he concludes that the *natural will* "is neither a power nor a will, but rather an inclination of the will, being a tendency by which it tends passively to receive what perfects it."[236] The created human nature necessarily seeks its own perfection.[237]

In his *Lectures on Romans* (1515–16), Luther taught that "it is sheer madness to say that man can love God above everything by his own powers."[238] To whom was he responding? Wilhelm Pauck pointed to Duns Scotus, a medieval theologian, and Biel, a Renaissance nominalist theologian. Luther asked these "pig-theologians" to "give proof of what

---

233. Scotus, *Will and Morality*, 153.
234. Scotus, *Will and Morality*, 153.
235. Scotus, *Will and Morality*, 155.
236. Scotus, *Will and Morality*, 155.
237. Scotus, *Will and Morality*, 156.

238. Luther, *Lectures on Romans*, 129. Latin text: "*Quocirca mera deliria sunt, que dicuntur, quod homo ex viribus suis possit Deum diligere super omnia,*" in Luther, *Die Römerbriefvorlesung*, 274.

you say, namely, that it is possible to love God 'with all one's strength' [Luke 10:27] naturally [*naturaliter*], in short, without grace!"[239] Luther summed up the issue "in a nutshell" in *The Bondage of the Will*, when he wrote that by biblical commands "man is shown what he ought to do, not what he can do."[240] In other words, *ought* did not imply *can*. But did not Scotus mean to say what humans *ought* to be able to do in a state of innocence? It was a question of what Scotus meant in his day when he spoke of what was reasonably expected of human nature, created in God's image, indeed, what a human being ought therefore to do, naturally speaking. Scotus argued, "I say that to love God above all is an act conformed to natural reason, which dictates that what is best must be loved most . . . as a first practical principle of action, this is something known per se, it is self-evident . . . For something must be loved most of all."[241]

For Scotus, the human intellect concludes,

> Something must be loved in the highest measure . . . Therefore, natural reason dictates that the infinite good be loved above all. Consequently, the will can do this by its purely natural endowments, for the intellect could not rightly dictate something to the will that the natural will could not tend towards or carry out naturally."[242]

But did Scotus mean to say that even after the fall, a human being can actively love God above all else by his own powers? No, not at all. Scotus made it clear that he was speaking of humans in a state of innocence, before the fall. Scotus argued, "I concede the conclusion that by purely natural means any will could love God above all, at least as human nature existed in the state in which it was instituted."[243] But Luther did not want to make a distinction between before and after the fall. Nor did he provide nuance to what a newly created human being ought to be able to do. Luther wrote:

---

239. Luther, *Lectures on Romans*, 129. Latin text: "*Probate, quod dicitis, 'ex totis viribus' Deum diligi posse naturaliter, sine denique gratia*," in Luther, *Die Römerbriefvorlesung*, 275.

240. Luther and Erasmus, *Luther and Erasmus*, 188–89.

241. Scotus, *Will and Morality*, 276.

242. Scotus, *Will and Morality*, 281.

243. Scotus, *Will and Morality*, 283. Latin text: "*Concedo conclusionem, quod ex puribus naturalibus potest quaecumque voluntas, saltem in statu naturae institutae, diligere Deum super omnia*," in Scotus, *Ordinatio* D27, 72 (line 53).

> Now, here we are speaking not only of the first man, but of any and every man . . . But if that man, even when the Spirit was present, was not able with a new will to will a good newly proposed to him (that is, obedience), because the Spirit did not add it to him, what should we be able to do without the Spirit in respect of a good that we have lost?[244]

Again, Scotus clarified that he was speaking of what a newly created human being ought to be able to do. "I say that God can be loved above all not only by charity, but also by one's natural endowments, at least in the state in which nature was instituted."[245]

The confusion for Luther came from the translation and understanding of the Latin idiom underlying the terms "can" and "naturally" (*posse* and *naturaliter*). For Luther, "ought" did not imply "can." For Scotus, "ought" is what he meant by "can." In classical Latin, *Deus diligendus est* was in the form of a passive periphrastic conjugation or gerundive plus *sum*. It conveyed the idea of a necessary, obligatory action, not simple futurity. But in medieval Latin usage, Scotus qualified the construction by adding the notion of *naturaliter*, which in his argumentation meant "ought." Think of it in the modern sense when one says, "Naturally, that is, of course I love my parents." Thus, that God ought or must be loved above everything (*Deus diligendus est super omnia*) implies that he can be loved above all else, *at least* in one's original state of innocence.

So, what did Scotus and Luther mean by *naturaliter*? For Scotus, the medieval meaning of the term was deduced from what he argued was self-evident. Given the supremacy and infinite worth of God our Creator, it was self-evident that God was to be loved above all else. Therefore, people could love God above everything else naturally, that is, by their own powers. But Luther, and Gabriel Biel as well, filled the terms *naturaliter* and *posse* with the Renaissance humanist understanding of the day. So what had happened in metaphysics, epistemology, and linguistics between Scotus's day and Luther's to cause such a misunderstanding of terms? Scholars have argued that the Latin idiom of Renaissance humanism and the Protestant Reformation had undergone a "revolutionary paradigm shift." There were "new conceptions and redefinitions." The Protestant Reformation was "above all a metaphysical and epistemic

---

244. Luther and Erasmus, *Luther and Erasmus*, 187.

245. Scotus, *Will and Morality*, 286. Latin text: "*Dico, quod non solum ex charitate potest Deus super omnia diligi, sed ex naturalibus saltem in statu naturae institutae*," in Scotus, *Ordinatio* D27, 80 (line 70).

revolution."[246] Carlos Eire pointed to the long tradition, beginning with sixteenth-century Catholics, of calling the Reformation a revolution. For instance, Eire referred to Frederic Seebohm's book *The Era of the Protestant Revolution* (1874), to which one could add Edward Maslin Hulme's book *The Renaissance, The Protestant Revolution and The Catholic Reformation in Continental Europe* (1915). In Eire's assessment, the plurality of "Reformations of the sixteenth and seventeenth century" indicated "a massive paradigm shift, but it is far more accurate to see the Reformations as a series of intertwined paradigm shifts."[247]

In his chapter on "Justification," Antonie Vos compared the language of Scotus and Luther and their different understanding of the qualifying term *naturaliter*. Vos noted that "the Age of the Renaissance" indicated "a huge language shift." He observed that little historical attention has been given to the fact that a "paradigm shift elicits a language shift."[248] As a result, the term *naturaliter* had shifted and become a qualification of natural human powers. *Nature* had become a fundamental order of reality in Renaissance humanism. Pauck noted that "In manner and method of theological argument," Luther retained in his lectures a "'modernist' orientation" of mind in his "general view of God and the world" as well as "in his psychological conceptions."[249] It was, therefore, the Renaissance humanist and nominalist idea of human autonomy that Luther read and rejected in these terms used by Scotus and Biel.[250]

In sum, although Scotus made it clear that he spoke of human beings' natural abilities before the fall, and Biel spoke of a general concurrence with human beings' abilities both before and after the fall, Luther would not consider human beings' natural abilities, whether before or after the fall, to be pertinent to the discussion of one's salvation.

---

246. Eire, *Reformations*, 746.

247. Eire, *Reformations*, 746. For more in Eire on revolutions and paradigm shifts, see 744–47.

248. Vos, *Theology of Scotus*, 265. For a fuller treatment of this shift in language, see Vos's chapter 6, 236–74.

249. Luther, *Lectures on Romans*, li.

250. For a fuller treatment, see Vos, *Theology of Scotus*, 236–74.

The Lutheran Book of Concord (1577)

The *Book of Concord* gave the definitive formulation of what Lutherans "believe, teach, and confess." Its publication marked the beginning of a time of stabilization in Lutheran faith and practice, despite continued squabbling. Three years later, in 1580, The Lutheran *Book of Concord* was published, which included the confessions of the Lutheran Church. "Orthodoxy thus prevailed in Lutheran Germany after 1580, despite some dissent."[251]

Of the four main authors of the *Book of Concord*, Jakob Andreae (1528-90), a Gnesio-Lutheran and professor of theology at Tübingen, and Martin Chemnitz (1522-86), a Philippist, who as pastor of the church of St. Aegidi lectured on Melanchthon's *Loci Communes*, there are two to whom Robert Kolb draws attention on the problem of predestination, namely Nikolaus Selnecker (1532-92), professor of theology at the Universities of Jena (1562-68), Leipzig (1568-70), Helmstedt (1571-74) and again Leipzig (1574-89); and David Chytraeus (1530-1600), professor of theology at the University of Rostock (1561-1600).[252] The question of whether one should even preach on the topic of predestination was often raised. Chytraeus and Selneker believed that the intent and result of teaching the doctrine of predestination was to console believers. This viewpoint was taken up in the Epitome, Article Eleven of the *Book of Concord*: "The doctrine of God's eternal election is profitable and comforting to the person who concerns himself with the revealed will of God."[253]

In a short treatise, Chytraeus defined the following terms: "necessity," "divine determination," "fate," "contingency," "human powers," and "free choice."[254] To serve the purposes of the previous discussion, I shall focus on his use of the term "human powers." The starting point of his discussion on human powers (*de viribus humanis*) was the original state of creation, that is, the first created humans in whom God "implanted the powers of the soul." The highest (*summa*) of the powers was "the mind, that is, the intellect or *ratio*, in which shone the illustrious knowledge (*notitia*) of the true God." He added, "Right judgment and the wisdom of the law ran congruent with the divine mind, discerning good and evil." Right judgment and the law "were the norm and rule of all action."

251. Eire, *Reformations*, 568.
252. Kolb, *Bound Choice*, 182-97.
253. Tappert, *Book of Concord*, 495.
254. For a fuller treatment, see Kolb, *Bound Choice*, 194-95.

HISTORICAL AND THEOLOGICAL INTRODUCTION 57

Indeed, the first created "will [*voluntas*] was turned toward God."[255] And human nature was such that the "will freely [*sponte et libere*] chose or rejected the dictates of the mind or the law of God."[256] Notably, Chytraeus said that "even though the freedom and command of the will was greatly impeded after the fall [*post lapsum*], there remained some part in external actions and in the reason and judgment of things."[257]

Crucially, "When therefore inquiry is made into human powers [*viribus humanis*] or free choice [*libero arbitrio*], let young people, at the height of their human powers, with passions and cravings, inquire whether people can rightly love God in this corrupt nature, discern good from evil, and see the way of eternal salvation."[258] Let them inquire "whether the will and heart can [*possint*] seriously love, obey, seek and obtain God?"[259]

Chytraeus recognized distinctions between various levels of necessity and that necessity (*necessitas*) was a "relative" term whose "foundation was some cause, especially an efficient cause, begetting something immutably."[260] The terminus (*terminus*) was the thing to which the effect or result was related, such as obedience was related to the command to obey. He noted the Aristotelian maxim that what is necessary is immutable or that which cannot be otherwise than it is (*quod aliter se habere non potest*).[261] Chytraeus defined another level of necessity, the implicative necessity of the necessity of consequence (*necessitas consequentiae*), as follows:

> The necessity of consequence is of those things and propositions, which by their own nature are mutable and contingent, but do not change—although in the beginning they could be changed—for they are either determined by God, or are foretold, or follow from causes, which do not change. For either something follows certainly on account of a logical connection [*dialecticam connexionem*], which is nevertheless contingent by virtue of its nature, or it is impossible. Or when something

---

255. Chytraeus, *Piae et Utilliss*, 60. The original pagination consisting of letters is cumbersome at best. Therefore my numbering begins with the title page as 1.
256. Chytraeus, *Piae et Utilliss*, 61.
257. Chytraeus, *Piae et Utilliss*, 62.
258. Chytraeus, *Piae et Utilliss*, 63.
259. Chytraeus, *Piae et Utilliss*, 63–64.
260. Chytraeus, *Piae et Utilliss*, 3.
261. Chytraeus, *Piae et Utilliss*, 4.

happens or has happened, contradictory things cannot be true at the same time.²⁶²

Chytraeus had been a student of Melanchthon, and it is not surprising that some of the wording recalled Melanchthon's definition of necessity of consequence, terms that described the implicative necessity of a proposition as a "logical connection" (*dialecticam connexionem*). Chytraeus gave biblical examples of necessity of consequence, such as, "Was it not necessary that the Christ should suffer?" (Luke 24:26) and "It was necessary that temptations come" (Matt 18:7).²⁶³ He cited Chrysostom on this point, who explained that these things were necessary not because of corrupted free choice (*arbitrij libertatem*), not because necessity imposed itself, but because Jesus foretold that it would come entirely from the evil will of human beings. These things happened "not because God has foreseen them, but because the human will was incurable."²⁶⁴

Crucially, Chytraeus noted the significance of the sharp distinction that the scholastics made between the necessity of consequence and the necessity of the consequent.

> For if the proposition is true, that God foreknows or orders beforehand that David will rape Bathsheba, then necessarily it follows that David will rape Bathsheba and murder Uriah. Nevertheless, the necessity of the consequent does not follow from that cause, namely, that David would simply and necessarily be an adulterer and murderer. For David could have abstained from adultery and unjust punishment.²⁶⁵

Chytraeus made the point that the necessity of the consequent would mean that David was an adulterer and murderer and, as such, was not free, nor by implication responsible, but bound to commit adultery

---

262. "*Necessitas consequentiae est earum rerum aut propositionum, quae sua natura mutabiles et contingentes sunt, sed non mutantur, vel quia sic a Deo determinatae, vel praedictae sunt, vel quia sequuntur ex causis, quae non mutantur, cum tamen initio mutari potuissent vel quia propter dialecticam connexionem certo sequitur aliquid, quod tamen sua natura contingens vel impossibile est, vel quia cum res fit aut facta est contradictoria simul vera esse non potest*," in Chytraeus, *Piae et Utilliss*, 22–23.

263. Chytraeus, *Piae et Utilliss*, 23.

264. Chytraeus, *Piae et Utilliss*, 23.

265. "*Nam si hac propositio vera est, Deus praescit vel praedixit Davidem rapturum esse Bathsabeam et interfecturum Uriam: necessario consequitur hac: David rapiet Bathsabeam et interficiet Uriam. Nec tamen inde sequitur necessitas consequentis, videlicet, quod David simpliciter necessario futurus sit adulter et homicida, potuisset enim David ab alterius conjuge et cade injusta abstinere*," in Chytraeus, *Piae et Utilliss*, 25.

and murder. "The necessity of the consequent action or state of affairs would itself be necessary, by its very nature." Such sheer necessity would mean that the state of affairs "cannot be otherwise than it is."²⁶⁶ Such an absolute necessity he rejected if applied indiscriminately to all talk of necessity.

Of interest to this study was the *Book of Concord*'s standpoint on the issue of whether one could love God above all else with one's own natural powers. In the Epitome, article two on "Free Will" asks, "Can man *by his own powers [ob er vermöge, aus seinen eigenen krefften / an propriis viribus possit]*, before he is reborn through the Holy Spirit, dispose and prepare himself for the grace of God?"²⁶⁷ The reply was, "It is our teaching, faith, and confession that in spiritual matters man's understanding and reason are blind and that *he understands nothing by his own powers [nichts verstehe aus seinen eigenen krefften / nihilque propriis viribus intelligere possint]*, as it is written in 1 Corinthians 2:14."²⁶⁸

The "Antitheses" stated that the Lutherans rejected the "so-called Stoic philosophers and Manicheans who taught that whatever happens must so happen and could not happen otherwise, that man always acts under compulsion." They also rejected the error of the "Pelagians who taught that by his own powers, without the grace of the Holy Spirit, man can convert himself to God." They also rejected the error of the "Semi-Pelagians who teach that man by virtue of his own powers could make a beginning of his conversion but not complete it without the grace of the Holy Spirit." Nor did they accept that even once the Holy Spirit had offered grace to man through preaching the word that "man's will is forthwith able by its own natural powers to add something to help, cooperate, to prepare itself for grace, to dispose itself."²⁶⁹ They accepted, however, "Luther's statement that man's will in conversion behaves 'altogether passively.'"²⁷⁰

The "Solid Declaration" of Article Two on "Free Will" gave more insight into the controversy that existed leading up to the *Book of Concord*

266. "*Vocant igitur necessitate consequentis consequens seu res ipsa, sua natura necessaria est, et aliter fieri aut se habere non potest*," Chytraeus, *Piae et Utilliss*, 25.

267. Tappert, *Book of Concord*, 469. German and Latin source texts, respectively: Dingel, *Die Bekenntnisschriften der Evangelisch-Lutherischen Kirche*, 1228, 1229.

268. Tappert, *The Book of Concord*, 470. German and Latin source texts: Dingel, *Die Bekenntnisschriften der Evangelisch-Lutherischen Kirche*, 1228, 1229.

269. Tappert, *Book of Concord*, 471.

270. Tappert, *Book of Concord*, 472.

between the Gnesio-Lutherans (followers of Luther's teaching legacy) and the Philippists (followers of Melanchthon).[271] The Lutherans asserted that the Philippist party erroneously taught that

> *although by his own powers* [*Doch hab er noch so viel naturlicher krefften / tamen tantum adhuc ipsi virium naturalium*] and without the gift of the Holy Spirit man is unable to fulfill the commandment of God, to trust God truly, to fear and to love him, man nevertheless still has so much of his natural powers prior to his conversion that he can to some extent prepare himself for grace and give his assent to it, though weakly, but that without the gift of the Holy Spirit he could accomplish nothing with these powers but would succumb in the conflict.[272]

In sum, it was the Philippist claim that one's "natural powers" remained intact, even prior to one's conversion, that the Gnesio-Lutherans overruled and the Philippists surrendered in the *Book of Concord*. Luther had taught that after the fall and prior to conversion, "not a spark of spiritual powers has remained or exists in man."[273] Furthermore, "although man's reason or natural intellect still has a dim spark of the knowledge that there is a God . . . nevertheless, it is so ignorant, blind, perverse" that even the most learned "cannot by their own powers" understand and accept the gospel as truth.[274] "But before man is illuminated, converted, reborn, renewed, and drawn by the Holy Spirit, *he can do nothing in spiritual things of himself and by his own powers* [*kan er vor sich selbst und aus seinen eignen, naturlichen krefften in geistlichen sachen / ex sese et propriis naturalibus suis viribus in rebus suam nihil inchoare, operari aut cooperari potest*]."[275] According to Pauck's identification of source texts, it was Luther's reading of Scotus and Biel—as if these two theologians from two different theological contexts used the term *naturaliter* in the same manner—that set Luther off. "They said, namely, that when the will is subject to synteresis, it is, only slightly to be sure, 'inclined toward the good.' And this tiny motion toward God (of which man is naturally capable) they

---

271. For a general introduction to the controversy, see Eire, *Reformations*, 564–68.

272. Tappert, *Book of Concord*, 520. German and Latin texts: Dingel, *Die Bekenntnisschriften der Evangelisch-Lutherischen Kirche*, 1346, 1347.

273. Tappert, *Book of Concord*, 521.

274. Tappert, *Book of Concord*, 521–22.

275. Tappert, *Book of Concord*, 525. German and Latin texts: Dingel, *Die Bekenntnisschriften der Evangelisch-Lutherischen Kirche*, 1356–59.

imagine to be an act of loving God above everything!"²⁷⁶ That is, even fallen human beings retained vestiges of the image of God and thereby natural God-given endowments.

Albert Pighius and John Calvin on Free Choice

It is not often that Protestant Reformation history texts went to the front lines, as it were, to give space to the other side of the arguments. The formidable opponent of Calvin is no doubt lesser known and therefore deserves a brief introduction. The Dutch mathematician and theologian Albert Pighius (1490–1542) was born in Kampen, the Netherlands. He studied theology in Louvain from 1507 to 1517 and, according to Lane, he was an "Erasmian humanist."²⁷⁷ Thereafter he studied in Paris. In 1522, his former teacher at Louvain, Adrian Florents, became Pope Adrian VI. Pighius then followed him to Rome. He returned to the Netherlands and in 1535 became provost and archdeacon of St. John's Church at Utrecht. As a delegate to the colloquies at Worms and Regensburg, it is likely that Pighius had picked up Calvin's *Institutes* (1539) while at the Worms colloquy, and that the two met each other while in Worms.²⁷⁸

Calvin had stated in the 1539 edition of the *Institutes* that grace abolished free choice. Pighius saw Calvin as an easy target. He attacked. In 1542, his book *On The Free Choice of Man and Divine Grace in Ten Books* (*De Libero Hominis Arbitrio et Divina Gratia, Libri Decem*) saw the light of day, the same year in which he died, at the end of December. In 1543, Calvin responded with *The Bondage and Liberation of the Will: A Defence of the Orthodox Doctrine of Human Choice against Pighius* (*Defensio Sanae et Orthodoxae Doctrinae De Servitute et Liberatione Humani Arbitrii Adversus Calumnias Alberti Pighii Campensis*). Calvin dedicated

---

276. Luther, *Lectures on Romans*, 130. On the meaning of "synderesis," see Muller, s.v. "synderesis": "The innate habit of the understanding that grasps basic principles of moral law apart from the activity of formal moral training; a concept from Aristotle, used by the medieval scholastics as a synonym for the patristic term *scintilla conscientiae*," in Muller, *Dictionary*, 351. On Biel's concept of synderesis, see Oberman, s.v. "scintilla conscientiae": "The spark of the conscience. A natural inclination toward good and away from evil. This is not an act or habit of the will but the voice of natural law speaking through the dictates of right reason," in Oberman, *Harvest of Medieval Theology*, 475. On Biel, see Oberman, *Harvest of Medieval Theology*, 65–67.

277. Calvin, *The Bondage and Liberation of the Will*, xvi.

278. For a brief biography of Pighius by Lane and Davies, see Calvin, *The Bondage and Liberation of the Will*, xvi–xviii.

his book to Melanchthon. Indeed, he wrote a letter to Melanchthon on February 16, 1543, in which he told him as much. Pighius had brought seven complaints against Calvin. First, if God controls all things in life, why bother with how we live? Calvin replied that God's providence works through us.[279] Second, why punish crimes if they happen by necessity? Reply, necessity does not violate the human will and evil it commits.[280] Third, your teaching on necessity undermines law and order. Reply, God works through secondary causes.[281] Fourth, necessity undermines religion. Reply, indeed, "everything that happens happens of necessity, as he had ordained." Therefore, the Reformers teach complete trust in God.[282] Fifth, does necessity make God the author of sin? Reply, God can even use bad human actors to accomplish his good purposes.[283] Sixth, original sin implies that nature is evil. Reply, "Luther and all of us define nature in two ways." Namely, there is a difference between the perfect original creation and the abuse thereof.[284] Seventh, Protestant doctrine exposes God to ridicule. Reply, "ought" does not imply "can." People are not excused from doing what God asks, even if they cannot do it on their own. The Law accomplishes its task. It exposes sin.[285]

Calvin noted that Pighius had claimed that all the church fathers affirmed free choice. But what did Pighius mean by "free choice"? Calvin said that Pighius defined the "force and meaning of the expression" in terms of "choice" (*arbitrium*), which was to be understood as "choosing" (*electione*) or, better, "will" (*voluntas*). Pighius called "free" (*liberum*) that which is "autonomous [*sui juris est*] or its own master [*aut sui ipsius habet potestatem*]." That is, "doing whatever it does in such a way that it does

---

279. Calvin, *The Bondage and Liberation of the Will*, 36. Latin text: Calvin, *Ioannis Calvini Opera Quae Supersunt Omnia*, 6:255–56.

280. Calvin, *The Bondage and Liberation of the Will*, 37. Latin text: Calvin, *Ioannis Calvini Opera Quae Supersunt Omnia*, 6:256.

281. Calvin, *The Bondage and Liberation of the Will*, 38. Latin text: Calvin, *Ioannis Calvini Opera Quae Supersunt Omnia*, 6:257.

282. Calvin, *The Bondage and Liberation of the Will*, 38–39. Latin text: Calvin, *Ioannis Calvini Opera Quae Supersunt Omnia*, 6:258.

283. Calvin, *The Bondage and Liberation of the Will*, 39–40. Latin text: Calvin, *Ioannis Calvini Opera Quae Supersunt Omnia*, 6:258.

284. Calvin, *The Bondage and Liberation of the Will*, 40. Latin text: Calvin, *Ioannis Calvini Opera Quae Supersunt Omnia*, 6:259.

285. Calvin, *The Bondage and Liberation of the Will*, 41. Latin text: Calvin, *Ioannis Calvini Opera Quae Supersunt Omnia*, 6:259.

not do it of necessity [*non necessario*], but is able not to do it [*sed possit non facere*]."²⁸⁶

Calvin wanted to avoid the illusory term "free" because of its connotation, namely, that a person "has both good and evil within its powers, so that it can by its own strength choose either one of them [*sub potestate sua bonum et malum, ut alterutrum eligere suapte virtute queat*]." It is important to understand that for Calvin, "freedom and bondage are mutually contradictory" terms.²⁸⁷ He therefore proceeded to sort out the distinct meanings of four different claims about the will, namely, that the will was "free, bound, self-determined, or coerced." First, he said that most people understand a "free" will to mean that the will "has in its power [*in sua potestate*] to choose good or evil." He acknowledged that this was Pighius's definition, too. Second, "a bound will" is "held captive" to evil desires "because of its corruptness." Such a will "can choose nothing but evil." This is the case even if the enslaved will chooses so "of its own accord and gladly," without any "external impulse" driving it. Third, the "self-determined" will "directs itself" when not "forced or dragged unwillingly." And fourth, the "coerced" will cannot incline to one of two opposite choices "of its own accord," nor by "internal movement." It is "forcibly driven by an external impulse." Calvin agreed to the third sense, that "man has choice and that it is self-determined." In this way he thought to exonerate God from the charge that he is the author of evil. Thus, if evil is done, Calvin imputed the cause to a mortal's own "voluntary choosing."²⁸⁸

After ruling out "coercion," option four, Calvin weighed in on option one and denied that "choice is free." The will is driven by "innate wickedness," and therefore "of necessity" "cannot seek anything but evil." This description dovetailed with the second option, the bondage of the will. "For where there is bondage, there is necessity [*ubi enim servitus, illic necessitas*]."²⁸⁹

---

286. Calvin, *The Bondage and Liberation of the Will*, 67–68. Latin text: Calvin, *Ioannis Calvini Opera Quae Supersunt Omnia*, 6:279.

287. Calvin, *The Bondage and Liberation of the Will*, 68. Latin text: Calvin, *Ioannis Calvini Opera Quae Supersunt Omnia*, 6:279.

288. Calvin, *The Bondage and Liberation of the Will*, 69. Latin text: Calvin, *Ioannis Calvini Opera Quae Supersunt Omnia*, 6:280.

289. Calvin, *The Bondage and Liberation of the Will*, 69. Latin text: Calvin, *Ioannis Calvini Opera Quae Supersunt Omnia*, 6:280.

Indeed, following the second description of the will, Calvin could then locate "the necessity to sin precisely in corruption of the will." Thus, only then could one understand how Calvin reasoned that the will was self-determined to sin. It was due to its bondage. "Now you see how self-determination and necessity can be combined together," he said, "a fact which Pighius tries to conceal when he thinks man's freedom consists of acting (whether well or badly) without necessity."[290]

Calvin vigorously denied a key principle of the simultaneity of human potency in eliciting acts of the will, a principle that was crucial to Pighius's argument. Pighius argued that "free will exists naturally in man." That is, that the will moved itself, and had "all its actions under its control, so that man wills and does each action in such a way that he has at the same time the power not to will it and not to do it." Pighius ascribed this freedom to Augustine.[291] But Calvin disagreed. He cited Augustine's *City of God*: "The human will takes the initiative in doing evil, but in doing good it is the will of the Creator which takes the initiative, whether in making that which did not exist before or in remaking that which had fallen."[292] Calvin noted that Augustine had retracted his earlier view that "what we will is under our own control." In his *Retractions*, Augustine wrote, "'But this power to live well we also receive from above, when the will is prepared by the Lord.'"[293] Building on his own appeal to Augustine, that humans have no "innate ability of free choice" to assent to the gospel, Calvin wrote, "God bends our heart so that we assent to the gospel. That assent is properly called ours, but doesn't derive from us."[294]

In an excursus on coercion versus necessity, Calvin replied to the complaint that where there is no free choice, there is no virtue and praise nor blame for sin. He argued that "God is good of necessity, but he obtains no less praise." God cannot but be holy; nevertheless he is most deserving

---

290. Calvin, *The Bondage and Liberation of the Will*, 70. Latin text: Calvin, *Ioannis Calvini Opera Quae Supersunt Omnia*, 6:280.

291. Calvin, *The Bondage and Liberation of the Will*, 103. Latin text: Calvin, *Ioannis Calvini Opera Quae Supersunt Omnia*, 6:303.

292. Calvin, *The Bondage and Liberation of the Will*, 104. Latin text: Calvin, *Ioannis Calvini Opera Quae Supersunt Omnia*, 6:304. See Augustine, *City of God*, 523.

293. Calvin, *The Bondage and Liberation of the Will*, 105. Latin text: Calvin, *Ioannis Calvini Opera Quae Supersunt Omnia*, 6:305.

294. Calvin, *The Bondage and Libeation of the Will*, 120. Latin text: Calvin, *Ioannis Calvini Opera Quae Supersunt Omnia*, 6:314. God's grace "sweetly and powerfully bends the human will." See Schaff, *The Evangelical Protestant Creeds*, 591.

of praise. Likewise, "the Devil is evil of necessity, but no less culpable."[295] Pighius argued, however, that God differs from mortals and therefore to argue from the principle of transfer did not hold. Calvin replied that "it is not contrary to reason for a quality which exists of necessity nevertheless to be deemed worthy of praise or censure."[296]

Calvin worked out his argument as follows. He opposed Pighius's argument that God's works *ad extra* are contingent, "that God does not do or will of necessity anything at all which is outside himself [*Deum nihil aliorum omnium a se necessario agere aut velle, sed mere libere*]."[297] From Pighius's book, he finished the sentence with "but purely freely [*sed mere libere*]."[298] Calvin's starting point was to inseparably link God's righteous character with God's works *ad extra*. That is, for Calvin, God's nature is necessarily righteous and therefore his works *ad extra* are too. Pighius, on the other hand, separated God's nature from God's will. Even so, Pighius disavowed the nominalist's extreme teaching on the freedom of the divine will. Pighius said, "Will is inferior to nature." That is, God is good and righteous by nature, not by his willing to be so. With this Calvin was fundamentally in agreement with Pighius, namely, that "God is good by nature." But Pighius was puzzled by what appeared to him to be Calvin's teaching, namely, that "God wills to be righteous of necessity."[299] Indeed, Calvin argued that "God is what he is by nature in such a way that he wills to be so, and he also wills what he wills in such a way as to have it naturally." Calvin made what he called a "circular connection" between God's attributes of goodness, wisdom, power, and righteousness and included God's will to form a bond of necessity. "Since, then, God wills to be whatever he is, and that of necessity, there is no doubt that just as he is good of necessity, he also wills to be so." In this state Calvin found God to be "so far removed from coercion and to the greatest

---

295. Calvin, *The Bondage and Libeation of the Will*, 147. Latin text: Calvin, *Ioannis Calvini Opera Quae Supersunt Omnia*, 6:333.

296. Calvin, *The Bondage and Liberation of the Will*, 147. Latin text: Calvin, *Ioannis Calvini Opera Quae Supersunt Omnia*, 6:333.

297. Calvin, *The Bondage and Liberation of the Will*, 147. Latin text: Calvin, *Ioannis Calvini Opera Quae Supersunt Omnia*, 6:334.

298. Calvin, *Ioannis Calvini Defensio Sanae et Orthodoxae Doctrinae de Servitute et Liberatione Humani Arbitrii*, 385a. This edition includes the first six books of Pighius's *De Libero Hominis Arbitrio et Divina Gratia* on pages 331–450.

299. Calvin, *The Bondage and Liberation of the Will*, 147. Latin text: Calvin, *Ioannis Calvini Opera Quae Supersunt Omnia*, 6:334.

degree willing [*voluntarius*]," that is, free if understood in the sense of "self-determined."[300]

In sum, Pighius's main thesis was that God is not good because he wills to be good. God is good, and essentially so. Nevertheless, Pighius made a distinction on the ontological level between the necessity of the divine nature, on the one hand, and the modal status of the contingency of divine willing in his works *ad extra*, on the other. As seen above, in Pighius's view, "God does not will works *ad extra* of necessity, but purely freely." Pighius grounded the contingency of human willing on the contingency of divine willing. Indeed, it is possible that God not will, the same that he wills. But quite naturally, God cannot will what is unrighteous. Ironically, Pighius's ontology of contingency would also be used and expounded by later Reformed scholastics, theologians whom I shall explore below in the next section.

Calvin appears to have rejected the notion that God can will things *ad extra* contingently. Furthermore, he clearly rejected a supposed dual dimension of necessity and contingency. Calvin's starting point was to define necessity, according to Aristotle, as "a fixed, steady state in which a thing cannot be otherwise than it is [*Statam esse ac firmam stabilitatem, ubi res aliter esse non potest*]. The existence of alternative possibilities is always the opposite of necessity." Since God is good necessarily, Calvin "deduced from this that he wills the good as necessarily as he does it." God is not coerced. "Of his own accord and voluntarily he tends to that which he does of necessity."[301] Although God is necessarily inclined to do what he does, for Calvin it is equally true that what is voluntary when speaking of God is compatible with what is necessary. Indeed, he himself said, "What is voluntary is not so different from what is necessary that they cannot sometimes coincide."[302]

On the anthropological level, Calvin taught that "the human race" lost the freedom with which it was endowed by its Creator, falling into "wretched bondage." Much like Luther, Calvin taught, "We say that man in this state of bondage is not endowed with a free ability to choose both good and evil so that he could conform to whichever he pleased [*ut ad*

---

300. Calvin, *The Bondage and Libeation of the Will*, 148. Latin text: Calvin, *Ioannis Calvini Opera Quae Supersunt Omnia*, 6:334.

301. Calvin, *The Bondage and Libeation of the Will*, 149. Latin text: Calvin, *Ioannis Calvini Opera Quae Supersunt Omnia*, 6:335.

302. Calvin, *The Bondage and Libeation of the Will*, 149. Latin text: Calvin, *Ioannis Calvini Opera Quae Supersunt Omnia*, 6:335.

utrumlibet accommodare sequeat]."³⁰³ Where Pighius differed from Calvin was not in whether the human race had fallen, but whether it had retained intact the original "natural endowments" of freedom *ad utrumlibet,* freedom to choose one of two opposites. For Calvin, the natural endowments of the human race were corrupted and supernatural gifts [*supernaturalibus donis*] lost.³⁰⁴

Calvin intended by the title of his book to indicate a fundamental opposition between *liberation* and *bondage.* Written at the age of thirty-three, Calvin was yet young but would only nuance his views a bit throughout his life.

6. Post-Reformation Scholasticism and Providence

Lutheran

David Chytraeus

Before moving forward in time with later post-Reformation Lutheran and Reformed scholastic formulations of the doctrine of God, I wish briefly to return to Chytraeus to highlight his views of basic features of the doctrine of God. Unlike Luther, Chytraeus made use of the distinction between the *necessity of consequence* and the *necessity of the consequent.* Like so many theologians, Chytraeus wished to exonerate God from the charge that he was the author of evil and to exonerate Lutheran teaching on election and predestination from the charge that it was necessitarian. In the same brief treatise examined above, Chytraeus made it clear that "whatever God determines or foreknows to be future, these things happen with certainty and necessity." But as for what kind of necessity, these things happen by "the necessity of consequence," not by "the necessity of the consequent." For although God "foresees what is going to happen," these things do not happen by a "simple" and "absolute" kind of necessity, which is what *the necessity of the consequent* would entail. The reason that something does not happen by a simple necessity is because quite often

---

303. Calvin, *The Bondage and Liberation of the Will,* 184. Latin Text: Calvin, *Ioannis Calvini Opera Quae Supersunt Omnia,* 6:360.

304. Calvin, *The Bondage and Liberation of the Will,* 186. Latin Text: Calvin, *Ioannis Calvini Opera Quae Supersunt Omnia,* 6:361.

"it is mutable in its very nature, and could be other otherwise than it is. Nor would its opposite have been impossible."[305]

One important feature of the doctrine of God that repeatedly appears in this section is the development of the terminology concerning the "knowledge of God." Chytraeus began a new section entitled "divine determination," which he formulated as,

> An action of the divine mind, by which God sees all things, even comprehending future events all together, whether good or evil, by which he aids the good while permitting what is evil, establishing its limits and boundaries, further than which it will not be permitted.[306]

As Muller noted, "In the older language of theology and philosophy, a *determinatio*, including a causal determination, did not need to indicate a matter of absolute necessity, but only the appointement or ordination of the terminus ad quem."[307] For Chytraeus, the wisdom or knowledge of God (*Sapientia* or *Scientia Dei*) "refers to God's knowing all things, eternal and temporal, past, present, and future, good and bad." The foreknowledge (*praescientia*) of God "refers to the action of the divine mind by which he foreknows and foresees all future good and evil, both necessary and contingent." Divine providence (*providentia*) "is the action of the divine mind that not only comprehends all things and foresees the future, but also preserves the nature of things." And finally, the decree of God (*dectretum Dei*) "is the action of the divine mind that actually arranges and orders future events according to God's good pleasure."[308]

What is one to make of these different formulations? Chytraeus himself said that these terms are all "cognates," synonyms "concerning

---

305. "Quaequnque, Deus determinat seu praescit futura esse, ea certo et necessario evenient, sed necessitate consequentiae, quia Deus ea praevidet eventura esse: sed non simpliciter et absolute necessario, seu non necessitate consequentis, quod saepe sua natura mutabile est, et aliter se habere potuisset, nec contradictarium illius simpliciter fuisset impossibile," in Chytraeus, *Piae et Utilliss*, 33–34.

306. "De divina determinatione, quae est actio mentis divinae, qua Deus omnia cernens, cunctos etiam futuros eventus, sive bonus sive malos prospicit, ad bonus adjuvat, malos autem permittit et terminos ac metas constituit quo usque sit permissurus," in Chytraeus, *Piae et Utilliss*, 26–27. Here I am following Kolb's translation of these select terms in Chytraeus's treatise but making my own slight but important adjustments. See Kolb, *Bound Choice*, 193.

307. Muller, *Dictionary*, 89–90.

308. Kolb, *Bound Choice*, 193. Latin text: Chytraeus, *Piae et Utilliss*, 27–28.

those who are to be saved and inherit eternal life."[309] Notably, each formulation after the head term "divine determination" speaks to and addresses the fount or "source" of God's action. Again, Chytraeus himself made this remark about these terms being like synonyms. Although it appears at first that he has conflated the terms *scientia, praescientia,* and *providentia,* leaving little room for distinctions between divine knowledge, divine willing, and divine foreknowledge following and based on divine willing, we shall see below that Chytraeus did draw on a distinction made by Prosper of Aquitaine between divine foreknowledge and divine determination.

Chytraeus set forth a duality of decrees. He taught that the decrees were twofold. Some decrees were decreed "simply and without any conditions, depending solely on the will of God." For instance, "God decreed from eternity to create the world, to send the Son, to establish the church." Other decrees were "conditional and mutable," such as in the case in the book of Jeremiah. The LORD said, "If a nation turns from its evil, I will relent of the disaster that I intended to do to it" (Jer 18:8). Chytraeus believed that these examples demonstrated that "the foreknowledge and disposition or divine decrees are not a matter of Stoic fate, nor are all things that are foreseen and foretold by God simply and absolutely immutable and necessary."[310] What was at stake was whether God was responsible for evil. Chytraeus drew on and found useful the distinction that Prosper of Aquitaine made between "divine foreknowledge and divine predestination."[311] After establishing the fact that there are no "temporal distinctions" or moments of time to be perceived in God, Prosper concluded that God foreknows and predestines "at the same time whatever things were to be done by an actor himself."[312] Nevertheless, Prosper wished to make a distinction and taught that *to know* is not *to predestine*. Therefore, God's knowledge could not be the cause of the actor's action. "God can [*potest*], therefore, have foreknowledge [*praescientia*] without predestination. Predestination [*praedestinatio*], however, cannot be [*non potest*] without foreknowledge [*praescientia*]." As Kolb points out, Chytraeus found these distinctions in terminology helpful in countering "the argument attributed to Boethius, Lorenzo Valla, and Luther in

---

309. Chytraeus, *Piae et Utiliss,* 27.
310. Kolb, *Bound Choice,* 193. Latin text: Chytraeus, *Piae et Utilliss,* 29.
311. Chytraeus, *Piae et Utiliss,* 30. See Kolb, *Bound Choice,* 193.
312. Chytraeus, *Piae et Utiliss,* 30.

De servo arbitrio," that absolute necessity made God the author of both good and evil.[313] Crucially, Chytraeus did not end up conflating divine determination with divine knowledge. He made a distinction between divine determination and divine knowledge, between predestination and foreknowledge, formulations that later Lutheran and Reformed theologians would develop further, to which I now turn.

Johann Gerhard

The editors of the Lutheran theologian Johann Gerhard's (1582–1637) *Theological Commonplaces* (1611) trace its origins to the monthly formal disputations that he oversaw in Coburg, beginning in 1607. As was the custom, a list of theological and philosophical theses, in Latin, was published prior to the university disputations. Theses on topics such as creation, providence, and election, for instance, were collected and published as *Aphorisms*. The *Aphorisms* represented a stage in the development of the *Theological Commonplaces* and reflect the kind of topics disputed at the universities.[314] The following eight *Aphorisms* on providence appeared under Commonplace IX. Gerhard began with the general truths concerning the created order and ended with human action, both good and bad.

> (1) Ordinarily divine providence preserves the course of nature which it has established. Thus the heavenly Father "makes the sun shine and the rain fall" (Matt 5:45).
>
> (2) Although divine providence generally acts through means, let us not cling to them but always look back to their First Cause. Second causes are of no effect unless God helps them. "Unless the Lord builds the house, those who guard it labor in vain" (Ps 127:1).
>
> (3) Divine providence can also carry out its works extraordinarily without means. In this way Moses was preserved for forty days and forty nights without food (cf. Exod 24:18).
>
> (4) Even if the secondary causes are present in actuality, divine providence can still hinder and change their effect. He saved three witnesses who were as though in the fire in Babylon (cf. Dan 3:19–27).

---

313. Kolb, *Bound Choice*, 193–94.
314. Gerhard, *On Providence*, xii.

(5) From secondary effects divine providence can produce an effect other than what their property produces. In this way He produced water from a rock (Exod 17:5–7).

(6) Brute animals not only are subject to the providence of God but also either by natural instinct or in some other way feel and in some ways confess God's sustenance and preservation. "These all look to You to give them their food" (Ps 104:27).

(7) The entry into, the advancement through, and departure from human life are directed in particular by the providence of God.

(8) The providence of God concurs differently in relation to good actions of men than in relation to their evil actions.[315]

As for good spiritual actions, God commands, approves, and drives those who are born again "in such a way that He himself causes and works them through the Holy Spirit." They are driven in such a way that "one's will cooperates [synergizes, συνεργεῖ] through powers that are not of nature but are given by the grace of the Holy Spirit, and it is an active or cooperative instrument." But "As to evil actions, on the other hand, God does not command nor will nor aid them, nor does he drive people to them."[316]

Three Acts of Providence: The First

In its wider scope, Gerhard said that the providence of God included three acts. The above eight aphorisms were an attempt to display the kinds of acts the providence of God included, in particular, in the third act of divine providence. The first act was "the foreknowledge of God" whose meaning included three things: (1) the "foreknowledge of things" that are known, (2) "the will and concern to foresee (for the will is the beginning of every action)," (3) and "the action itself by which matters are taken care of and governed." Briefly, he said providence consisted in "foreknowledge, purpose, and administration, control."[317]

Furthermore, "God considers all things in a permanent, fixed, and unchanging 'now.'" He transcends time. There is no past or future in God.

---

315. Gerhard, *On Providence*, 74–78.
316. Gerhard, *On Providence*, 78.
317. Gerhard, *On Providence*, 51.

His "ability to see all things is subject to no change," which he argued John of Salisbury said so beautifully.[318] For this reason, even the word *"foresee"* is inadequate and misleading. Moreover, the scholastics correctly argued that "God knows all other things outside Himself distinctly."[319] On the question whether "God understands all other things outside Himself through ideas of them," he answered in the affirmative, citing Seneca (ca. 3 BC-AD 65), Augustine, and Jean Gerson (1363-1429). As Aquinas pointed out, "'According to His essence, God is the likeness of all things. Therefore an idea is nothing other than the essence of God.'" And Gabriel Biel expressed it as follows: "'In the case of God, ideas exist not subjectively and in reality but objectively, because the creatures that God understands are not in Him in reality and subjectively.'" That is, "All things are in God objectively, according to power, eminently.'"[320] To the question, "Does God know singular things?" Gerhard answered, "It would be a disgrace to deny this."[321] To the question whether "God knows infinite things?" he answered, "God is infinite, God knows himself, therefore, God knows infinite things." He then gave a lengthy quote from Augustine's *City of God*, book 12, chapter 19, the end of which said, "His wisdom is simply manifold and uniformly multiform. With His incomprehensible comprehension He comprehends all things incomprehensible." Then Aquinas, "God knows the things which are in the power of God or the potential of His creation, and yet these things are infinite. Therefore God knows infinite things."[322] Gerhard concluded with a twofold distinction in God's knowledge that later Reformed theologians also made much use of. He cited the distinction as made by William of Auxerre (ca. 1150-1231) in his *Summa Aurea*, book 1, chapter 48, "'The knowledge of God with respect to all possible things is called 'intuitive' or the knowledge of simple understanding. With respect to those things which are, have been, or will be, it is called 'the knowledge of vision'; with respect to things to come, it is called 'foreknowledge.'" Gerhard added that as concerns future things, God sees them as "truly present."[323]

---

318. Gerhard, *On Providence*, 52.

319. Gerhard, *On Providence*, 53.

320. Gerhard, *On Providence*, 54-55. On divine ideas and exemplar causality, see Fisk, *Edwards's Turn*, 167-89.

321. Gerhard, *On Providence*, 56.

322. Gerhard, *On Providence*, 57.

323. Gerhard, *On Providence*, 57.

To the question whether "the foreknowledge of God is unchangeable," Gerhard, contrary to necessitarianism, said that although it is "sure and immutable," this fact "does not remove every contingency from things, nor does it bring about an absolute necessity."[324] For this reason, one must understand that there are two kinds of necessity:

> The one is *of the consequent* [*consequentis*] (which some call absolute; others, *preceding*; and still others, *simple*), which arises out of the necessity of the necessary link of cause and effect.[325]

The second kind of necessity is:

> *Of the consequence* [*consequentiae*] (which they also call *of hypothesis*, *following*, and *conditional*), which stems from the act of existence and pertains by nature to contingent things that are still called necessary either because they follow from causes which do not change, though they could have changed by their own nature, or because, when they exist, they cannot at the same time not exist. You see, *everything that exists must exist because of the very fact that it does exist.*[326]

In other words, explained Gerhard, in the case of the necessity of the consequence, even though causes act contingently and freely, God still has foreknowledge of these acts. There is no irreconcilable difference. He added that "metaphysical philosophers warn that this is not called a necessity properly speaking inasmuch as it must be evaluated from its proximate cause, but not from the act of existence."[327]

Furthermore, Gerhard added that "the Scholastics" exerted much effort to explain how God has "determinate and necessary knowledge of future contingent things."[328] Aquinas thus explained that immediate contingent causes can have contingent effects, even though the First Cause was a necessary cause. But then God's knowledge of them is necessary, he held. Biel explained that "'the freedom of a second cause is sufficient to preserve the contingency, because it is enough that one required cause be free.'"[329]

---

324. Gerhard, *On Providence*, 57–58.
325. Gerhard, *On Providence*, 58.
326. Gerhard, *On Providence*, 58.
327. Gerhard, *On Providence*, 58.
328. Gerhard, *On Providence*, 58.
329. Gerhard, *On Providence*, 58.

But Gerhard then asked how one reconciled God's infallible knowledge with the contingency of future things? He then quoted Scotus (*Sent.* 1, dist. 39) who gave several opinions. Some, said Scotus, said that God views the whole movement of time as present to eternity, an eternal now. But Scotus himself held, according to Gerhard, that "'The divine will, which is the first rule of contingent things, first determined contingent things before the divine understanding understands them.'" But Gerhard admitted that Scotus's claim baffled him. Notably, Scotus's claim would make God's knowledge of future contingents contingent upon God's determinate will. Gerhard seemed to understand this and returned to Aquinas, who said that future contingents should be considered contingent in themselves, and when as yet undetermined by God's will, God knows them as they exist in themselves. Gerhard then gave the explanation of William of Occam (ca. 1287–ca. 1347) in which he said that God's intuitive knowledge of himself and all things is like unto ours. Just as we know things present as true, contingent, and infallibly so, without turning contingency into necessity, so too "'God's knowledge does not impose necessity on future contingent things.'"[330] Gerhard found Occam's explanation to be simple and true. Gerhard then turned to Biel, who explained that God knows future contingents contingently. But Gerhard then added, "However, these ideas are in need of careful interpretation, for God knows contingent effects necessarily and not contingently."[331] But then again, he concluded that although free and contingent causes result in effects that are necessary, it is "not with necessity of the consequent but with necessity of the consequence; not absolute necessity but hypothetical necessity." Indeed, God sees all things, past, present, and future "in the absolute 'now' of eternity."[332]

For Gerhard, God sees and knows when and how "the power to act shall turn in causes that act contingently and freely." Nevertheless, God's visionary knowledge in no way imposes absolute necessity on his creatures. For, "in His creation some things were endowed with the ability to act freely."[333] Gerhard added a brief note about the contingency of things. The fall of Adam and Eve in Eden supposes the contingency of things. For praise and blame to be at all meaningful supposes the contingency of

---

330. Gerhard, *On Providence*, 58–59.
331. Gerhard, *On Providence*, 59.
332. Gerhard, *On Providence*, 59.
333. Gerhard, *On Providence*, 59.

things. Nevertheless, God is no "disinterested spectator of what happens in the world." The bottom line is that "divine foreknowledge" of what happens in no way imposes "absolute necessity, nor is every contingency or freedom thereby abolished."[334]

Before turning to the second act of providence, I wish to note that Gerhard addressed two questions that are very relevant to this study and deserve our attention. First, whether God's foreknowledge brings about the necessity of sinning? Second, whether all things are fated by necessity? Can human beings, thus, be excused from sinning since they live in a world controlled by necessity and does not fate make God the author of sin? To the first question, Gerhard said, "All the less should we say that divine foreknowledge inflicts on people a fated and necessary need to sin." In what might appear at first to be counter intuitive, he cited Jerome, who commented on Ezekiel 3 that "It is not the case that we must do what God has foreknown just because God knows what is going to happen. Because He is God, He knows what we are going to do of our own will." Likewise Augustine, in *City of God* book 5 chapter 10, who said that when someone sins, "neither fate nor fortune nor anything else but the man was going to sin."[335] In other words, one sins of one's own accord. In the case of Judas, God foreknew his betrayal and foresaw that it was voluntary. Furthermore, "the foreknowledge of God does not impose an immutability on things from the standpoint of before [*a priori*] but only from the standpoint of after [*a posteriori*]. That is, when God knows that a things exists, it has to exist." Crucially, even so, with respect to an event's own cause and nature, it "could exist otherwise" than it does.[336] And God also knows that contingency.

For the above reasons, Gerhard said that he could not approve of what Calvin wrote in his "(*Instit.*, bk. 3, ch. 23, sect.9): 'By the ordinance of God (whose equity is unknown to us but is quite sure to Him), a necessity of sinning is imposed upon the reprobate.'" Nor "Piscator (*Disp. de praedest.*, p. 11: 'By virtue of divine counsel, it could only have happened that our first parents sinned.' Nor Bucanus (*Locus* 14, p. 136): 'What men and angels do, they do out of necessity, because God has decreed it to happen by His providence.'"[337]

---

334. Gerhard, *On Providence*, 59–60.
335. Gerhard, *On Providence*, 60.
336. Gerhard, *On Providence*, 60.
337. Gerhard, *On Providence*, 61.

In support of his opinion, Gerhard gave another lengthy quote from Augustine's *City of God* "*De civ. Dei*, bk. 5, ch.9," which I quote but in part.

> We are not afraid that we are not doing willingly what we do willingly just because He whose providence is infallible foreknew that we were going to do it . . . Thus He who foreknew al the causes of things could not have been ignorant of our wills, which are among the causes that He foreknew as the causes of our deeds.[338]

To the second question, about so-called fated necessity, Gerhard gave three replies:

(1) The proponents of this position incorrectly conflate divine foreknowledge with divine predestination, decree, and will. In support of his reply, he quoted Augustine who wrote, "(*De praedest. sant.*, ch. 10): 'Predestination cannot exist without foreknowledge, but foreknowledge can exist without predestination.'"[339] Once again, Gerhard noted the confusion surrounding the meaning of "fore" in the word "foreknowledge." To clarify, he quoted the commentary of Ludovicus Vives (1493–1540) on Augustine's *City of God*, "(*De civ. Dei*, bk. 5, ch. 10): 'The thing that makes this debate more difficult is that some people imagine that the future is to God the way it is to us.'" But there is no passing of time in the mind of God, nor awaiting the future. Again, the foreknowledge of God imposes no "absolute necessity of acting," nor does it violate human freedom to act since that freedom is also "in the order of causes which God foreknew."[340]

(2) The proponents of this position disallow the use of the distinction between the necessity of the consequent and of the consequence on the grounds that they are "philosophical." But Gerhard argued that the use of these terms did not function as some kind of proof, nor did they introduce some new article of faith beyond Scripture. He then turned the question around on them and asked why they introduced "the fated necessity" of "the Stoics" into the discussion.[341]

---

338. Gerhard, *On Providence*, 61. I referred to this passage from Augustine's *City of God*, 190–91, above, under the section: "Logica Moderna and Medieval Scholastic Distinctions."

339. Gerhard, *On Providence*, 62.

340. Gerhard, *On Providence*, 63.

341. Gerhard, *On Providence*, 64.

(3) The proponents of this position hold that just as God's attributes are absolutely necessary, so all things happen by absolute necessity. But Gerhard replied that they incorrectly associate God's infallible foreknowledge of things with the imposition of absolute necessity upon things. This is because the "evil actions of men do not arise from God's foreknowledge. Rather, these must be evaluated on the basis of their proximate cause." He then cited "Scotus (*Sent.* 1, dist. 45, q. 5)," who argued that people know innately that God is a necessary being, regardless of whether he wills things outside himself or not. "However, if He were to will necessarily, He would be unable not to will the things which do not exist outside of Himself."[342] In other words, if on their supposition, God wills things necessarily, outside God as in God, then so must he will all possible things that do not and may never exist, such that they would necessarily come into being and exist outside God. Gerhard said that his more simple reply was that God acts freely even in the good things that he does. In other words, if one were to ask whether "God can do what he has done better than he did?" he cited Scaliger, who replied, "God can do otherwise, because in supreme power is also included lesser power."[343]

Three Acts of Providence: The Second

"Predetermination or end purpose" is the second act of divine providence. "For whatever God does in time He has decided to do from eternity."[344] That God foresees implies not only knowledge but also the will to provide (Eph 1:11). By "end purpose" is meant not only God's plan of salvation set forth in Christ, but also "the preservation of His creatures."[345] But "should the purpose of God be referred also to the sins of people?" No. In this case, the reverse does not hold. "The things that God does not do in time He has not decreed to do from eternity." God has not decreed and it was not his eternal purpose that human beings fall. But the remedy for the fall "has been decreed by God from eternity and arranged in Christ." Indeed,

---

342. Gerhard, *On Providence*, 64.
343. Gerhard, *On Providence*, 64–65.
344. Gerhard, *On Providence*, 66.
345. Gerhard, *On Providence*, 66.

"God in time permitted man to fall."[346] Thus, Gerhard would say that God decreed to permit humans to fall which differs from saying that God decreed the fall. But he warned that by speaking of "a decree to permit evil deeds" one "must understand the word 'decree' to refer not to the evil deeds themselves, but to those good ends which God knows how to elicit from them by His wisdom and goodness."[347]

Three Acts of Providence: The Third

The third act of divine providence is "control," whereby God "sustains and governs" all things "wisely, freely, powerfully, and well." This act of God's "providential care deals with all things which exist and occur in the world," referring to Colossians 1:17 and Hebrews 1:3.[348] Concerning erroneous views of the objects of providence, Gerhard cited Clement of Alexandria, Cyril of Alexandria, and Augustine as telling that "there were some who thought that 'the highest parts of the world are governed by divine providence, but the lowest part of earth and the closer atmosphere in which winds and clouds rise up are driven rather by accident and chance.'" As I reported above in the section, "Maimonides: A Medieval Jewish Guide to Views on Providence," Gerhard also referred to Maimonides's view, expressed in the *Guide for the Perplexed*, "(*De direct. perplex.*, ch. 136): 'No individual corruptible things are in the province of divine providence except humans, because of their intellect, which is incorruptible.'" But Gerhard noted that Scripture gives a comprehensive view of God's providence, extending to our earth and weather: "'Matt 5:45 He makes His sun rise and sends rain on the just and the unjust.'"[349]

Gerhard divided this third act into two parts, namely, "preservation and governance."[350] Briefly, he said that *preservation* is, according to Scaliger, "'the continuation of existence,'" which included humans' God-given "essence, properties, and power to act." There is therefore "a constant 'inflowing'" of God's preserving power. "It is in God that we move (Acts 17:28)."[351] As for *governance*, God's particular concern is for

---

346. Gerhard, *On Providence*, 67.
347. Gerhard, *On Providence*, 67.
348. Gerhard, *On Providence*, 69.
349. Gerhard, *On Providence*, 69.
350. Gerhard, *On Providence*, 71.
351. Gerhard, *On Providence*, 71.

all human beings, and he is especially concerned for the church "and all the true members of the church." Gerhard noted that although all has been created "for man's sake," according to Scaliger's explanation, "Man, as the most beautiful compendium of the entire universe, is God's particular concern."[352]

Seven Ways Divine Providence Concurs with the Evil Actions of Human Beings

First, Gerhard noted that God "concurs in evil actions" by the simple fact that he foreknows and sees them.[353] Second, he acknowledged that Acts 17:28 would seem to implicate God in evil action since it is God who sustains us and in him we live and move and have our being. But "a careful distinction must be made between the doing or action itself and the fault of the action. An action as action is not a sin." It is the "defect in the action" that is sin. As Augustine explained, the cause of someone limping lies not in the strength of muscle but in the dislocated leg. Furthermore, the defect is not to be traced to some universal or First Cause. Once again, one must look to the near or proximate cause of one's evil action.[354] Third, God concurs in evil "by permitting" it. Though "God does not will sin, yet He does not hinder it, and that is His permission." But there are different end purposes involved. "Permission applies to sin itself." But God's will "applies to a useful end," that which God in his wisdom will produce out of the situation. Gerhard noted that Lombard "(*Sent.* 1, distinctions 45–46)" followed Augustine's argument, "Permission properly implies the negative act of not willing."[355]

Gerhard further divided *divine permission* into "seven causes or ways" of divine permission which "Damascenes (*Orth. fid.* bk. 2, ch. 31) listed from Nemesius." Briefly, the seven ways of divine permission are: (1) calamities may make latent virtue known; (2) disgraceful acts, such as the crucifixion, can be salutary; (3) a thorn in the flesh can temper pride; (4) "dire straits may serve as a warning"; (5) calamities may serve God's

---

352. Gerhard, *On Providence*, 73.
353. Gerhard, *On Providence*, 79.
354. Gerhard, *On Providence*, 79.
355. Gerhard, *On Providence*, 80.

greater glory; (6) the blood of martyrs may be the seed of the church; (7) and slipping into one sin may serve to correct other affections.[356]

The fourth way that God concurs in evil action is "by abandoning." This applies to all sin except that of Adam and Eve in Eden. God removes the hedge around those who flee from him. Damascenus established two kinds of abandoning: (1) as in the case of Christ's complaint (Ps 22:1), (2) and a "final and condemnatory" abandoning, as in the case of incorrigible sinners. Fifth, God concurs in evil "by handing one over to Satan." Sixth, God concurs in evil "buy setting the limits beforehand," as in the case of Job. Lastly, the seventh way God concurs in evil actions is "by eliciting good from them," as in the case of Joseph.[357] Another instance of the seventh way is the passion of Christ. Gerhard pointed out an important distinction made by "Leo (Sermon 16 *de passione Domini*)."

> The Jews' will to kill did not come from the same source as His [Christ's] will to die, nor did the savageness of their crime and the long-suffering of the Redeemer come from one and the same spirit. You see, the Lord did not send the impious hands of raging people upon Himself, but He allowed them. He did not compel them to it by foreknowing that it would happen, though He had taken up flesh for this very purpose.[358]

In sum, God's permission is not to be understood as giving tyrants approval to sin. Permission is always subject to the seven ways of divine permission outlined above. As Gerhard quoted Augustine, "Whether this [sin] happens in some other explainable way or in an inexplicable way, God is just and good; that is, He is not a cause of sin." God is not the orderer nor author of evil wills. But God can "bring back inordinate wills" and turn them to good.[359]

God Is Not the Cause of Sin

Gerhard devoted his entire chapter 10 to this important topic, which follows on the heels of the *seven ways* in which God concurs in evil action without compromising his good and just character. The bulk of the chapter takes up controversial statements and situations in Scripture,

---

356. Gerhard, *On Providence*, 80–81.
357. Gerhard, *On Providence*, 81–83.
358. Gerhard, *On Providence*, 81–83.
359. Gerhard, *On Providence*, 86–87.

situations such as the command to sacrifice Isaac, Joseph sold into slavery by the will of God, the hardening of Pharaoh's heart, God's command to Shimei to curse, and so forth. I wish to reserve many of these Scripture passages for my dialogues in part 2 of this book. In what follows, I wish to showcase in summary fashion Gerhard's most salient points.

Gerhard once again affirmed that "God does not will nor command nor approve nor aid sin itself according as it is such, and much less does He force or drive people to it or impose upon them a necessity to sin by some immutable decree (Ps 5:4; 1 John 2:16; Deut 25:16; Zech 8:17; Wis 11:24; 1 John 1:5)."[360] If God punishes sin, does that make him the author of sin? No. Technically speaking, punishment is not evil. Moreover, the original cause of sin is in the sinner. The original cause of mercy is in God. God is an avenger only after humans are first sinners. Representative of the early church fathers, "Basil wrote a complete oration entitled 'God Is Not the Author of Sin' [*Quod Deus non sit auctor peccati*]." Gerhard also took issue with what he called the "vulgar arguments" of some "Calvinists," such as Zwingli, Calvin, Beza, and Zanchi. Representative of these was Peter Martyr, whom he cited, and who wrote, "God inclines and drives the will of the ungodly to serious sins (Martyr, *Commentary on Romans*, f. 38)."[361]

Gerhard outlined four objections to his view and gave replies. First, he rejected the Calvinist's use and application of a distinction between God's "hidden will" and his "revealed will" to explain why God is not the author of sin. For Gerhard, their use amounted to "contradictory wills in God."[362] For Gerhard, theological distinctions must be based on Scripture. Gerhard, however, was not opposed to the scholastics' very different use of this distinction, namely, as "a distinction not of things but of vocabulary (Thomas, *ST* part 1, q. 19, art. 11; Biel, *Sent.*, bk. 1, dist. 45, q. 1)."[363] Second, citing Zwingli, it will not do to claim "that God is not bound by the law" when it comes to what sin is. God's own righteousness is mirrored in the law.[364] Third, he rejected the claim that sinners were merely defective instruments of the sin committed. But how then did one explain the first sin in Eden? Fourth, he rejected the notion that if sin

---

360. Gerhard, *On Providence*, 88.
361. Gerhard, *On Providence*, 90.
362. Gerhard, *On Providence*, 90.
363. Gerhard, *On Providence*, 91.
364. Gerhard, *On Providence*, 91.

were committed with good purpose and intent, it was acceptable, since it was from God. Again, how did one apply this to the first sin in Eden?[365]

Gerhard also opposed the use by "Calvinists," such Beza and Peter Martyr, of the term "incline" to mean that God "inclines the will of the wicked." That is, that God inclines with a kind of "internal impulse" by which he moves people to actual sin. This idea Gerhard opposed.[366]

Despite his calling out some Calvinists on their positions on providence, Gerhard was not opposed to all Reformed theologians. For instance, he approved the statement of Franciscus Junius Sr. (1545-1602) who wrote in "*De peccato Adae*, q. 1, ch. 4, 'No necessity to fall was imposed by God on our first parents.'" And of Musculus, who wrote in "*Loci comm.*, p. 975: 'It is our responsibility simply to give our omnipotent and just God freedom of will and righteousness, so that He wills or does nothing evil—in fact, is not even able to do evil—for how could the inestimable goodness of the divine nature want, love, or do anything evil?'" He said he also approved of such statements made by "Sebastion Castalion, Antonius Corranus, William Perkins, and others."[367]

Reformed

Leiden University

Notably, the Reformed professor of theology at Heidelberg (1584-92) and Leiden (1592-1602), Franciscus Junius Sr., affirmed the two distinct kinds of necessity, discussed above, in his 1598 Leiden theses *On the Providence of God*. He wrote that the necessity of consequence was a hypothetical necessity, and the necessity of consequent was an absolute necessity. "Of those we call necessary, there are two genera. For some are necessary absolutely and per se, by what they call a necessity of the consequent, others by hypothesis, a necessity of consequence."[368]

Along with professors Lucas Trelcatius Sr. (1542-1602) and Franciscus Junius Sr. at the University of Leiden, Franciscus Gomarus (1563-1641) was professor of theology at Leiden (1594-1611), at Saumur

365. Gerhard, *On Providence*, 92.
366. Gerhard, *On Providence*, 107-08.
367. Gerhard, *On Providence*, 107.
368. "*Eorum quae necessaria vocamus, duo sunt genera. Alia enim sunt per se et absolutè necessaria, necessitate (ut vocant) consequentis: alia ex hypothesi, necessitate consequentiae*," in Junius, *Opuscula Theologica Selecta*, 159.

(1614–18), then at Groningen (1618–41). Gomarus was born in Bruges, present-day Flanders, Belgium. He studied in Strasbourg, Neustadt, Oxford, then Cambridge in 1583. In Cambridge he earned his master's degree, *magister artium* (1584). Gomarus was a member of the Synod of Dordt and auxiliary translator of the Dutch Bible, the *Staten Vertaling* (1637).[369]

In Leiden on January 21, 1595, Professor Gomarus presided over disputation *Theses Theologicae De Providentia Dei* that were defended by the respondent Jacobus van Miggrode. The theses on divine providence systematically set out the basic features of the doctrine of God. Antonie Vos has said that these theses had "great programmatic value." First, thesis 5 stated,

> This decree comprehends indefinite foreknowledge (*praescientiam indefinitam*), which they call the knowledge of simple understanding (*simplicis intelligentiae*), and prefinition (*praefinitionem*) or predestination, but then generally understood.[370]

How did they understand the "fore" (*prae*) in the term "*fore*knowledge?" As we have seen, theologians also spoke of God's foreknowledge as God's foresight. Thus, God sees the state of affairs in question. But in this case, does God see future states of affairs in reality or does God see possible states of affairs? The first word, "indefinite," will help us answer the question. That he was speaking of possibilities is indicated by the term "indefinite" (*indefinita*), that is, possible states of affairs that had yet to be defined or determined by God's will as future states of affairs in the reality of this world. Furthermore, this foreknowledge was prior in order to God's will—for if it were not prior to God's will it would not be indefinite, but definite. Thus, *foreknowledge* was God's knowledge of *a priori* possible states of affairs. Furthermore, in Gomarus's 1605 cycle of similar theses on providence, he made it clear in thesis 6 that technically speaking the

---

369. For a previous treatment of some of these basic features of the doctrine of God, see Fisk, "Divine Knowledge at Harvard and Yale."

370. "Decretum hoc complectitur praescientiam indefinitam (quam simplicies intelligentiae vocant) et praefinitionem seu praedestinationem generaliter sumptam," in Gomarus, *Theses Theologicae de Providentia Dei*, 4. See Vos, "Reformed Orthodoxy in the Netherlands," especially 143; see too Vos's earlier essay on these theses by Gomarus in Vos, "Scholasticism and Reformation," especially 110–15. I have largely followed Vos's translation into English, but with slight adjustments. Note that Vos in his chapter contribution to the Brill Companion may confuse the reader since he calls thesis 6 "thesis 4," 142.

word "knowledge" (*scientia*) better suited God's infinite knowledge than the word "foreknowledge" (*praescientia*). The latter was more suitable for accommodating the human understanding of what Scripture calls God's "foreknowledge" of future events. Gomarus also indicated that the other term commonly associated with "to foreknow" was the verb "to foresee" (*praevidere*). But, he said, to *foresee* was not suitable for describing the infinite knowledge of God. The suggestion that God *foresees* the future suggested temporality in God which was something Gomarus wanted to avoid. "God, for whom nothing is future, does not foresee but simply sees that which is present."[371] Thus the expression "God's knowledge of simple understanding." Second, thesis 6 stated,

> Indefinite foreknowledge [*praescientia indefinita*] in God is the most perfect knowledge of the universal and individual states of affairs that can obtain [*quae fieri possunt*].[372]

It is clear from this thesis that God's *indefinite* knowledge is all-encompassing, including all possible states of affairs, both universal and individual. The modality of possibility is entered in with the use of *posse*, that is, what can, or is possible. Vos indicates that this theory of possibility belonged to the tradition of Duns Scotus. Third, Gomarus brought God's will and predestination into discussion in thesis 7, which stated,

> Prefinition is the act of the will of God by which from foreseen states of affairs, he has predefined the creation and governance of the world.[373]

Thesis 5, above, made it clear that by the lesser-known term "prefinition" Gomarus also meant "predestination," which, as seen here, referred to the act of God's will. Once again, it is crucial to understand that Gomarus did not mean to identify "foreseen" with future time-indexed events, as if God had to then respond to them by his will. Nor do future events dictate God's will. For this reason it was important to clarify what Gomarus meant by "foreseen," and what he understood to be God's knowledge of *possible* states of affairs, not factual states of affairs.

---

371. Gomarus, *Theses Theologicae de Providentia Dei*, 4. See Vos, "Reformed Orthodoxy," 142.

372. Gomarus, *Theses Theologicae de Providentia Dei*, 4; See Vos, "Reformed Orthodoxy," 142.

373. Gomarus, *Theses Theologicae de Providentia Dei*, 4. See Vos, "Reformed Orthodoxy," 143.

Franeker University

In 1623, William Ames (1576–1633) published what would be the first edition of his *Marrow of Theology* (*Medulla Theologica*). Ames was a professor of theology at Franeker University 1622–32. Interestingly, according to Ames's auction catalogue, he owned a copy of Gomarus's *Conciliatio doctrinae orthodoxae*.[374] Like Gomarus, Ames spoke of the first of God's twofold knowledge in terms of "simple understanding" and of "all things universal and particular." Ames's theses twenty-five and twenty-six clearly indicated two kinds of divine knowledge, structurally, or conceptually, locating the divine will after the first and prior to the second. In the chapter on the decree and counsel of God, he stated the first kind of knowledge in thesis 25:

> The knowledge of simple understanding refers to all possible things, i.e., all things universal and particular which may be brought into being through the most perfect knowledge in God.[375]

Ames formulated the second kind of knowledge of God in thesis 26:

> The knowledge of vision is the knowledge of all future things, whether they are necessary in their own nature, or free, or contingent.[376]

Crucially for the position and function of God's will between these two kinds of knowledge, Ames explained the position of the will in thesis 27:

> The things which God knows through the knowledge of simple understanding he knows by his all-sufficiency, but those things he knows through the knowledge of vision he knows by his efficiency or by the decree of his own will.[377]

The implication of these theses is that on the conceptual level of the first kind of knowledge, there is divine freedom as to what states of affairs God will actualize and bring out of the realm of possibility into the realm of futurity. Ames made this clear in thesis 34:

---

374. Sprunger, *The Auction Catalogue of the Library of William Ames*, 12; Gomarus, *Conciliatio Doctrinae Orthodoxae*, 159.
375. Ames, *Marrow of Theology*, 96.
376. Ames, *Marrow of Theology*, 96.
377. Ames, *Marrow of Theology*, 96.

> [God's] will is truly free, because whatever it wills it wills not by necessity of nature but by counsel.[378]

As to whether events and human decisions outside God, made in time, impose themselves upon God's knowledge and will in any way, Ames clearly said in thesis 36 that God's freedom "precedes them in principle." Moreover:

> What God wills to do outwardly he wills not out of natural necessity but by preceding choice, for there is no necessary connection between the divine nature and such acts.[379]

Furthermore, in thesis 28, Ames denied any kind of "middle knowledge" (*scientia media*) in God, by which he said that some (the Jesuits and Arminians) say that God knows "hypothetical" future contingents "before the decree of his will." Ames rejected this third kind of knowledge since it "supposes that events will happen independently of the will of God and also makes some knowledge of God depend on the object."[380] With the negative of one significant term, "omnivolent," we can summarize Ames's position. He said in thesis 47 that although God is "omniscient and omnipotent, it cannot be said that he is omnivolent."[381] For if God were, then he would have to will into existence all that he knows could be, by necessity of nature. But that is not the case.

Utrecht University

Gisbertus Voetius (1589–1676) also taught a twofold knowledge of God when preparing a disputation about "The Knowledge of God" (*De scientia Dei*).[382] In the opening lines, he referred to the first kind of knowledge as God's "necessary knowledge" of all possibilities, a knowledge which precedes God's will:

---

378. Ames, *Marrow of Theology*, 97.
379. Ames, *Marrow of Theology*, 97.
380. Ames, *Marrow of Theology*, 96.
381. Ames, *Marrow of Theology*, 99; Goodwin also says this, in Goodwin, *Exposition of Ephesians*, 216; so too Charnock, in Charnock, *Existence and Attributes of God*, 2:22.
382. On these theses, see Vos, "Reformed Orthodoxy," 146–51. Also Beck, "Gisbertus Voetius (1589–1676): Basic Features of His Doctrine of God."

God's necessary knowledge is the knowledge that structurally (or by way of conceiving) precedes every act of God's will.[383]

Voetius explained that there are a variety of ways to distinguish the two kinds of divine knowledge, as "necessary and free, simple understanding and vision, indefinite and definite, speculative and practical." On the latter two terms, what is speculative is what God can know. What is practical is what God knows to be factually actual. Thus, like Gomarus, he also called it "indefinite" and, like both Gomarus and Ames, "simple." Voetius continued in the opening paragraph to explain God's maximally omniscient knowledge of himself:

> And by this God knows himself in himself and by himself in a first, immediate and maximally necessary act, and consequently all possibilities, not in themselves, but in his own nature as their necessary ground.[384]

This formulation follows from the very nature of God's necessary being and knowledge. Notably, this is an act, an all-sufficient necessary act. It consists of all that is necessarily true of God considered in himself. This knowledge is not knowledge of future things as they are in themselves, but rather it is the *ground* of all possible things, things that God can bring into existence in time, but does not have to. As examples, Voetius mentioned Matthew 3:9, where we read Jesus saying that "God is able from these stones to raise up children to Abraham." And Matthew 26:53, where we read Jesus saying, "Do you think that I cannot appeal to my Father, and he will at once send me more than twelve legions of angels?"

How did Voetius formulate the second kind of divine knowledge? As indicated above, Voetius also called this second kind of knowledge "free," "definite," and "visionary."

> Free knowledge is that by which God knows determinately after the decree of his will all existent states of affairs, in whichever temporal indexation they may be, whether present, past, or future.[385]

---

383. "*Necessaria est, quae omnem, voluntatis actum ordinae naturae antecedit*," in Voetius, *Selectarum Disputationum Theologicarum*, 246.

384. "*Et hac Deus primo actu immediato, et maxime necessario cognoscit se ipsum in se ipso et per se ipsum. Deinde, omnia possibilia, non in seipsis sed in sua essentia tanquam causa ipsorum necessaria*," in Voetius, *Disputationes selectae theologicae*, 246.

385. "*Libera scientia est qua post decretum suae voluntatis cognoscit determinate res omnes existentes, in quacunque temporis differentia sint, sive praesentis, sive praeteriti,*

The pattern of the contingency of states of affairs, contingent upon the determining decree of God's will, becomes clear in Voetius's formulation. What is determined by God's decree of the will is the time-indexation of future events that will come about in the course of time in this world. Voetius joined the above-mentioned Reformed theologians in setting out a knowledge and will-based paradigm and ontology of genuine contingency. Consider Vos's statement on the importance of this kind of radical contingency:

> The *necessity-contingency* pattern is characteristic of the whole of the doctrine of God, which is the core of Christian thought, and the doctrines of the *ordo salutis* are anchored in such a doctrine of God which radically interprets God's activity as contingent activity.[386]

After receiving an appointment as professor of Hebrew and practical theology at the University of Frankfurt an de Oder in 1667, and a professorship in 1670 at the University of Duisburg, upon the recommendation of the senate of Utrecht University, June 12, 1677, Petrus Van Mastricht (1630–1706) succeeded his teacher Voetius and was appointed professor of theology and practical theology, beginning the "Dutch" phase of his career with his inaugural oration at Utrecht University September 7, 1677.[387]

Over his lifetime, Van Mastricht presided over many disputations and published many editions of his major theological work, *Theoretico-Practica Theologia*. He prepared students to discuss controversial topics such as those which came up when debating the providence of God. It is evident from his theological work, for he said as much, that Van Mastricht had consulted Ames's *Marrow of Theology* when he made his own formulations of the twofold knowledge of God. In Van Mastricht's chapter on "The Intellect, Knowledge, and Wisdom of God" (*De intellectu, scientia, et sapientia Dei*), he used the now familiar terms of "God's simple knowledge of understanding" and "pure possibilities" to describe the first kind of knowledge and "God's knowledge of vision" to describe the second.[388] Like Ames, Van Mastricht also denied that there was a third kind of divine knowledge:

---

sive futuri," in Voetius, *Disputationes selectae theologicae*, 247.

386. Vos, "Reformed Orthodoxy," 149.
387. Neele, *Petrus Van Mastricht*, 227–31.
388. "*Duplex nomen obtinet: scientiae naturalis, seu simplicis intelligentiae, qua,*

Whether there is in God a third kind of knowledge, what they call middle knowledge, besides natural foreknowledge or knowledge of simple understanding on the one hand, and free or knowledge of vision on the other?[389]

In part 2, chapter 10, I will explore in more detail the theory of "middle knowledge" (*scientia media*), as originally proposed by the Jesuit Luis De Molina (1535–1600). The content of the chapter arises from a 1717 Harvard commencement day disputation that denies that there is a third type of divine knowledge in God which was called *middle knowledge*. I also will examine the counterarguments of Reformed theologians.

The following eight questions (*quaestiones*) give an idea of the debated issues about providence in general. The answers to the question were either given or implied by Van Mastricht in the text.[390]

Quaestio 1. "Whether there is such a providence of God, by which he foresees individual and all things, according to the council of his will?" Indeed, there is. In his answer to the second objection, Van Mastricht said, "Divine providence destroys neither contingency nor our free choice."[391]

Quaestio 2. "Whether there is such an influx of divine providence, by which God physically predetermines all causes, by all means, to act?"[392] Van Mastricht said the Reformed position answered yes, since Scripture testified that "in him we live and move and have our being" (Acts 17:28). Furthermore, God's providence is said to determine contingents in a way that guards both God's independence

---

circa pure possibilia . . . scientia libera seu visionis," in Van Mastricht, *Theoretico-Practica Theologia*, 146 (§ 14).

389. Van Mastricht, *Theoretico-Practica Theologia*, 148: "*An praeter praescientiam naturalem, seu simplicis intelligentiae, et liberam, seu visionis, in Deo sit scientia aliqua tertia, quam mediam appellant?*"

390. These eight *quaestiones* have been slighty revised but were previously published in Fisk, "Petrus Van Mastricht and Freedom of the Will," 113–14.

391. Van Mastricht, *Theoretico-Practica Theologia*, 395: "*An detur talis Dei providentia, qua omnibus et singulis prospiciat, secundum consilium voluntatis suae?*" Van Mastricht adds *libere* in his explanation. In refuting objection 2, Van Mastricht speaks of contingency: "*Nec divina providentia contingentiam tollit, aut arbitrii nostri libertatem*."

392. Van Mastricht, *Theoretico-Practica Theologia*, 395–96: "*An in providentia, talis detur influxus Dei, quo physice praedeterminet omnes omnino causas ad agendum?*"

and sovereignty, on the one hand, and human freedom and dependence, on the other.[393]

Quaestio 3. "Whether the influx of divine providence removes contingency from all states of affairs, and urges severe necessity?"[394] No, it does not.

Quaestio 4. "Whether the influx of divine providence removes or violates human free choice?"[395] No, it does not.

Quaestio 5. "Whether the predetermining influx makes God the author of sin?"[396] No, it does not.

Quaestio 6. "Whether there is some general concurrence and indifference toward all creatures in divine providence, which is determined by each individual creature according its proper nature, and from human beings according to their choice?"[397] No, it does not.

Quaestio 7. "Whether or not divine providence concerns sin, except by neutral/idle permission, or mere withholding/absence thereof?"[398] No, it does not.

Quaestio 8. "Whether divine providence constitutes an unchangeable end and limitation of human life?"[399] No, it does not.

Van Mastricht saw at least four overall objections to the Reformed doctrine of providence that students would have to overcome in their debates. First, that necessity and freedom were irreconcilable. Second, that

---

393. Van Mastricht, *Theoretico-Practica Theologia*, 395–96. "*Sua providentia dicatur determinare contingentia.*"

394. Van Mastricht, *Theoretico-Practica Theologia*, 396: "*An influxus ille providentiae divinae, e medio tollat omnem rerum contingentiam, duraque urgeat necessitate?*"

395. Van Mastricht, *Theoretico-Practica Theologia*, 397: "*An influxus ille providentiae divinae, tollat aut laedat libertatem arbitrii humani?*"

396. Van Mastricht, *Theoretico-Practica Theologia*, 398: "*An influx ille praedeterminans, Deum faciat auctorem peccati?*"

397. Van Mastricht, *Theoretico-Practica Theologia*, 398: "*An in providentia divina detur concursus aliquis generalis et indifferens in omnes creaturas, qui determinetur a singulis creaturis pro sua quaque natura, et ab homine pro sua arbitrio?*"

398. Van Mastricht, *Theoretico-Practica Theologia*, 399: "*An circa peccatum providentia divina, non occupetur, nisi oitiosa permissione, seu mera anergeia?*"

399. Van Mastricht, *Theoretico-Practica Theologia*, 400: "*An providentia divina constituat immobilem terminum et modum vitae humanae?*"

the divine predetermining influx made God the author of sin. Third, that human free choice was violated. Fourth, that if Reformed theologians removed all indifference from the divine-human equation, then free choice would cease to be. As to the concurrence of the divine and human wills and the divine influx, Van Mastricht's overarching reply was that no one can escape from the clear implication of the teaching of Scripture that "in him [God] we live and move and have our being" (Acts 17:28). Furthermore, the *pre* in the teaching of the divine *pre*determining influx did not point to a chronologically conceived cause and effect relation, but rather to the sovereign priority of God and his real interaction with and present involvement in the actual course of this world. Moreover, that God governs and sustains the world at every moment, that we live and move in him, that he can effect change in this world, in no way implicates God in the evil moral actions of people. That is, God's *physical* predetermination (Q.2) pointed to God's ability to work in the physical dimension of this world, but it differed from the moral dimension of evil human action. All the good that humans produce, as it were, is in concurrence with God's will. In this sense, God stands asymmetrically behind good and evil and is therefore not the author of evil, as alleged.[400]

Synopsis of a Purer Theology (Synopsis Purioris Theologiae)

The editors of the recent bilingual edition of the *Synopsis Purioris Theologiae* (1625) call the *Synopsis* a "handbook of scholastic Reformed theology," a "seminal treatise of Reformed scholasticism." The origins of the *Synopsis* were public disputations conducted at Leiden University between 1620 and 1624. The four principal authors of the 1625 *Synopsis* were Johannes Polyander (1568-1646), two newly appointed professors in 1619, Antonius Walaeus (1572-1639) and Antonius Thysius (1565-1640), and a year later Andreas Rivetus (1573-1651).[401]

The first disputation over which Rivetus presided was disputation eleven "On the Providence of God."[402] The disputation followed naturally after the topic of "The Creation of the World" since God provides and

---

400. On this issue, see Fisk, "Petrus Van Mastricht and Freedom of the Will," 113-115; also, Fisk, *A Book of Faith Seeking Understanding*, 39-42; on providence, predetermination, previous motion, see Ames, *Marrow of Theology*, 107-110.

401. Te Velde, *Synopsis Purioris Theologiae*, 1-2.

402. Te Velde, *Synopsis Purioris Theologiae*, 261.

cares for the creation he has established. Unlike Gerhard's three acts of providence, Rivetus proposed a "two-fold act" of providence. "The one is eternal, the other is within time."[403] Taken together, he espoused "the preexistent structural ordaining, in God's mind, of things towards a goal." This he called the "practical knowledge of God" whereby from eternity he preordained everything and in time directs them to their goal, namely, the glory of God. Notably and conceptually, the working of God's intellect and will are distinct but inseparable.[404]

As seen before, Rivetus highlighted a key biblical passage that he said makes the inescapable claim about our lives, that "in him [God] we live and move and have our being" (Acts 17:28), and that God's providence pertains not only to the heavens above but also to each particular thing on earth. God is the one who has the power to effect change in the heavens and on earth.[405] The old adage that Gerhard held also held true for Rivetus, namely, "God does nothing within time which He had not decreed from eternity." God pays attention to the smallest of details. He is the master architect, the most worthy craftsman. "Architects state that large stones cannot be laid well without small ones (so says Plato)."[406]

Although God has endowed human beings with intellect and free will, they do not act independently of God, the First Cause. Rivetus "traced" every creature's action, both its "manner and completion," back to God. There is therefore a divine concurrence of wills. The human will represents created freedom, but this freedom arises from and shares in a concurrence with divine, thus, uncreated freedom. "The notion that the functioning of divine providence destroys the freedom of the created will is so far from the truth that the will cannot exist at all without it." Again, both the manner and completion of human action "depend upon the effective working of the divine will." God establishes free choice. He does not destroy it.[407]

Furthermore, Rivetus counters the claims of those who argue that God only works in and through secondary causes, as if he endowed them with power to act on their own without any sovereign impulse, influx, or

---

403. Te Velde, *Synopsis Purioris Theologiae*, 261.
404. Te Velde, *Synopsis Purioris Theologiae*, 263.
405. Te Velde, *Synopsis Purioris Theologiae*, 265.
406. Te Velde, *Synopsis Purioris Theologiae*, 267.
407. Te Velde, *Synopsis Purioris Theologiae*, 269.

incitation by the First Cause, God. God moves the created human will.[408] God moves his creatures such that they act in accordance with their own nature. God's concurrence is such that "he directly influences the action of the created being, so that one and the same action is said to proceed from the first and the second cause," as if it were one completed action.[409]

Here the classic question of whether God is the author, actor, or producer of evil arises. Rivetus asked "whether sins, too, fall under divine providence." He replied that God neither procures nor provides for sin. But certainly sin and evil do not fall outside God's governance. "He foresees sins in advance, and wills to permit them." Since God has prior knowledge of sin, he can direct the course of events to "some universal or particular good." This may be to display God's glory, mercy, or justice. But formally speaking, evil is the absence of good, and therefore God does not provide for evil in this sense. But in a "relative sense," since this is God the Father's world, he provides for and ultimately governs the scope and measure of evil. Just not evil as evil.[410]

Rivetus made a distinction between God's "effectual" working and God's "permissive" working. The first applies to all things that fall under God's general and specific providential care: the "moral good" and both "civic and spiritual virtues." As the "highest good" (*summum bonum*), God is "the author and source of all good."[411] Moreover, Scripture attests to the second, that is, the *permissive* working of God. This includes both God positively permitting something and God merely not hindering something. Some Scripture references he gave for the first and second, respectively, were "And we will do this, if God permits" (Heb 6:3) and "Therefore God gave them up in the lusts of their hearts" (Rom 1:24). Rivetus acknowledged that "permission for all sins" fell under "God's providence," as stipulated above. Indeed, God does not merely permit or allow things to happen. Rather, "God both wills and directly decrees the permission, and ordains it for some good purpose that is greater than that of which the absence is the evil that is permitted." God's will, thus, "is not idle" in his works of permission. God is not a neglectful Father.[412]

---

408. Te Velde, *Synopsis Purioris Theologiae*, 273.
409. Te Velde, *Synopsis Purioris Theologiae*, 271.
410. Te Velde, *Synopsis Purioris Theologiae*, 277.
411. Te Velde, *Synopsis Purioris Theologiae*, 277.
412. Te Velde, *Synopsis Purioris Theologiae*, 279.

Part 1 has served the purpose of introducing and explaining scholastic distinctions in the historical context of disputation. Many of these distinctions appear in the formulation of theses and *quaestiones* of the New England colleges' commencement broadside sheets that will be the subject of each chapter in part 2. Without a knowledge of the medieval, Reformation, and post-Reformation use of the scholastic terminology it would be difficult if not impossible to discern its importance and signification for the colleges' curricula, not to mention why the students are learning the art of disputation in the first place.

Part II

NEW ENGLAND DISPUTATIONS ON PROVIDENCE

1. Immutability

WHETHER THE IMMUTABILITY OF THE DECREE DENIES
THE FREEDOM OF A CREATURE?
DENIED BY RESPONDENT FRANCIS GOODHUE.[1]
RECTOR SAMUEL WILLARD
1702 HARVARD QUAESTIONES 14

I ATTENDED THE AFTERNOON commencement day exercises at Harvard in Cambridge, July 1, 1702, presided over by Samuel Willard (1640–1707), the acting vice president (1701–07), and pastor of Third Church Boston. In my quest to understand how theologians defended God against the charge that he is the author of evil, and that all that unfolds in this world happens by necessity, I was keen on listening to the student respondent and talking to Vice President Willard after the ceremony. There was a man, however, in the audience, who appeared very agitated. After the ceremony, he came to where Vice President Willard and I were standing and introduced himself.

1. Willard, "Harvard 1702, Original." "4. *An immutabilitas decreti tollat libertatem creaturae? Negat Respondens Franciscus Goodhue.*" For the catalog of commencement broadsides, see Harvard University, "Commencement Theses, Quaestiones, and Orders of Exercises, 1642–1818." All translations in this and subsequent chapters are mine.

"Allow me to introduce myself. I am Mr. Keith, a missionary from Scotland. I am very troubled by what I think is a 'dangerous opinion' that I heard today," he said. "The respondent's reply to the *quaestio* listed on the broadside sheet strongly implied that Adam's fall in Eden could not have been avoided, that God decreed the fall, and Adam disobeyed necessarily."[2]

"I fear that you may have misunderstood some of the more technical points and terms used by the respondent. Have you been trained in scholastic terminology? Why not tell me your chief concerns," said Vice President Willard.

"My concern is the degree to which you subordinate human beings to God. My own thesis is that 'God, who is the First Cause of all created beings, doth not determine the will of man, so that he necessarily produceth any sinful action.'[3] The problem I have with your commencement *quaestio* and disputation is that your understanding of God, as the First Cause, implies that God causes people to act, and as such, when people sin, ultimately, God is the actor causing people to sin. That makes God the author of sin," said Mr. Keith.[4]

"Let me respond, if you will. Consider the following proposition, 'That the fall of Adam, by virtue of God's decree, was necessary.'[5] What is your first impression?" he asked.

"I hear the word 'necessary' and it sounds as if Adam's fall was necessitated by God's decree. And if not, then you run the risk of implying that God's decree failed in some sense, or was impeded. And surely you do not mean to say that, do you?" said Mr. Keith.

"Not at all. When I say, 'by virtue of,' in English, I am thinking of the underlying Latin idiom, namely, *vi* and its meaning.[6] The little word *vi* means force, power, energy, and virtue. It points to the cause that can produce an effect, and in this case, that God can produce a physical, though not moral, effect in this world. This last point is an important distinction to make. You do believe that God can act and move upon the human soul and spirit, even quicken and awaken the human spirit,

---

2. Keith, *Refutation*, 1. See too Fisk, "Que Sera, Sera. The Controversial 1702 Harvard Commencement *Quaestio* on Whether the Immutability of God's Decree Takes Away Human Freedom of the Will."

3. Keith, *Refutation*, 3.

4. Keith, *Refutation*, 3.

5. Willard, *Brief Reply*, 9.

6. Willard, *Brief Reply*, 9.

without being held responsible for human action?" asked Vice President Willard.

"Before you reply," he continued, "let me also address your concern about the 'necessity' of the decree. There are several distinctions to be made. First, there is a difference between God's works *ad intra* and *ad extra*. Most people only dwell on the latter. That is because it affects them as human beings. Their lives, their ability to make choices, and so on. But I like to remind my students," he said, "that God's eternal decrees fall under God's works *ad intra*. Strictly speaking, these works *ad intra* are 'immanent' acts of God and do not directly affect you and me.[7] That is, they are not at all conditioned by God's omniscient knowledge which includes knowledge of you and me, that is, a knowledge of our possible existence, but not actual existence. For on the level of immanent acts, there is as yet no time-indexed number of days appointed for you and me in futurity. In one of my lectures to my congregation, I taught that 'there is the residue of the Spirit with him. There are innumerable possible beings, which shall never have existence.' As for God himself, 'he never was without this decree,' that is, the *immanent* decree.[8] So, on the foundational level of immanency, God always approves of all the very best things that he can possibly do, without actually decreeing to do them all. Whatever God purposes to do in time, he first decrees in eternity. Consider this, 'God himself is not more ancient than his decree.' If you ask me what figures into determining what God decrees, I would answer, 'the mere good pleasure of God.'"[9]

"Now, here is a bridge to the acts of God *ad extra*," he continued, "under which fall the 'transient' acts of God. Of the possible beings that could be, it is the 'decree that appoints which of them shall be.' By God's decree, 'they pass from possibility to futurition.' The decree includes 'the manner of production, time, and means.'[10] But this decree 'lays no forcible necessity on the creature; but only a certainty as to the event.'"[11]

"The second distinction that I wish to make," he continued, "concerns what is called 'hypothetical necessity.' Theologians refer to this kind of necessity as a 'necessity of infallibility.' Quite simply, it is necessarily

---

7. Willard, *Compleat Body*, 102.
8. Willard, *Compleat Body*, 251.
9. Willard, *Compleat Body*, 252.
10. Willard, *Compleat Body*, 102.
11. Willard, *Compleat Body*, 103.

the case that the result of God's decree shall follow. Necessarily, a prophecy in Scripture shall come true," he said.

"I must say, that when I hear the word 'infallibility,' I think of an absolute necessity. But I think theologians are quick to distinguish the two from each other," I said.

"Most certainly," said Vice President Willard. "Infallible necessity or hypothetical necessity are not at all absolute. Remember, what is absolute stands alone and apart from any qualification or condition. The adjective, *absolute*, points to the unrestricted and free sense of necessity. But in the case of a *hypothetically* necessary proposition, the result or consequence that follows, only follows in a restricted sense. That is, there is an implication about what logically follows which is built into the way a proposition is composed. Let me give an example. 'It is hypothetically necessary that if you are married, you have a spouse.' But whether you are married or not is a hypothetical. And if you are married, then having a spouse is merely a necessity of the consequence of being married. Wouldn't you both agree?" he asked.

"I am not ready to concede my point that your defense of the immutability of God makes God the author of sin," said Mr. Keith. "I see no other way out than that God's will must be conditioned by the choices and circumstances of my fellow human beings."

"Let me make another important distinction that may help you," said Vice President Willard. "Some of God's acts are 'natural' and some are 'voluntary.'[12] I dare say that many people unwittingly confuse the one with the other."

"But are not all God's *natural* acts also voluntary, that is, will-based?" I said.

"That is true. 'God is a most free agent, and his will is himself.' So in that sense you are correct. 'But yet all God's voluntary acts are not natural.' Though God cannot act contrary to his nature, there are many things he does, which 'if he had not done them, or had done otherwise,' would not have been contrary to his nature.[13] God is not omnivolent. He does not will all that he can will. And not all that he does will to come about is necessary. Let me be clear. The *natural* acts of God are necessary. The voluntary acts of God are 'consequently contingent.'[14] Let me test you

---

12. Willard, *Compleat Body*, 250.
13. Willard, *Compleat Body*, 250.
14. Willard, *Compleat Body*, 250.

to see if you can tell the difference between natural and voluntary acts of God. As to God's acts *ad intra*, if I say, 'The Father eternally begets the Son,' and as to acts *ad extra*, if I say, 'Fire burns.' Which are they, natural acts or voluntary acts?" he asked.

"Natural acts," I said.

"Correct," said Vice President Willard. "And the reason they are natural, that is, necessary, is because there is no alternative possible object of choice. That the Father eternally begets the Son is absolutely necessary.[15] Likewise, that fire burns is the one natural and necessary determination of God for fire. That fire burns does not change and vary from one day to the next. Now let me test you again. If I say, 'God cannot but be himself,' which is it, a natural necessity or is it voluntary?" he asked.

"It is naturally and necessarily so," I said.

"Correct again. And if I say, 'God is Creator and Redeemer.' Naturally or voluntarily?" he asked.

"Voluntarily," I said. "For God 'might not have willed to make a world or to have made it thus,'" I said.[16]

"Precisely. Not only was God at liberty to create and redeem the world, but supposing that God wills to create, it was, then, a 'hypothetical necessity that the world must be.' God does not change his mind once he decrees. The transient acts of God do not change God. That which is new is the newly established relation between God and the newly created people, places, and things. Furthermore, to create or not was 'arbitrary with him whether he would have thus willed.' That which is natural is beyond mere choice. That which is voluntary is a matter of God's choice, that is, 'an act of liberty' that is thus 'not compatible with absolute necessity.'[17] To choose is to elicit an act of the will. When speaking of God's choice and freedom '*ad opposita*,' God either accepts or rejects the object presented to his mind to choose. Or God gives preference to one among many choices. In the freedom *ad opposita*, God's liberty is such that he is indifferent to the one over the other. So the object before God's mind does not compel God, rather God is internally determined by the council of his good pleasure and goodwill. That which seems good to God to do he does," he said.[18]

---

15. Willard, *Compleat Body*, 250.
16. Willard, *Compleat Body*, 250.
17. Willard, *Compleat Body*, 250.
18. Willard, *Compleat Body*, 250.

"If I may interrupt you," said Mr. Keith, "it sounds as if you are saying that God deliberates within himself about that which he is going to do. But how can that be since God is pure act?"

"Now you have touched on the nub of the issue. Indeed, God does not deliberate about his *natural* actions. But God is a rational being and he does deliberate about *voluntary* actions which we also call 'contingent actions.' God's will is a most reasonable faculty of power. But that is not to say that there are successive moments of time that pass as is the case when human beings deliberate. The distinction I made before about God's 'transient' acts comes into play here. The works of God 'out of himself are contingent, or acts of liberty.' I am speaking here of acts concerning creation and providence. Thus, that God be Creator and Redeemer is a 'relative' and contingent matter," he said.[19]

"When you engaged with the respondent you admitted that God is 'the physical cause of sinful human action,' but you denied that he is the moral cause thereof. Then you hid behind another distinction and said that 'God only determines the will of man to the material of the action, but not to the formal thereof,'" said Mr. Keith.[20]

"There is a grand distinction to be made between God's *physical* action that is a power to effect things in the reality of this world, on the one hand, and holding God accountable for the *moral* actions of human beings, on the other. First, I wish to make it clear that human beings like you and me are dependent upon God, not at all independent. The Scripture clearly says, 'For in him we live and move and have our being,' (Acts 17:28). You and I are what scholastics call secondary causes. God is the First Cause.[21] And there is a concurrence of our wills. But we must not confuse God's physical power, which is able to quicken and awaken our faculties, with our moral choices. We dare not implicate God in our sinful human actions. God's physical powers work at a different level, a substrate level, when moving upon our souls.[22] The physical and the moral are of different kin. The Lord Jesus taught his disciples to pray, but that does not mean that the Lord is responsible for some prayers which he himself calls 'prayers of abomination' (Prov 28:9).[23] When you and I

---

19. Willard, *Compleat Body*, 250–51.
20. Keith, *Refutation*, 3.
21. Willard, *Brief Reply*, 11, 12, 27.
22. Willard, *Brief Reply*, 20–21.
23. Willard, *Brief Reply*, 13, 38.

persuade ourselves to go forward with sinful action, the moral dimension of action belongs to us alone," he said. "Let me ask you, who was morally responsible for Jesus the Messiah's crucifixion?"

"Both Jew and Gentile, both Herod and Pontius Pilate," I said. "Peter said to the Israelites, 'this man, handed over to you according to the definite plan and foreknowledge of God, you crucified and killed by the hands of those outside the law,' (Acts 2:23)."

"Indeed. Now you see why the distinction between the physical and the moral dimension is so important. Although God *predetermines* the centurion's decision to one action, namely, to pierce Jesus' side, the movement of God on his faculties is not prior in time, but only in a causal priority and structural order of nature. But it is the centurion's will that actually produced the moral action," he said. "God thus stands asymmetrically behind virtue and vice."

"You said that God is the First Cause. Does that not make him ultimately responsible for sinful human action?" asked Mr. Keith.

"Not at all. Although God moves upon and quickens the faculty of the human will, it is not the created will per se that sins, but rather the defective use of the will that results in sin. Imagine a rider of a lame horse. The jockey may whip and stir up the horse to go. But the defect lies with the lameness of the horse."[24]

"Despite, or perhaps I should say with, these scholastic distinctions, it seems to me that you make God 'a law to himself,'" said Mr. Keith.[25]

"Not at all. Let me ask you another question. Allowing for the distinction between the physical and the moral dimension, to which dimension would you attribute temptation and persuasion to commit sin?" asked Vice President Willard.

"To the moral dimension, of course," he said.

"Actually, if God were to tempt and persuade someone to commit sin, he would be implicated on both levels, or in both dimensions, in both the act and the moral character of the act, that is, in both the material and the formal sense of action. But again, God's influx and quickening movement on the physical substrate level of reality does not implicate God in the moral character of human action. Think of Jesus foretelling that Peter would deny him three times. Did Peter blame Jesus' prophecy

---

24. Willard, *Brief Reply*, 25.
25. Keith, *Refutation*, 4.

for his denials? No, he did not. Peter wept bitterly," said Vice President Willard.[26]

"I hold that the essence of human free choice lies not only in independence but also absolute indifference," said Mr. Keith. "How do you understand the essence of free choice?"

"The essence of liberty 'is rooted in *lubentia rationis, primario et formaliter*, that is, liberty is primarily and formally rooted in the lubency or readiness of the will to act.'[27] The Reverend Charles Morton and I share similar views about rational lubency. He taught students at Harvard that 'Reformed philosophy places the liberty of the will not in indifference to opposites (willing or not willing, nilling or not nilling), but in a rational spontaneity.'[28] The readiness of the will to act means that the will is master of its own acts. As the Franeker University professor William Ames taught in his *Marrow of Theology*, 'Man of his own accord freely fell from God.' As a matter of fact, Ames also taught that even after the fall, formally speaking, 'freedom of the will essential to man's nature remains' intact.[29] But on the material level of freedom, the ability to attain the good that we will to achieve is fallen and in bondage," said Vice President Willard.

"I recall you asking the respondent, Francis Goodhue, to discuss necessity and freedom in the divided sense and in the compound sense of the terms. You and the respondent claimed that Adam could have not fallen in the divided sense of necessity and freedom."[30]

"Indeed. Let me explain a couple of important distinctions in this regard. If I were to propose to you that you could both be guilty and justified at the same time, what would you say?" asked Vice President Willard.

"I would say that that is a logical contradiction. Technically, the problem is that you are applying the predicate *guilty* to *justified*," said Mr. Keith.

"Excellent. That is the result of reading the proposition in the compound sense. But now suppose that I propose to you that although you

---

26. Willard, *Brief Reply*, 21. On whether it was in Peter's power to deny or not to deny Christ, see the disputation in the year 1465 in Louvain, Belgium, De Rivo, "A Quodlibetal Question on Future Contingents"; For the underlying Latin, see Baudry, *La Querelle Des Futurs Contingents*, 70–78.

27. Willard, *Brief Reply*, 14.

28. Williams, "Ethicks and Pneumaticks," seq. 9. For a fuller account, see Fisk, *Edwards's Turn*, 227–29.

29. Ames, *Marrow of Theology*, 114, 119.

30. Keith, *Refutation*, 6.

are declared justified, it is possible that you be guilty. How would you respond?"

"I am guessing that you will say that it is possible in the divided sense. But you will have to explain this sense to me."

"Indeed, I will. You will note that I used a comma to divide the proposition into two parts. In this way I avoid applying the predicate to both terms and ending up in a contradiction. So, at the *moment* in eternity when God declares you justified, it is *possible* at the same moment that you be condemned. This is not at all to say that God may possibly change his mind at a later *moment* and reverse the declaration of justification. No, God's decree is immutable.[31] There is another distinction that I wish to make. Briefly, there is a conceptual difference between a 'first act' (*actus primus*) and a 'second act' (*actus secundus*)."[32]

"Scholastic theologians," continued Vice President Willard, "abstract two acts of will from the concept of the will. If you recall, I mentioned a structurally ordered *order of nature*. According to that order, in a first act, God moves upon and quickens our soul's passive faculties. This prepares the way for the second act, whereby you and I exercise our wills.[33] God is acting at the physical level of reality, 'enabling us to comply with his invitation.'[34] This is how God engages with us and moves upon our souls' faculties and it explains why he is the 'author and finisher of our faith.'[35] Formally speaking, the second act freely belongs to you and me.[36] In the first act, God acts in the physical dimension of reality and infuses a principle of grace in what we call 'regeneration.' There is no active concurrence or participation on our part in this first act. In regeneration, when you and I believe, we are in a sense completing what God has begun. Once again, as the Franeker professor Ames taught, although 'God determines the infusion of the principle of grace in the first act, you and I retain our freedom in the second act.' As I explained above about the Latin word *vi*, Ames also uses the word *vi* to point to God's efficacious power and movement upon our soul's faculties. It points to God as the cause who produces an effect. Nevertheless, formally speaking, you and I

---

31. Willard, *Compleat Body*, 466.
32. Willard, *Brief Reply*, 15.
33. Willard, *Compleat Body*, 819.
34. Willard, *Compleat Body*, 819.
35. Willard, *Compleat Body*, 819.
36. Willard, *Compleat Body*, 458.

'do not lose our freedom or potency to opposite acts.'[37] But to your point, Mr. Keith, there is no absolute indifference on our part in the second act. The only kind of necessity that there is as we move from the first act to the second act is, as we said earlier, an infallible and thus implicative necessity, not an absolute necessity," he said.[38]

"Still, I must protest. 'If Adam's fall was necessary,' or the angels' fall for that matter, they would have an excuse, since 'necessity has no law.' In other words, how can you sentence someone under the law for wrongdoing, if that person was compelled and coerced against his or her will?" asked Mr. Keith. "Furthermore, I think it better that the students of 'the College of Cambridge in New England' not hear or be taught the doctrine which says that 'God determines creatures to sinful actions.' Clearly, with this doctrine you are giving students an excuse to sin, 'by virtue of God's decree.'"[39]

"Let me remind you," said Vice President Willard, "that people, places, and things are not necessary in themselves, that is, by nature. You must remember that there is a prior hypothetical necessity or supposition, and that is what determines things to be one way and not another. The people, places, and things about which we are talking are, themselves, 'mutable and contingent.' Hypothetical necessity does not 'alter the nature of the thing itself, but only gives us reason to conclude of the event, that it shall certainly be so. This is usually called necessity of infallibility.' And so we argue that 'if God had purposed a thing to be, it shall not be frustrated, because his purposes are unchangeable. But this purpose doth not, itself, alter the nature of the thing, nor obstruct its natural acting, nor lay any compulsion upon it.'[40] You must realize, Mr. Keith, that 'philosophers and logicians' subordinate causes, one to another, and order causes as either essential or contingent.[41] The Leiden professor Adriaan Heereboord, in

---

37. "*Gratia illa infusa non determinat voluntatem proprie nisi in actu primo: ita ut libertas quaedam remaneat ad actum secundum; qui licet infallibiliter sequatur motionis efficacis vi; libertatem omnem tamen aut potentiam ad contrarium non tollit,*" in Ames, *Rescriptio Scholastica*, 136.

38. Ames, *Rescriptio Scholastica*, 147.

39. Keith, *Refutation*, 6–7.

40. Willard, *Brief Reply*, 10.

41. Willard, *Brief Reply*, 19; cf. Scotus, *A Treatise on God as First Principle*, §1.3, §§1.15–1.16, §2.33, §3.6. Scotus says, "something causes contingently," in 4.15, and "I do not call everything contingent which is not necessary and which was not always in existence, but only that whose opposite could have occurred at the time that this actually did. That is why I do not say that something is contingent but that something is caused contingently," in §4.18.

the *Meletemata* or philosophical disputations that our students at Harvard recite, reminds us that 'the most noble question of all' is to ask what the root and First Cause of contingently ordered second causes is. Is it God's will, or, as you would have it, the human will? He answered that the root and First Cause of contingency in things is God's will itself."[42]

"Before you leave," continued Vice President Willard, "let me end our conversation with a practical application of some things that we have discussed. Prayer matters. But so too God's moving upon our souls and quickening them on the *physical* level. God is the one who enables us to request the one thing that God himself has engaged with himself to do. God empowers us in the physical dimension and reality of our souls that we may pray, with God being immediately present and active in our lives. 'What comes to pass in time, is no other but what he had appointed before all time, in the days of eternity; and for this very reason all God's works are said to be known to him, Acts 15:18.'"[43]

The correspondence between Vice President Samuel Willard and Mr. George Keith, who was in attendance at the 1702 Harvard commencement, took place immediately following the commencement, between 1702–04. The Willard-Keith correspondence affords scholars the opportunity to observe the kind of dialogue and argumentation that took place at commencements between the rector, the student respondent, and at times learned members of the audience, for whom commencement broadside sheets were printed and distributed, often at the cost of the graduating class. The last comments by Vice President Willard about God's will being the root of contingency intrigued me, and I decided to attend the 1704 Harvard ommencement in order to learn more from Vice President Willard about the notion of God's will being the root of all contingency.

---

42. Heereboord, *Meletemata*, 66; for more, see Fisk, *Edwards's Turn*, 144–48.
43. Willard, *Compleat Body*, 91.

2. Contingency

Whether the Root of Contingency in Second Causes be God's Will Itself? Affirmed by Samuel Wiswall.[1] President Samuel Willard 1704 Harvard Quaestiones 14

As planned, I attended the afternoon commencement day exercises at Harvard in Cambridge, July 5, 1704. Vice President Samuel Willard presided over sixteen *quaestiones,* one of which captured my attention, "Whether the root of contingency in second causes be God's will itself." The respondent, Samuel Wiswall, affirmed that it is so. After the commencement exercises, I talked to both Vice President Willard and Mr. Wiswall and engaged them in conversation about what appeared to me to be their strong appeal to the Franciscan tradition of emphasizing the central role of God's will.

"It appears that you teach a will-centered versus an essence- or nature-centered theology at Harvard," I said. "Could you explain to me the importance of rooting contingency in God's will itself?" I asked.

"Certainly," said Vice President Willard. "The Franciscan theologian John Duns Scotus (1266–1308) sets out the argument for contingent causality most profoundly in *Lectura I 39*, and less so in *A Treatise on God as First Principle*.[2] In *Lectura I 39*, Scotus not only shows that there is contingency in things created, but explains how it is the case. He sets out

---

1. Willard, "Harvard 1704, Original." "14. *An radix contingentiae in causis secundis sit ipsa Dei voluntas, affirmat respondens Samuel Wiswall.*"

2. Scotus, *Contingency and Freedom, Lectura I 39*, 96, 102, 104.; Scotus, *A Treatise on God as First Principle*, §4.18; Wolter and Frank, *Scotus on the Will and Morality*, 9–11.

his theory in three steps: 'There is contingency in things, God is the cause of contingency in things, and it is God's will which is the cause of contingency in things.'[3] He argues that if there is a finite being that is caused, then there is an infinite being. But suppose I say, 'If there is an infinite being, then there is a finite being.' Is that proposition valid?" asked Vice President Willard.[4]

"No," said Mr. Wiswall, "The conclusion does not follow necessarily. The premise that there is an infinite being stands on its own. I see then that if there is a contingent being, then some other being is necessary."

"Precisely. Scotus proceeds to argue from binaries, such as, infinite and finite, contingent and necessary. Now which is the lesser of the two binaries?" he asked.

"The finite is lesser than the infinite, and the contingent is lesser than the necessary," I said.

"Indeed. Now if I predicate finiteness of the subject *being*, what then will I conclude?" he asked.

"If there is a finite being, then there is an infinite being," I said. "And to avoid an infinite regress, then that finite being is caused by the first being at the head of the series of causes."[5]

"Correct. And based on what we just said, God's existence, as First Cause, does not necessitate the existence of secondary causes or beings. Let us look at the other binary, the contingent and the necessary. 'If there is a contingent being,' then there is a necessary being, namely, God. But does God's necessary existence 'entail the existence of other contingent beings (creation)?'" he asked.[6]

"No, not at all," said Mr. Wiswall. "But does Scotus apply the term 'contingent' to the realm of possibility or the realm of 'factuality?'" he asked.

"Excellent question. When Scotus uses the term 'contingent' he is talking about the realm of the *factuality* of beings. Thus far, as Scotus has led us to conclude, God's necessary existence does not entail the factuality of your existence and mine, " he said.

"Can you explain to us how it is the case that there is contingency in things?" I asked.

3. Scotus, *Contingency and Freedom*, Lectura I 39, 95.
4. Scotus, *Contingency and Freedom*, Lectura I 39, 96.
5. Scotus, *Contingency and Freedom*, Lectura I 39, 97.
6. Scotus, *Contingency and Freedom*, Lectura I 39, 99.

"In the second step, Scotus shows how it is that 'God is the cause of contingency in things.'[7] Now suppose there is a prior cause that necessitates, that is, necessarily moves a second cause. Does the second cause produce its effects contingently or necessarily?" asked Vice President Willard.

"I suppose necessarily, since the First Cause moved the second cause necessarily," I said.

"Indeed. Given a sequence of events, each occurs necessarily if the first is moved necessarily. But since in the first step Scotus showed that there is contingency in things as we know them, then if we back up we conclude that God contingently moves secondary causes and thus God is the cause of contingency in things," he said.

"God thus endows all created things with contingency," I said.

"Precisely. Now let us move to the third step. Scotus shows how it is that 'God's will is the cause of contingency in things,' a thesis which is the source of today's *quaestio*. Scotus inquires 'what it is in God by virtue of which he contingently moves what is.'[8] Now, by which faculty does God cause all that he causes, the intellect or the will, and why?" asked Vice President Willard.

"I suppose that God's will would never act contrary to God's intellect. For that would imply an imperfection in God's intellect. Certainly God knows what ought to be done, which way to act. So there is no practical intellect in God as there is in you and me," I said.

"Precisely the reasoning of Scotus himself. But Scotus says that though there be no practical knowledge in God, there is 'theoretical knowledge.'[9] Remember, God always knows the good that ought to be done. But that which God actually does is a 'theoretical' question. In fact, Scotus says, the question is a neutral question, as in the proposition, 'stars are even in number.'[10] Once God's will acts and assigns the number, then the proposition is either true or false. Now let me ask you, if God knows what he knows essentially and necessarily, can God's knowledge be the source and cause of contingency?" he asked.

"Based on that which we just said, no. For necessary causes produce necessary effects. Therefore, God's knowledge, that is, intellect, cannot be

---

7. Scotus, *Contingency and Freedom*, Lectura I 39, 102–03.
8. Scotus, *Contingency and Freedom*, Lectura I 39, 104.
9. Scotus, *Contingency and Freedom*, Lectura I 39, 104.
10. Scotus, *Contingency and Freedom*, Lectura I 39, 106.

the cause of the contingency in things in the realm of factuality," I said. "Thus, God's will must be the cause of contingency in things."[11]

"Precisely. God's will does not act contrary to his intellect, but neither does God's intellect operate like ours by guiding that which God wills. Thus, God's intellect presents, as it were, a neutral proposition to God's will, and his will can be said to act of its own accord. God's will passes things out of the realm of possibility into the realm of futurity," he said.[12]

"Does Scotus tell us about how our own human will is a cause of contingency?" I asked.

"Indeed he does. He also tells us how our human will differs from God's. He analyzes a threefold division of human freedom. He looks at human freedom to opposites (*ad opposita*) in terms of opposite acts, opposite objects, and opposite effects. Our freedom as regards opposite acts means that our will is an active potency in regards 'to willing and not-willing, loving and hating.'[13] Our freedom as regards opposite objects, which as Scotus points out still involves an act of the will, which means that our will is an active potency to love or hate the same person. Or it can mean to love this person, not another," he said.

"It seems as if, in the freedom of opposite acts as regards an object, the will has a potency to oppose itself (to love or to hate the same person). And in the second example, the potency of the will remains the same, to love. It could love another, but chooses to love this one over that one," I said. "But does not the example of the will's ability to oppose itself entail the mutability of the human will, and therefore a certain kind of imperfection?" I asked. "And if so, then we cannot attribute an imperfection to God's will, and therefore here is a clear difference between our will and God's will," I said.[14]

"Indeed it does, and Scotus takes note of this as regards freedom to opposite acts. You and I can love someone one day and hate them the next. This is, thus, a mutability expressed over time, successively. We cannot will both to love and to hate the same person at the same moment. Neither can God. But as regards opposite acts, God, you, or I can will to

---

11. Scotus, *Contingency and Freedom*, Lectura I 39, 105–06.

12. Scotus, *Contingency and Freedom*, Lectura I 39, 107; see Scotus's other arguments for contingency in Scotus, *A Treatise on God as First Principle*, §§4.12–4.18.

13. Scotus, *Contingency and Freedom*, Lectura I 39, 108; Scotus, *Scotus on the Will and Morality*, 9–10.

14. Scotus, *Contingency and Freedom*, Lectura I 39, 110–11.

love someone with the *possibility* at that same moment that we will not to love that same person. To state the possibility of acting otherwise at the same moment is not a contradiction and differs from what we just said about not both willing to love and to hate the same person at the same time. For the one act is factual, the possible act is not. I can say that this applies to God, as well as to you and me, since it does not imply an imperfection or mutability. I am speaking, thus, of the *contingency* of God's willing, not mutability. Crucially, in Scotus's argument, contingency differs from mutability."[15]

"What is freedom as regards opposite effects?" I asked.

"Briefly, this has to do with the will's potency to produce opposite effects. For instance, you and I can will to love or hate something without producing the desired result. We can thus separate this third freedom as regards effects from the second freedom as regards objects. But in the case of God, I cannot imagine that his act of will fails to produce the intended result," he said.

"Could you explain what Scotus means when he speaks of freedom as regards opposite acts and opposite objects in relation to the simultaneity of a factual act of the will, on the one hand, and a non-factual possibility of an act of the will, on the other?" asked Mr. Wiswall.

"You will recall that we spoke earlier about an actor loving someone one day and hating that person the next day," said Vice President Willard. "In this case Scotus says that the human will is 'successively related to opposite objects, and this possibility and contingency result from its mutability.' Let us a consider a proposition that Scotus himself puts forth. 'Something white can be black.' In what sense can this be true?"[16]

"Something white today can be black tomorrow," said Mr. Wiswall.

"Indeed. In the same way, if we pay attention to the divided sense of the terms of a proposition, we can say, 'The will loving him, can hate him,' to use Scotus's example.[17] With our mutable wills, while loving someone today, we can hate him or her tomorrow. Here we see *diachronic* freedom at work. The contingency of whether the actor will love or continue to hate the next day is clearly discernible. But note the importance of the terms of contingency, namely, the opposite terms of love and hate, each

---

15. Scotus, *Contingency and Freedom, Lectura I* 39, 111; Scotus, *Scotus on the Will and Morality*, 10.

16. Scotus, *Contingency and Freedom, Lectura I* 39, 114.

17. Scotus, *Contingency and Freedom, Lectura I* 39, 114.

at different successive moments of time. Note too that not only are there opposite acts of the will, but also opposite objects," he said.

"But did we not discuss earlier the idea of loving someone with the *possibility* at that same moment of not loving that same person?" I asked.

"Indeed. Scotus speaks of this 'logical possibility' in terms of non-successive acts of the will. 'For at the same moment the will has an act of willing, at the same and for the same moment it can have an opposite act of willing.' Consider the proposition Scotus puts forth: 'There can be a world.'[18] Let me ask you: Does the proposition claim that there is a factual world?" he asked.

"No, it does not," I said. "And yet, it is valid to say that a world *can* exist, even if it does not. But this proposition is about an ontology of possibility and contingency, is it not?" I asked.

"Indeed. Scotus has used this proposition to set up further talk about freedom and contingency. You will recall the proposition from earlier in our discussion, 'The will loving him can hate him.' If read in a compound sense, it results in a contradiction, since the reader applies the predicate to the whole proposition. But it is not a contradiction to read the proposition in the divided sense of the terms, applying the predicate to only one of the terms. Thus, 'At the same moment the will elicits an act of loving him, at the same and for the same moment it can have an opposite act of willing, namely, an act of hating him.' Scotus, thus, argues along the lines of 'logical possibility' and 'real potency.' The language of 'at the same and for the same moment' exemplifies Scotus's theory of 'synchronic contingency.'[19] Returning to the example we previously discussed, I can say, 'There is a world in which I now factually stand, but at and for this same moment, it is possible that there be no world. Thus, contingency says that what now is, *can* not be or be otherwise than it is," he said.

"So, how does Scotus relate this distinction to freedom of the will, and how does it support his argument for God's will as the cause of contingency in things created?" I asked.

"If it is possible that you will something otherwise than that which you in fact will, your will is free, is it not? In other words, it is possible that you not-will something at the same moment that you do will something," he said.[20]

---

18. Scotus, *Contingency and Freedom, Lectura I 39*, 116.
19. Scotus, *Contingency and Freedom, Lectura I 39*, 119.
20. Scotus, *Contingency and Freedom, Lectura I 39*, 123.

"This is the language of 'synchronic contingency' about which you were talking, isn't it?" I said.

"Indeed. Now I understand that you would like me to move on and talk about seventeenth-century theologians who are studied and whose disputations are recited in the Harvard curricula, theologians such as Adriaan Heereboord. But before I do that, I would like us to look at another important distinction that Scotus makes between the potency to will and the act of the will itself. That is, the will itself should be thought of as separate and apart from the eliciting of an act of the will. If we conflate the two, we lose the freedom of the will. Heereboord, to whom we will turn in a minute, also realizes the importance of this distinction. Now the will is prior to the act of the will, 'by nature,' as the scholastic terminology says. By 'nature' or by 'order of nature' has nothing to do with nature, earth, wind, and sky. Rather, by 'order of nature' refers to a structural ordering of the faculty of the will as being prior to the moment of eliciting an act of the will. 'Hence,' says Scotus,

> It [the will] is contingently related to willing and has a contingent relation to not-willing at that moment at which it elicits a volition; not because it had a contingent relation to willing at an earlier moment, for then it was not a cause, but because now, when it is the cause which elicits an act of willing, the will has a contingent relation to the act, so that willing at a, it can not-will at a.[21]

"For Scotus," he said, "whether human or divine, it is the 'real potency' to will that is the cause which passes something out of the realm of possibility into the realm of factuality. That is, the will actualizes that which was merely possible into something factual," said Vice President Willard.[22]

"Scotus has been talking about human freedom and hereby laying the groundwork to return to talking about divine freedom. Surely, given the doctrine of God's simplicity and the fact that God is pure act, there can be no succession of moments in time, no diachronic contingency, as you called it earlier. Tell us, then, how God's will is free and the cause of contingency?" I asked.

"Certainly. You will recall the imperfection and mutability that we saw in the human will as regards freedom to opposite acts, that the will's

---

21. Scotus, *Contingency and Freedom, Lectura I* 39, 118.
22. Scotus, *Contingency and Freedom, Lectura I* 39, 118–19.

ability to oppose itself entails the mutability of the human will from one moment to the next, and therefore a certain kind of imperfection. As we go forward in our discussion, keep in mind that contingency differs from mutability. Now God, who is pure act, cannot exercise freedom as regards opposite acts, as humans can. God's will has 'one single volition, and therefore it can will opposite objects by one single volition.' Unlike human volitions, God's single volition is unlimited as regards opposite objects. God hereby enjoys unlimited freedom.[23] And in regards to today's *quaestio*, remember, God is immutable. Which fact is another reason why whatever God wills, he wills in one act of willing. Nevertheless, this fact does not limit God from willing, in one pure act, that one object of his will take place in the course of this world at one moment, and another opposite act take place at another moment. Hereby God achieves in one single divine and eternal 'moment' that which humans only can achieve from one moment to the next," he said. "Thus the possibility of the mutability of the human will from one day to the next."[24]

"If I understand you correctly," I said, "Scotus has shown that the separation of the will from the act elicited by the will establishes the freedom of the will. And it establishes the contingency in the effects that are willed. When Scotus says, 'at that moment and for that moment at which it [the will] has a volition with respect to something, it can not-will (*nolle*) and can have an opposite act,' he is speaking of a contrary simultaneous freedom of the will to not will. Likewise, God's will, 'although it cannot have opposite acts (because his will is identical with its volition),' yet in eternity his will wills (*velle*) 'by one single volition' that you and I, for instance, are born in time, and in eternity it is possible that his will wills (*velle non esse*) that you and I not be born or it is possible that his will not-will (*nolle esse*) that you and I be born. Thus as concerns God's will itself, his will 'can produce and not produce an object,'" I said.[25]

"Precisely. There is thus a difference between being able to produce and actually producing. To sum up what has been said, with both God and human beings, at the moment of willing, we can say that simultaneous alternatives are possible. However, unlike with human beings, with God there is but one eternal moment of willing. Perhaps this is why Scotus uses the syntactical device of the divided sense, about which we

---

23. Scotus, *Contingency and Freedom, Lectura I 39*, 124.
24. Scotus, *Contingency and Freedom, Lectura I 39*, 124–25.
25. Scotus, *Contingency and Freedom, Lectura I 39*, 126, 128.

talked earlier. The example of Scotus now appears all the more striking, when he said, concerning one eternal divine moment, not two successive moments, 'The will loving him, *can* hate him,' that is, at that moment and for that moment at which God's will has a volition with respect to him," he said.

"I believe that you were going to say something about the first act (*actus primus*) and the second act (*actus secundus*), two acts which Scotus mentions in this context," said Mr. Wiswall.

"Indeed, I was," said Vice President Willard. "These two distinct acts represent two states of contingent reality. You and I are created in God's image. God has endowed us with a faculty of the will, a natural potency to elicit an act of the will. God can act and move upon our created wills. He can quicken our wills. We are connected with God in this way and also dependent upon him for our powers to act. This is where we begin to talk about the faculty of the will. This describes the state of the first act. A state of readiness, as it were. Thus, in Latin we say, *in actu primo*. The state of the second act, as you can imagine, is where the action is. In the second state or act, we say that the will elicits an act. The will is in the state of actually working, thus in Latin we say, *in actu secundo*. Now in God, who is pure act, that is, in his intra-trinitarian operations and productions, we say that God is 'fully actualized.' In God, however, although we can abstract and conceive of a distinction between these two acts, the two states or acts are inseparably one. For instance, God not only possesses omniscience, in the first act, but he also actually knows what he knows, in the second act," he said.[26]

"Before talking about the Leiden professor Heereboord and his *Meletemata*," he continued, "whose philosophical disputations students rehearsed while at Harvard, let me briefly say a word about another source for the Harvard curriculum, from another Leiden professor, namely, Franco Burgersdijk. His *Institutio logicarum* (1626) was studied by Harvard students. Listen to what he said about possible and contingent propositions. 'A possible proposition is that which when it is false, can be true.' On the contrary, 'An impossible proposition is that which when it is false cannot be true.' Then he gives the examples of propositions: 'the sun stands still, fire does not burn, a virgin birth.' Let me ask you, are those biblical examples of propositions impossible?"[27]

---

26. Scotus, *God and Creature*, 513; Scotus, *Contingency and Freedom, Lectura I* 39, 127; s.v "actus primus" and "in actu," in Muller, *Dictionary*, 11, 165–66.

27. Burgersdijck, *Institutionum Logicarum*, 133–34 (Pagination from 1651

"It certainly seems so," I said, "without divine intervention."

"Perhaps that is why Burgersdijk says that these are examples of hypothetical propositions (*secundum quid*). In reality, he says, these do not differ from contingent propositions. Then he says, 'It is said that that which is possible is that which is not, but can be.' On the other hand, he says, 'Contingent is that which is, but *can* not be.' From these propositions, you see how a Scotistic reading can derive both contingency in a diachronic sense of from one moment to the next, and contingency in a synchronic sense of simultaneous alternatives at the same moment," he said.

"Does Professor Heereboord teach students in the *Meletemata* or philosophical disputations, number 18, *De contingentia*, about God's will as the source of contingency in things?" I asked.[28]

"Indeed he does," he said. "Heereboord addresses the question of whether God contingently causes things to be. As in the Franciscan tradition of Scotus, he teaches that God acts contingently in his works *ad extra*. But, nevertheless, Heereboord sees this as entirely compatible with claiming that whatever God causes to come about in time, both the means and the end, cannot be impeded or hindered. The philosophers of Coimbra, the Jesuits, opposed what they saw as the unacceptable implications of such teaching. For them, to say that God acts contingently implies an imperfection in God, and mutability.[29] You will recall that we talked about this accusation earlier and how to resolve it."

"I also recall that two years ago at commencement we discussed what Heereboord called 'the most noble question of all,' namely, the one we have been discussing today," I said.

"Indeed. Since you and I are dependent upon God, even the secondary causes of our wills are rooted and grounded in God's will. Remember, God as the First Cause endows and quickens the faculty of our will to be able to act. You and I can act with simultaneous alternative possibilities, which we now understand better, having thoroughly discussed Scotus's teaching on this matter. For Heereboord, given God's sovereignty over first and second causes, means and ends, even contingently produced outcomes and effects, come about in dependence upon God and his will.

---

edition). Translation mine.

28. Heereboord, *Meletemata*, 66. Translations mine. On this topic, see Muller, *Post-Reformation Reformed Dogmatics*, 3:403–04; on Heereboord and contingent causality, see Fisk, *Edwards's Turn*, 144–48.

29. Heereboord, *Meletemata*, 66.

There is no independently contingent reality in Heereboord's philosophical worldview," he said. "For if there were, one could conclude that our wills, as secondary causes, impeded God's will, which I am sure you would agree is unacceptable," he said.[30]

"Does this mean that, for Heereboord, there are no effects produced that are necessary?" I asked.

"Not at all. He also holds that there are secondary causes, such as fire that burns, which necessarily operate the way they are designed to. Although the laws of nature are contingently caused, that does not mean that those laws function one way one day and another the next," he said.

"Does Heereboord also hold to two distinct states of acting, a first and a second?" I asked.

"Indeed he does, in the sense that we discussed earlier. And much like the Scotistic tradition, he distinguishes between the will as free to act and the actual act itself. According to Heereboord, what the Jesuits, Remonstrants, and Arminians oppose is God's efficacious moves upon our faculties in the first and second acts. They jealously guard the notion of an independent, self-determining, yet co-operating will in the second act as the only way to preserve human freedom. For Heereboord's opponents, there is no previous, sovereign act of God in the first act such that the second act infallibly follows. They hold to a "simultaneous concurrence" of God's will and ours. In that way, they believe they give you and me genuine freedom. But the cost they pay, according to Heereboord and other Reformed theologians, is to cast aside God's sovereign will by grounding and rooting human activity in the human will. Their account of things results in human activity informing God's will and knowledge and is a case of the very necessity they wish to avoid. Heereboord nicely explained the Reformed position when he said that God imparts in the first act the potency humans will use in the second act. Power, thus, 'contingently sprouts and descends from God,'" he said.[31]

"I recall that Franeker professor William Ames taught students what appears to be a Scotistic understanding of simultaneity and synchronicity, namely, that 'in the moment of time in which the act is determined to one choice or object, the individual retains true sovereign power,' or is master of his or her own will, 'if he or she were to will otherwise.'"[32]

---

30. Heereboord, *Meletemata*, 66.
31. Fisk, *Edwards's Turn*, 146.
32. Fisk, *Edwards's Turn*, 146.

"Indeed. The difference between the Reformed and the Remonstrants, Arminians, and Jesuits on this point about a simultaneous concurrence of wills (divine and human) is that God is the primary source of contingent causality for the Reformed. The question is, Does God act because we act or do we act because God acted? It is the latter. As St. John said, 'We love because he first loved us' (1 John 4:19)," he said.

"If I may sum up," he said. "God as First Cause acts contingently in his acts *ad extra* and therefore the succeeding sequence of events moves contingently all the way down and includes secondary causes, such as human volitions. Let me give an example from Heereboord about God's works *ad extra*. He asks us to imagine a series of causes, A, B, C, and D. God is the First Cause, A. If B is moved by A, necessarily, so is C by B, and D by C. But if A moves B contingently, then B moves C contingently, and so on down the line of proximate causes.[33] Today's Harvard *quaestio*, argued before our esteemed audience, took up what Heereboord called the most *noble* question. The respondent learned well how to answer the question from reciting Heereboord's disputations. Mr. Wiswall affirmed that the root of contingency in secondary causes is God's will itself," said Vice President Willard.

My attendance at the 1704 Harvard commencement and discussion with Vice President Willard at that time about contingency had introduced me to the important topic of the concurrence and intersection of God's will and ours. I wished to learn more about the topic, especially since it was a major topic of debate between Reformed theologians, on the one hand, and Jesuits, Remonstrants, and Arminians, on the other. My opportunity came at the Harvard 1715 commencement, where they discussed at length the concurrence of God's will and human freedom.

---

33. Heereboord, *Meletemata*, 67; for a fuller treatment, see Fisk, *Edwards's Turn*, 148.

3. *Concurrence*

WHETHER THERE IS A CONCURRENCE OF PRIMARY
AND SECONDARY CAUSES IN EVERY ACTION?
AFFIRMED BY NATHANAEL APPLETON.[1]
PRESIDENT JOHN LEVERETT
1715 HARVARD QUAESTIONES 1

IT WAS COMMENCEMENT DAY at Harvard College, and I attended the ceremonies in Cambridge. I had taken up lodging along the Charles River. Having obtained a copy of the commencement broadside sheet beforehand, I studied the list of sixteen questions to be debated and was particularly intrigued by the first question about the concurrence of God's will and ours in all human action. There was a nasty quarrel over whether God concurs even with the evil actions of men and women, and, if so, in what sense, in what ways?

The Reverend President John Leverett (1662–1724) addressed the learned audience and commenced with examining the young candidate for the master's degree.[2] He addressed Nathanael Appleton, "Please explain whether or not God concurs with human action, and, if so, whether that includes evil human action as well."

"Esteemed Reverend President, as is common knowledge and held by all, the Scripture testifies of God that 'In him we live and move and have our being' (Acts 17:28). That 'It is God who is at work in you, enabling you both to will and to work for his good pleasure' (Phil 2:13). And

---

1. Leverett, "Harvard 1715, Original."

2. On the election of John Leverett to president of Harvard College, see Morison, *Harvard College in the Seventeenth Century*, 550–56. For a description of the Harvard commencement program, see John Noble, "An Old Harvard Commencement Programme, 1730."

that 'The LORD has made everything for its purpose, even the wicked for the day of trouble' (Prov 16:4). We cannot escape from the truth that God is very much involved in our lives. In accordance with Scripture, we teach that God is the First Cause and that therefore he is the one who stirs, awakens, moves, and enables secondary causes, such as you and me, to act. Even so, God concurs in a much different way in relation to the evil actions of men and women than in relation to the good actions of men and women," said Appleton.

"Would you care to elaborate on that difference?" asked President Leverett. "And please include in your answer an explanation of the difference it makes whether we speak of God concurring only in secondary causes or in both first and secondary causes."

"Thank you for your questions. Let me reply by saying that God does not stand idly by when sin and evil happen. He does not take a hands-off approach. Nor is God somehow above the law, invoking some kind of immunity clause. Not at all. God's relation to the evil actions of men and women can be explained as follows. If an injured horse limps, it is not because of some divine design defect that can be traced back to God as First Cause such that he must assume responsibility for the limping horse. Nor is it the case that God himself cripples the horse. The horse limps because the horse and rider injured tendons and impaired the leg. Likewise, humans sin due to a defect in the will, an abuse of the will. Even though God endows men and women with the ability to choose either good or evil, it is their wills that choose. Our endowment by God of many blessings, talents, gifts, and abilities is not the cause of sin. As a matter of fact, we can even turn the worship of God into something utilitarian, something useful for us to achieve our own ends and goals. Worship, then, is no longer disinterested love for who God is, but self-interest. So you see the problem of evil lies within our darkened hearts and abusive wills. God commands worship, but the nearest cause of the twisting of worship for our own ends lies within us as secondary proximate causes. Not God, as First Cause," he said.

"Now," said Appleton, "let me add something about God concurring in both the first and secondary causes. There are those who claim that the only way to keep God far away from any responsibility for sin and evil is to argue that God only comes alongside human actors and merely works alongside their own powers to act. They don't see humans as mere secondary actors, but as sole initiators of their acts. They dismiss the idea of

God as the First Cause who stands behind all that happens in this world, both good and bad. Who moves us and enables us to act."

"What is at stake for their view?" he continued. "Those who argue in this way wish to establish human independence from God as the First Cause. But they wrongly identify God's endowing and enabling us to act in the physical dimension of this world with the evil of our actions in the moral dimension of this world. In order to exonerate God from any involvement in sin, they teach that humans initiate acts on their own, without God, the First Cause, giving the initial impulse or stirring to act. When they take this step they unwittingly fail to distinguish between the physical dimension of this world and the moral dimension of this world. Let me say it very bluntly. God can will to permit that evil happen or he can will not to hinder evil without ever willing evil as evil. To be clear, God does not will sin as sin, evil as evil."

"What is at stake for us gathered here today?" asked Appleton. "Our Father's world. This is our Father's world. The Father relates to this world as a Father to a son, as the Creator to the creation. But this imagery gives a mere sense of relation, a Father-son or -daughter relation. The Father provides for his creation and governs its vast scope, which includes evil," he said.

"Excellent. Well done," said President Leverett. "There are many ways in which God concurs with evil, yet without sinning thereby. I like what you said about this world belonging to our Father. He sustains the world, upholds it, cares for it, wills to permit rain to fall on the just and unjust. If God abandons us, it is not without cause. Please walk us through some of the most controversial Bible passages on this very topic. For many deny the sovereignty of God in his providential governance of this world. They do not admit that God moves in this world and in our lives as both the First Cause and primary mover as well as in secondary causes, in you and me. Even so, God guards the contingency and freedom of secondary causes," said President Leverett.

"Very well," said Appleton. "We read in the Bible how Paul instructed the Corinthian assembly 'to hand this man over to Satan' (1 Cor 5:5). One might be excused for thinking that Scripture approves of the church abandoning someone to Satan for destruction. It may appear that God's word condones sinful acts. On the contrary, as a just judge, God may order the abandonment of someone for the purposes of testing, examination, chastisement, or 'the destruction of the flesh,' as in this case. Note that the abandoning in this case is not for the destruction or murder of the person, but for the removal of the unrepentant sinner from the church assembly. When someone turns away from God, God may indeed justly surrender the person to Satan. As hard as that may sound, God is just and holy."

"What about the case of God 'putting a lying spirit into the mouth of these your prophets?' (2 Chr 18:22). Does this not implicate God in the sin of secondary causes?" asked President Leverett. "Would it not be better to distance God from stirring up these secondary acts of sinful men in order to preserve God's honor? Please explain."

"Let me attempt to exonerate God from the allegation that our teaching that God as First Cause concurs even with the evil of secondary causes implicates God in the sin and makes him to be the author, even actor, of sin. Although at first sight it is difficult to understand Ezekiel, who addressed this situation as follows, 'If a prophet is deceived and speaks a word, I, the LORD, have deceived that prophet'; nevertheless, Ezekiel immediately added, 'and I will stretch out my hand against him' (Ezek 14:9). Ezekiel explained that it was God's purpose that Israel no longer go astray. God warned Israel not to seek prophets to tell them what they wanted to hear, namely, that all was well. God said, when Israel returns to me, I will have achieved my purpose, namely, 'Then they shall be my people, and I will be their God, says the Lord God' (Ezek 14:11)."

"So, when God wills to permit a lying spirit to say, 'Peace, peace,' when there is no peace, it is a judgment upon Israel," said Appleton. "But God himself is not driving these prophets to lie and deceive. Jeremiah said of this, 'The prophets are prophesying lies in my name; I did not send them; nor did I command them or speak to them' (Jer 14:14). God clearly said that the lies come from within the prophets, not from God. 'They are prophesying the deceit of their own minds' (Jer 14:14). When people refuse to hear the truth, and want their ears only to be tickled with what they want to hear, then God may justly abandon them and even 'send them a powerful delusion' (2 Thess 2:11). Why? Because 'they refused to love the truth and so be saved' (2 Thess 2:10). I recall the scholastics who quoted Augustine: 'When you hear the Lord say, "I the Lord have deceived that prophet," you know that the one He permits to be deceived has earned it by his sins.'[3] In other words, God may will to permit the 'the father of lies' (John 8:44) to stir up trouble, but God's willing to permit differs from mere permission. It means that God maintains his sovereignty

---

3. Augustine, *De gratia et liberum arbitrium*, chapter 23, as quoted by Gerhard, *On Providence*, 99.

over this world and all secondary causes—this is our Father's world—yet our teaching absolves God from the allegation that if he governs both first and secondary causes in this world, he must somehow be the author, even actor, of sin."

The commencer Appleton's performance pleased President Reverend Leverett, Governor Joseph Dudley, as well as the assembled trustees. After the ceremonies, I walked with President Leverett in the college yard on his way to the Leverett estate. "You know," he said. "I defended the same question posed to me back in 1683 when I earned my master's degree. The question listed on the Harvard broadside and posed to me was, 'Whether There Is Concurrence of the Primary Cause with All Secondary Causes? Affirmed by John Leverett.'"[4]

"Tell me," I said, "what do you think is at stake in defending today's claim?"

"Reformed theologians distinguished between a *general concurrence* of primary and secondary causes and a *previous concurrence*. The respondent or commencer, as we sometimes call them, ably defended and affirmed from Scripture that there is a sovereign divine concurrence of wills without implicating God in sin as the author and actor of evil. But I want to add that Reformed theologians were especially keen on attributing to God a so-called *previous* concurrence, sometimes called divine *premotion* in the matter of the concurrence of primary and secondary causes. As should be clear by now, God is the First Cause, and he freely wills to move upon the human soul and in the concurrence of God's willing and human willing, God preserves the contingency of the his own First Cause right through the contingency of and completion of secondary causes. Remember, you and I are secondary causes, as are the laws of nature, etc. If God were to will necessarily, without alternate possibilities of willing at his disposal, then necessity would transfer to all the secondary causes, and one would end up in a necessitarian worldview. Now, scholastics abstracted two acts, whereby God awakens and enables the human will in the first act, and humans elicit an act of the will in the second act," said President Leverett.

"Indeed. I recall the discussion of first and second acts with President Willard when I attended the 1704 Harvard commencement. He presided over the question 'Whether the Root of Contingency in Second Causes be God's Will Itself?' The respondent Samuel Wiswall affirmed

---

4. "*An detur concursus causae primae cum omni causa secunda? Affirmat J. Leverett*," in Morison, *Harvard College in the Seventeenth Century*, 2:611.

that is was so. I learned that when Reformed theologians like Ames and Heereboord talked about a *previous* concurrence, the term pointed to God's sovereign acting from his own initial first act right through the completion of our second act. I see now that a so-called *general* concurrence of God's will and ours paves the way for rooting secondary human action in the human will. Thereby granting them great autonomy from God as First Cause. They think contingency sprouts in the human soul, but I recall that we teach that contingently sprouts and descends from God," I said.

"Contingency is an important teaching when trying to explain how God concurs with all secondary action," said President Leverett. "We have seen that there is an asymmetrical stance of God in relation to evil when juxtaposed with good. God's relation to evil is relative when compared to his direct relation to and cause of all good in this world through secondary causes. Many question the contingency of God's hardening the heart of Pharaoh. They wonder if that was not a case of God necessarily implicating himself in Pharaoh's sin. It is true that God told Moses to perform miracles before Pharaoh, and then said, 'But I will harden his heart, so that he will not let the people go' (Exod 4:21). We must recall that there is a certain natural remnant of hardness in everyone's heart. Even those who were followers of Jesus the Messiah had a certain slowness of heart or veil over their hearts. Did not our Lord Jesus say as much to the disciples on the road to Emmaus, 'How slow of heart to believe all that the prophets have declared!' (Luke 24:25). Are we not all in need of a heart of flesh to replace a heart of stone?"

"But what kind of hardness of heart did Pharaoh have?" I asked.

"Pharaoh had acquired a bad habit over time, the hardening of his heart," said President Leverett. "Scripture chronicles this acquisition of a hardened heart, telling us that when he saw the rain, hail, and thunder, 'He sinned once more and hardened his heart, he and his officials.' Note the phrase, *once more*, as in he kept on and thereby acquired a hardened heart. And now the tension between God's foreknowledge and forecasting of the hardening of Pharaoh's heart and Pharaoh's decision not to let God's people go. It is like our Lord Jesus when he forecasted Simon Peter's denials, and yet Peter in no way blamed God. Peter didn't think that he had no choice in the matter. That all was necessitated by God's will. No. '[Peter] went out and wept bitterly' (Luke 22:62). Regard the contingency of these two events in Scripture. God's foretelling that Pharaoh will harden his heart, and Pharaoh freely hardens his heart, and Jesus foretelling that Simon Peter will thrice deny him, and Peter freely denies the Lord.[5] Truly there is contingency from First Cause to last, all the way through these events. God's foretelling of Pharaoh's hardened heart, yet placing the blame squarely on Pharaoh; the foretelling of Simon Peter's denials, yet Peter freely acknowledging his guilt in the affair. No hint of fate playing out here, nor of Lady Fortune's forcing everyone's hand."

"I recall William Ames's teaching about the sovereignty of God in 'previous motion' and 'secondary causes' in his chapter in the *Marrow of Theology* on 'Providence.' He said, 'All secondary causes are predetermined to some extent by the force of this government. First, they are stirred to work by an influence, or previous motion.' He explained it by saying that God is the one who puts things into motion, a process that prior to God's action and movement upon the human soul was only 'potentially in the creature.' Second, Ames pointed to the Scripture passage about Shimei cursing King David. When Abishai wanted to take off the head of this 'dead dog,' David said, 'If he is cursing because the LORD has said to him, "Curse David," who then shall say, "Why have you done so?"' David concluded, 'Let him alone, let him curse; for the LORD has bidden him' (2 Sam 16:10). David thought that perhaps this was God's way of looking on his distress and that the LORD would bless him through it all. Ames put this passage forward as an example of God working through causes to accomplish his purposes." Third, Ames taught that God uses secondary causes to set 'limits and bounds' to all creatures' actions. As in the case of Satan and Job, Joseph and his brothers, Scripture passages which Ames mentioned."[6]

"I also recall the Lutheran scholastic Gerhard, who taught on this passage that David was 'speaking out of the true humility of his heart, recognizing the righteous judgment of God that because of his sins he deserved both the persecution of his son and this cursing from Shimei.' Would you not agree that the case of David and Shimei is like so many cases in the Hebrew Bible where God governs, even instigates, if I may use this word, the affairs of people only to the extent that these people deserve correction or punishment for sin? But God is not directly driving someone like Shimei to commit sin. For the Torah clearly says, 'You shall not curse a leader of your people' (Exod 22:28). Gerhard said that 'Shimei surely sinned very seriously in this action and was punished by God as a

---

5. I have in part adapted my discussion from Gerhard's in *On Providence*, 93–95.
6. Ames, *Marrow of Theology*, 110.

result.' For how could we say that Shimei sinned if he was merely fulfilling God's command? In many ways, the cases of Pharaoh and Shimei are similar. In both, God willed to stretch or extend the limits and bounds and thereby allow them both to carry out what was already festering in their hearts," I said.[7]

"Well said. Professor Ames also taught students about contingency and how it can be applied to Simon Peter's faith and denials," said President Leverett. "Consider the contingency of Peter denying the Lord. Until the Lord Jesus said anything to Peter about his three denials, Peter's faith or denials were a mere possibility. Indeed, it was always a possibility in the mind of God according to God's knowledge of simple understanding and of all possible states of affairs, a basic feature of the doctrine of God which Ames himself taught. Therefore, in the non-temporal and purely structural order of God's knowledge prior to God's decree of the will whereby he determines what he will permit to happen with Peter, the proposition 'Peter will deny the Lord' was a mere possibility. It had, as of yet, no temporal designation of if and when the proposition may happen. But, of course, once in time the Lord forecasted Peter's denials, necessarily Peter would deny the Lord. But the contingency of Peter's denials was real. That is, there was nothing in Peter's denial itself such that it had to happen, of necessity. Remember the adage, 'Whatever God does in time He has decided to do from eternity,' said the Lutheran scholastic Gerhard, or as the Presbyterian Stephen Charnock (1628-80) put it, "He wills or nills nothing to be in time, but what he willed and nilled from eternity."[8] Thus, since God decreed in eternity that Jesus would have this encounter with Peter and predict Peter's denials, it was going to happen. But it happened only as a consequence of the decree, or as is equally true, as a consequence of Jesus' prophecy. Ames, thus, taught that there was no absolute necessary connection between the terms of the proposition, "Peter" and "denial," or "Peter" and "faith," in God's knowledge of simple understanding and of all possibilities. In other words, the future contingent propositions of what would play out in time, such as 'Peter will believe' or 'Peter will deny the Lord,' had no determinate truth value assigned to it independent of God's decree.[9] I believe you learned about the teaching from President Willard at the 1704 commencement that the

---

7. Gerhard, *On Providence*, 97–98.
8. Gerhard, *On Providence*, 66; Charnock, *Existence and Attributes of God*, 1:326.
9. Fisk, "Divine Knowledge at Harvard and Yale."

root of contingency in secondary causes is God's will itself. Now, as we go our ways, ponder what the Presbyterian Stephen Charnock taught, 'Man hath a power to do otherwise than that which God foreknows he will do.'"[10]

As we ended our discussion, I thanked President Leverett for his generous gift of time. I told him that I anticipated meeting him again in the near future at another commencement day ceremony. Little did I know that only two years later we would meet again on the old college yard in Cambridge.

---

10. Charnock, *Existence and Attributes of God*, 1:450.

4. Middle Knowledge

WHETHER BESIDES THE KNOWLEDGE OF SIMPLE UNDERSTANDING
AND THE KNOWLEDGE OF VISION THERE IS ESTABLISHED
A CERTAIN THIRD MIDDLE KNOWLEDGE IN GOD?
DENIED BY NEHEMIAH HOBART.[1]
PRESIDENT JOHN LEVERETT   1717 HARVARD QUAESTIONES 4

IT WAS COMMENCEMENT DAY again at Harvard College in Cambridge. I took up residence in my former lodging along the Charles River. I met with President Leverett on his estate before the ceremonies to discuss the commencement day broadside questions. There was one question or problem, as it were, that fell under the doctrine of providence that I was eager to discuss with the president. The broadside question number four introduced the theory of a third kind of divine knowledge, called "middle knowledge" (*scientia media*) that the Jesuit Luis de Molina (1535–1600) had proposed. The respondent or commencer, as they called them, was Nehemiah Hobart. According to the broadside, he was going to oppose the idea of so-called *middle knowledge*.

"President Leverett, could you please explain to me what exactly middle knowledge is and why the respondent Mr. Hobart is set to oppose it in his argumentation today?" I asked.

"Certainly. Let me tell you in his own words how Molina defined *middle knowledge* and why he proposed such a novel idea. His major treatise on divine foreknowledge and providence is known, in short, as the *Concordia*. The full title was *The Compatibility of Free Choice with the Gifts of Grace, Divine Foreknowledge, Providence, Predestination, and Reprobation* (*Liberi Arbitrii cum Gratiae Donis, Divina Praescientia, Providentia, Praedestinatione et Reprobatione Concordia*, Part IV) (1588). A revised

---

1. Leverett, "Harvard 1717, Original."

edition was published in 1595. You can also find most of the *Concordia*, part IV in Molina's commentary on Aquinas's *Summa Theologiae*, First Part, published in 1592. This is how he defined *middle knowledge*:

> The third type is middle knowledge, by which, in virtue of the most profound and inscrutable comprehension of each faculty of free choice, He saw in His own essence what each such faculty would do with its innate freedom were it to be placed in this or in that or, indeed, in infinitely many orders of things—even though it would really be able, if it so willed, to do the opposite, as is clear from what was said in Disputations 49 and 50.[2]

"Before digging into the meaning of the many parts of this definition of *middle knowledge*, you will do well to remember that Molina called the first kind of divine knowledge 'natural' and the second 'free.' With this additional third kind of divine knowledge, *middle knowledge*—the subject of today's commencement disputation—Molina intended to reconcile once and for all human free choice and the contingency of things with divine foreknowledge. When asked if *middle knowledge* is the same as God's *natural* or *free* knowledge, Molina said no. *Middle knowledge* was not to be called *free* because, he said, 'it is prior to any free act of God's will.'[3] Now, it is crucially important to see that he positions *middle knowledge*, by way of conceiving it, after God's *natural* knowledge and prior to God's will, which will in turn is prior to God's *free* knowledge. Conceptually, thus, he called it *middle knowledge* because he positioned it between God's *natural* knowledge and God's *free* knowledge, and specifically between God's *natural* knowledge and God's will. And then pay close attention to what else he said. He added that this *middle* knowledge is not called 'free.' Why? 'Because it was not within God's power to know through this [*free*] type of knowledge anything other than what He in fact knew.'[4] In other words, God's *free* knowledge of God's free will knows in fact what the created free wills of human beings will do. Not hypothetically or conditionally, but absolutely and by the determination of God's will, God freely knows what he has determined to take place in time."

"But from the sounds of it, is Molina's understanding of God's *free* knowledge much different than the Reformed understanding of God's

---

2. Molina, *Concordia*, 168 (Disp. 52, §9). In addition to Freddoso's introduction, for a fuller treatment of middle knowledge and a Reformed response, see Beck, *Voetius on God, Freedom, and Contingency*, 300–51.

3. Molina, *Concordia*, 168 (Disp. 52, §10).

4. Molina, *Concordia*, 168 (Disp. 52, §10).

free knowledge?" I asked. "I presume that the respondent Mr. Hobart will answer my question."

"It is nearly the same," he said. "The big difference between Molina and the Reformed is in their definitions of *natural* and *middle* knowledge, and in Molina's conceiving of the position of *middle* knowledge as prior to God's will. But let's wait to talk about how the Reformed replied to Molina's *middle knowledge* until after the ceremony. Then we can discuss Mr. Hobart's defense of the Reformed position, which says that there is no need for any more than two types of divine knowledge. That much of an answer is already made clear in the wording of the question and answer on the commencement broadside sheet that you have. But first, there is much more to say about Molina's novel idea of *middle knowledge*."

"Take note of Molina's definition," he continued. "God has 'inscrutable comprehension of each faculty of free choice.'[5] Whose faculty of free choice was he talking about?" he asked.

"He was referring to human beings, like you and me," I said.

"Correct. Molina was shifting the focus of the root cause towards the free choice of men and women. Then he said this about *middle knowledge*, 'He [God] saw in His own essence what each such faculty would do with its innate freedom were it to be placed in this or in that' order of circumstances.[6] And he added that created innate freedom, like yours or mine, could will to do otherwise than it does. Now here is his crucial move. Molina places God's *middle knowledge* of what human innate freedom will do, prior to, by our way of conceiving it, God's willing of what will come about. In other words, God's *middle knowledge* concurs with the choice of human innate freedom *before* the decision of God's free will. Human choice therefore plays a decisive role in determining not only what God knows, but what God wills. There is not a concurrence of divine and human wills, but a concurrence of divine *middle knowledge* and human choice. Let me put it more precisely. *Middle knowledge* shifts the root of contingency away from God's will and places it squarely in the concurrence of innate human freedom with *middle knowledge*," he said.

"If I understand your explanation of Molina correctly, he said that before God wills to create you or me, and thereby endow us with innate freedom, he knows hypothetically what you and I would freely do in each

---

5. Molina, *Concordia*, 168 (Disp. 52, §9).
6. Molina, *Concordia*, 168 (Disp. 52, §9).

and every circumstance. The emphasis is placed on our innate freedom and free acts as well as on God's hypothetical knowledge," I said.

"Indeed," he said. "Molina made it clear that God's *middle knowledge*, as he put it, 'depends on the fact' that you and I would, in our freedom, 'do this or that, and not the other way around.'[7] In other words, not that what we do depends on God's *middle knowledge*, but rather that *middle knowledge* depends on what we do. Molina wanted to provide some nuance to his theory, and so he added that *middle knowledge* shares in part some characteristics of *free* knowledge. He sought to clarify that God does not know for sure by way of *middle knowledge*, 'absolutely, without any hypothesis,' what you and I will actually and 'in fact' do, given our 'created free choice.' That is because the characteristic of knowing what we will do belongs to God's *free* knowledge of what he knows will happen, after the fact, as it were. What happens in the course of this world depends on the concurrence of God's 'free determination of His will' and 'created free choice.'[8] You should not miss this point, namely, that for Molina, our hypothetical actions inform God's *middle* knowledge which in turn informs the determination of God's will."

"I am a bit confused by the meaning of the term 'free' in 'God's free determination of His will' and the 'free knowledge of God' in Molina's theory. Did he root the contingency of what happens in the course of our lives and choices in God's free will? Is that what he meant by free will and free knowledge?" I asked.

"No, not at all," he replied. "By *free* knowledge, Molina intended to say that God's knowledge is free in the sense of being open to the reality of what you and I will choose to do, in such and such circumstances, given the fact that we are 'endowed with free choice.' In other words, what we do 'does not stem from God's foreknowledge.' The reverse is true in Molina's theory. What God foreknows stems from what we freely choose to do. 'Nor does this fact stem from God's willing that the thing in question be done by that being,' said Molina. 'Rather, it stems from the fact that the being would freely will to do that thing.' In this sense Molina called God's knowledge and will 'free.' He said further that God's free knowledge 'depends on the fact that the being would in its freedom do this or that, and not the other way around.'"[9]

---

7. Molina, *Concordia*, 170 (Disp. 52, §10).
8. Molina, *Concordia*, 170 (Disp. 52, §10).
9. Molina, *Concordia*, 170 (Disp. 52, §10).

"So, in Molina's theory, the term 'free' was not used in the sense of God's freedom to sovereignly determine, according to his good pleasure, and without violating our wills, the choice of human beings with a kind of persuasive divine influx and movement upon our souls," I said.

"You are quite right," he said. "What you said sounds more like what the Reformed would say. But we will get to their theory shortly. Now, for Molina, not only did *middle knowledge* partly share some features of God's *free* knowledge, but also some features of God's *natural* knowledge. So, we see Molina partly conflating the three types of knowledge into one. He said this about *middle knowledge* sharing some features in common with God's *natural* knowledge, 'since it was prior to the free act of the divine will and since God did not have the power to know anything else.'[10] Indeed, as we have said, he positioned both *natural* and *middle* knowledge prior to God's will, by way of conceiving the order. But notice what he said about God 'not having the power to know anything else.' Molina has said that God's power to know your choices and mine, for instance, is limited. In his theory, it is not within God's power to know the things that could happen otherwise or contrary to what in fact will happen in concurrence with the human powers of free choice. Let us here state Molina's definition of God's *natural* knowledge:

> One type is purely natural knowledge, and accordingly could not have been any different in God. Through this type of knowledge He knew all the things to which the divine power extended either immediately or by the mediation of secondary causes, including not only the natures of individuals and the necessary states of affairs composed of them but also the contingent states of affairs—through this knowledge He knew, to be sure, not that the latter were or were not going to obtain determinately, but rather that they were indifferently able to obtain and able not to obtain, a feature that belongs to them necessarily and thus also falls under God's natural knowledge.[11]

"Take note of the limitation of the extent of God's power to know things. God's knowledge of the possibility of you and me doing otherwise than we in fact do appears unavailable to God in *natural* knowledge. This is because of the feature of *natural* and *middle* knowledge both being conditional, conditioned upon human freedom. The power to do otherwise belongs to you and me necessarily and is ours essentially, according

---

10. Molina, *Concordia*, 169 (Disp. 52, §10).
11. Molina, *Concordia*, 168 (Disp. 52, §9).

to Molina. On his account, since God's *natural* knowledge is prior, by our way of conceiving it, to God's *middle knowledge* as well as the free determination of God's will, God's *natural* knowledge does not include knowledge of the determination of the will, nor of God's *free* knowledge. Even though there is no temporal separation of moments from one type of knowledge to another, still, Molina wished to retain the indifference of whether states of affairs will obtain or not in the course of our lives in this world. Given this lack of knowledge, Molina added the third type of knowledge. In his theory he supposed that in this way he genuinely preserved human freedom and the contingency of things in this world."

"If I understand Molina correctly," I said, "always keeping in mind the non-temporal way of conceiving of *before* and *after* in regards to these types of knowledge, God does not know or see 'through his natural or middle knowledge, before the determination of His will, which part He Himself is going to choose' as he himself said."[12]

"Indeed," he said. "In this regard, Molina compared God and creatures, saying, just as you and I do not know beforehand that to which our wills will turn, since our minds are not infinitely greater than our essential being and will, 'so too neither does God know, before He determines His own will, which part it is going to be turned toward.' In fact, Molina said that he could not conceive how, 'before the act of His will,' God foreknew which part His freedom would turn toward. 'For if such knowledge existed, then He would in no way be able to choose the opposite part.' That is, God's will would be necessitated and determined to turn one way without the possibility of choosing otherwise. God's freedom was lost. Or so he thought."[13]

"But," I asked, "would not the Reformed say that in the very first type of God's knowledge, whether one calls it natural or the knowledge of simple understanding, God's all-sufficient knowledge includes all possible states of affairs that could be wrought through his absolute power? And is not this knowledge of God necessary since the object of God's knowledge is necessary, that is, in the sense that it is necessary to hold that God *can* produce more than he actually does? The Presbyterian pastor Stephen Charnock said as much. In fact, he made an important

---

12. Molina, *Concordia*, 171 (Disp. 52, §11).

13. Molina, *Concordia*, 171 (Disp. 52, §11).

distinction between God's absolute power and his ordinate power. The latter is linked to the act of God's will."[14]

"Well said. That is, God knows all possible states of affairs in virtue of his absolute power. But we will say more about this important distinction between God's absolute and ordinate power later. For now, let us continue our conversation about Molina's theory with Mr. Hobart, after the ceremonies," he said.

I agreed and went to take a seat in the audience. President Leverett introduced Mr. Hobart, who proceeded to explain Molina's theory. He related to the audience much of what we had discussed before the ceremony. President Leverett then asked the respondent the following question. "Could you tell us how Molina handled any objections to his theory?" he asked. "And could you begin to move from theory to practice, fleshing out the theory with examples?"

"Indeed," said Mr. Hobart. "Let us proceed to look at Molina's answers to those who raised objections to his theory. Some, like the Mercederian Francisco Zumel (1540–1607) and the Dominican Domingo Banez (1528–1604) questioned Molina's theory that God's knowledge is conditioned upon human action. The oft-cited examples were whether the Tyronians' and Sidonians' repentance was conditioned upon whether Jesus would work miracles in their midst as he had done in Chorozain and Bethsaida. And whether David's safety was conditioned upon whether Saul would descend upon the city of Keilah. Would the people of Keilah betray David into Saul's hands, out of fear? The Lord had said, 'Yes, they will betray you in such and such circumstances.' But David escaped, unharmed. Was that not a hypothetical, thought Molina? He found dangerous those who denied these hypotheticals. He believed that there must be 'middle ground between what is *absolutely future* and what is *merely possible*.'[15] He said that his opponents failed to make this distinction in order to avoid his theory of *middle knowledge*. He believed that the Bible passage in Matthew 11 about the Tyronians and Sidonians clearly spoke of conditional future repentance. He placed this kind of conditional knowledge on the line with *middle knowledge*.[16] Thus, prior, by way of conceiving it, to God's free will and God's *free* knowledge. Instead of seeing these so-called conditional circumstances as contingent

---

14. Charnock, *Existence and Attributes of God*, 1:411.
15. Molina, *Concordia*, 201 (Disp. 53, §6).
16. Molina, *Concordia*, 201–02 (Disp. 53, §§6–7).

states of affairs, flowing from God's decree of the will, and as such, the actual outcome as a necessity of the consequence of God's decree, Molina was convinced that everyone must conclude that these biblical examples fall under God's *middle knowledge*. Why? The reason is that Molina believed that in this way he could preserve genuine human freedom."

"If I may continue," said Mr. Hobart, "it is important to recognize that Molina believed that his opponents' doctrine of God's 'predetermination' and 'efficacious concurrence' robbed the Sidonians and Tyronians of their innate freedom to choose otherwise. He thought that his opponents must link any certitude of the repentance or rejection by the Sidonians and Tyronians to God's predetermination and efficacious concurrence, or lack thereof. For how else, he thought, could his opponents make any distinction between the actual response of the people of Chorozain and Bethsaida to Jesus' miracles and the hypothetical response of the Sidonians and Tyronians? For Molina, whether these people repent or not ultimately rests upon human free choice and consent. In his words, 'whether or not the faculty of choice that is moved and stirred' by grace 'wills to consent to and cooperate with it—as the Council of Trent clearly taught.'"[17]

"It seems that Molina was unable to conceive of the power we as humans possess to do otherwise than we in fact do," said President Leverett in reply. "That is, there is no incompatibility in our holding on the one hand to God's predetermination and efficacious grace, and on the other to our claiming that we always retain the power to do otherwise than we do. Even though we will never do otherwise. Was this not true of the power of our Lord Jesus while he was on earth? I think so. Allow me to quote Charnock, who said, 'Man hath a power to do otherwise than that which God foreknows he will do.'[18] Charnock wished to make the point that if something be future, it either rises up from itself or from God. But 'not from itself,' for 'then it would be independent and absolute.' Is that not an argument against Molina's theory, Mr. Hobart? Charnock said, 'The knowledge of God cannot arise from the things themselves, for then the knowledge of God would have a cause without him; and knowledge, which is an eminent perfection, would be conferred upon him by his

---

17. Molina, *Concordia*, 202–03 (Disp. 53, §7).
18. Charnock, *Existence and Attributes of God*, 1:450.

creatures."[19] And that would be unacceptable." The president then quoted Charnock again.

> But as God sees things possible in the glass of his own power, so he sees things future in the glass of his own will; in his effecting will, if he hath decreed to produce them; in his permitting will, as he hath decreed to suffer them and dispose them; nothing can pass out of the rank of things merely possible into the order of things future, before some act of God's will hath passed for its futurition.[20]

"Mr. Hobart, would you please explain Molina's theory of how God concurs with human action, both good and bad?"

"Certainly," he said. "Molina distinguished between three type of human actions. First, there are moral actions that only need God's 'general concurrence.' Suppose Peter were to say to Jesus, 'You are the Messiah.' All that was required for Peter to freely and indifferently say what he said was God's 'volition to create the whole order of things all the way up to Peter' speaking. This included God's concurrence with all the secondary causes from Peter's birth leading up to Peter's speech act. Quite naturally, it included God endowing Peter with a soul, the power to speak, and God agreeing to concur with Peter's speech act.[21] Crucially, Molina said,

> This concurrence is not a motion of God's *on* the faculty of choice by which He moves, applies, and determines it either to precisely *that* act of speaking or even to *some* act of speaking or other; instead it is an influence *along with* the faculty of choice, an influence that depends for its existence on the influence and cooperation of that faculty itself.[22]

"Notably," said Mr. Hobart, "God's general concurrence was 'intrinsically indifferent.'[23] For Molina, that meant that Peter was free to speak or not to speak. Molina wanted to make clear that Peter was the cause of the speech act. God foresaw Peter's free speech act 'on the hypothesis' that God would predetermine everything required for Peter to speak. All this was according to the good pleasure of God's will (*voluntas beneplaciti*). But Molina also stressed the point that all was in 'dependence on Peter's

---

19. Charnock, *Existence and Attributes of God*, 1:433.
20. Charnock, *Existence and Attributes of God*, 1:433.
21. Molina, *Concordia*, 242–43 (Disp. 53, §7).
22. Molina, *Concordia*, 243 (Disp. 53, §7).
23. Molina, *Concordia*, 243 (Disp. 53, §7).

free cooperation, which God foresaw to be forthcoming."[24] This way of speaking clearly explains Molina's theory of general concurrence."

"So, for Molina, God foresees, predetermines and concurs in a general sense with good human actions, but merely foresees evil human actions," said President Leverett.

"Yes. That is how I understand Molina," said Mr. Hobart. "He wanted to avoid any opinion that appeared to make God the author of evil. Let me skip over the second type of human action, which concerned God's concurrence with last minute confessions of faith, and proceed to talk about the third type of human action. How, for instance, did God concur with Peter's threefold denial of the Lord Jesus? He said that one should not approve of his opponents who did not want to speak of God's predetermination, efficacious concurrence, and directing of the human faculty of free choice in such cases, but would so speak of God's operations in the case of good human action.[25] Molina placed the blame for evil human action squarely upon the sinner's abuse of the will. Thus, in the case of Peter's denials, God provided everything needed, as I already explained earlier, for Peter to elicit an 'indifferent' act of the will to deny Christ. Indeed, God made provision by way of a 'predetermination to permit Peter' to deny Christ. Why? Molina explained:

> [It was] for the sake of the excellent end that God Himself intended by this permission, to perform the evil action that He foresaw would occur under those circumstances because of Peter's free choice—that is, a predetermination not to alter the circumstances or to confer on Peter other aids in the presence of which he would not lapse into that denial because of the same freedom of choice.[26]

Mr. Hobart finished by explaining that Molina accused his opponents of holding to the opinion that God predetermines, directs, and concurs with non-evil human actions in such a way that their free choice is violated and they have no power to act otherwise than they do. He attributed this to an "intrinsic efficacious" concurrence.[27] Molina thought that his opponents were forced to this conclusion, given that he could not conceive how they reconcile the certitude of God's foreknowledge

---

24. Molina, *Concordia*, 244 (Disp. 53, §7).
25. Molina, *Concordia*, 246 (Disp. 53, §9).
26. Molina, *Concordia*, 247 (Disp. 53, §9).
27. Molina, *Concordia*, 247 (Disp. 53, §10).

with human free choice. He thought that their scheme meant that God foreknew future human action in an absolute sense.

At this point, Mr. Hobart sat down and President Leverett closed the afternoon ceremony by inviting the distinguished guests to continue to enjoy the other festivities.

I was delighted that the three of us, the president, Mr. Hobart, and myself, continued the discussion about Molina's theory. I asked the president and the respondent to tell me about the Reformed response to Molina's theory of *middle knowledge*.

"Let me begin our time together," said President Leverett, "by turning to the Reformed professor Gisbertus Voetius at Utrecht University and a disputation of his on middle knowledge.[28] First, the twofold knowledge of God, known by various names, such as his knowledge of simple understanding and his knowledge of vision, was all-sufficient and encompassed the whole nature of objects of his knowledge. These two types of God's knowledge correlate to God's absolute and ordinate power. Like Charnock, Voetius held that it is the decree of God's will that passes objects out of a state of possibility into a state of futurition.[29] Second, it follows therefore that God cannot know a state of affairs in a conditional future state prior, by way of conceiving it, to God's will. One reason, as Molina himself acknowledged, is that God knows these possibilities indifferently.[30] God could have employed Judas in his service in the place of Paul. God could have ordained that David be handed to Saul by the people of Keilah. Prior to the will, these propositions have no determinate time indexation or truth value. Third, Molina's theory of an indifferent cause moving a self-determining human will, independent of God's sovereign influx will not do. What then is the source of God's knowledge of this cause?[31] In sum, Voetius's line of argumentation asked, How can a state of affairs achieve the state of futurition prior to the decree of God's will? And, mind you, that state of futurition might be that the event occurs in reality or not, given the accompanying conditional circumstances. For there is a difference between being in a state of futurition and being in reality.

---

28. Here I am following the work of Beck, *Voetius on God, Freedom, and Contingency*, 334–51.

29. Beck, *Voetius on God, Freedom, and Contingency*, 334–35.

30. Beck, *Voetius on God, Freedom, and Contingency*, 335.

31. Beck, *Voetius on God, Freedom, and Contingency*, 336.

"Now let us consider," said President Leverett, "what God told David about whether the people of the city of Keilah would betray him into the hands of Saul, if he were to stay, and what in fact David did. There is no incompatibility with God knowing in virtue of his *absolute* power—and telling David—that if he were to stay, the people would betray him, on the one hand, with God knowing, in virtue of his *ordinate* power, and predetermining that David will to flee. For God's ordinate power is joined to his will. What we can say about this case is, first, David always retained the power to do otherwise. Thus, his freedom was not violated. Second, although God's power is one, we can abstract two types of power. Charnock said, 'Absolute is that power whereby God is able to do that which he will not do but is possible to be done. Ordinate is that power whereby God doth that which he hath decreed to do, that is, which he hath ordained or appointed to be exercised.'[32] In this case, God had ordained that David flee. The Bible passage preserves both David's free choice and God's sovereignty in predetermining his flight to safety. Concerning God's sovereignty, we read, 'Saul sought him every day, but the LORD did not give him into his hand (1 Sam 23:14).'"

"There is, then, no need for *middle knowledge*," said Mr. Hobart. "Charnock made it clear that 'his ordinate power is a part of his absolute; for if he had not a power to do everything that he could will, he might not have the power to do everything that he doth will.' Like Voetius, he also stipulated the rules that govern God's absolute power. 'The object of his absolute power is all things possible; such things that imply not a contradiction, such that are not repugnant in their own nature to be done, and such as are not contrary to the nature and perfections of God to be done.'"[33]

"So there is no contradiction in holding, as Charnock did," said Mr. Hobart, "that 'by his absolute power, God might have given the reins to Peter to betray his Master, as well as to deny him.' Or consider Judas and Paul. As already mentioned, by his absolute power, God could have 'employed Judas in the same glorious and successful service, wherein he employed Paul.'[34] John the Baptist spoke of God's absolute power over possible states of affairs when he said, '"God is able of these stones to raise up children to Abraham"' (Matt 3:9). The difference between God's

---

32. Charnock, *Existence and Attributes of God*, 2:12.

33. Charnock, *Existence and Attributes of God*, 2:12. On this point, see Beck, *Voetius on God, Freedom, and Contingency*, 334.

34. Charnock, *Existence and Attributes of God*, 2:13.

absolute and ordinate power is clearly seen in the instance of Jesus' statement in Matthew 26:53, 54 when he said, "'My Father can send twelve legions of angels,' there is his absolute power.' But consider God's ordinate power. "'But how then shall the Scriptures be fulfilled, that thus it must be?' There is his ordinate power."[35] In other words, we must uncouple God's absolute power from his will. That is after all what 'absolute' means; that which is unconditional, unrestricted, and unconnected. "His power is free from any act of his will.' When God's power is 'joined with an act of his will, it is called ordinate.' His ordinate power 'is guided by his will and wisdom.'"[36]

"In sum, Charnock said, there were 'possibles,' 'factibles,' and 'actuals.' What is possible is 'the object of absolute power,' what is factible is 'the object of ordinate power,' and what is actually made or done is 'the object of preserving power.'[37] Molina's theory appears to confuse what is *possible* with what is *factible*, and what is *factible* with what is *actual*."

"To return to the case of Peter's denials," said President Leverett, "what Molina failed to understand was that the Lord Jesus' prediction in no way violated Peter's freedom, since he always retained the power to act otherwise than he in fact did. And this in no way undermines the certitude of Jesus' foreknowledge. Given Jesus' prophecy, the consequence was that Peter was going to deny the Jesus. No doubt about it. But the denial itself was not intrinsically necessary, as if uncoupled from Jesus' prediction and God's ordinate power. Even so, Peter retained the power to do otherwise than Jesus foreknew he would do. One has to distinguish between God's absolute power and his ordinate power and between Peter's power to will and the evil act he actually elicits to do."

"To Molina's point about predetermination and intrinsic necessity," he continued, "'Creatures have a power to act about more objects than they do.'[38] If that were not so, they would be intrinsically necessary agents. Likewise, God would not be free if he had not the power and ability to do more than he actually does. God would be 'a natural and necessary agent, which cannot be supposed of God.'[39] I think the warning that Charnock gives about this topic is appropriate to repeat: 'But what if the

---

35. Charnock, *Existence and Attributes of God*, 2:13.
36. Charnock, *Existence and Attributes of God*, 2:13.
37. Charnock, *Existence and Attributes of God*, 2:16.
38. Charnock, *Existence and Attributes of God*, 2:21.
39. Charnock, *Existence and Attributes of God*, 2:22.

foreknowledge of God, and the liberty of the will, cannot be fully reconciled by man? Shall we therefore deny a perfection in God to support a liberty in ourselves? Shall we rather fasten ignorance upon God, and accuse him of blindness, to maintain our liberty?' The bottom line is, God is not 'ignorant' and creatures are not 'necessitated.' Charnock wisely added,

> It is a cursed affectation that runs in the blood of Adam's posterity, to know as God, though our first father smarted and ruined his posterity in that attempt; the ways and knowledge of God are as much above our thoughts and conceptions as the heavens are above the earth (Isa 55:9).[40]

My time with President Leverett in Cambridge at the Harvard College commencement was very profitable. However, I still had many unanswered questions. The next year I attended for the first time the Yale College commencement. The thesis on the broadside that intrigued me was about contingent propositions. This would prove to be a great day of learning. I would meet up with Samuel Andrew, the second president *pro tem*, from 1707–19.

---

40. Charnock, *Existence and Attributes of God*, 1:450.

5. Contingent Propositions

A Proposition about the Past Can Be Contingent[1]

President Samuel Andrew 1718 Yale Logic Thesis 20

PRESIDENT SAMUEL ANDREW (1656–1738) welcomed me to New Haven and to Yale College. He gave me a tour, since it was my first time to visit. The year prior, in September, the commencement day exercises were conducted in the meetinghouse on the New Haven Green for the very first time. But this year, 1718, he proudly took me to see the college's first building, which had just been completed. The new building housed the now famous Jeremiah Dummer collection of books.[2] I asked President Andrew about the commencement day theses. In particular, I told him I was intrigued by logic thesis number 20, since I was interested in learning more about contingency. He assured me that I would not return home disappointed.

I entered the Yale College building with President Andrew, and he introduced me to Sir Daniel Newell, one of eight bachelor commencers listed on the commencement day broadside.

"I would like to introduce you to one of our students who is well prepared to discuss contingency with us," said President Andrew.

"Pleased to meet you," I said.

"He has an excellent notebook of commonplaces and definitions in theology, and he has rehearsed explanations of the Reformed classical tradition of contingency. I propose that the three of us meet after the

---

1. Saltonstall, "Yale College Commencement Broadside 1718." Logic thesis "20. *Propositio de praeterito, potest esse contingens.*"

2. Minkema and Levesque, *Jonathan Edwards Tercentennial*, 28–38.

exercises. But now we must ready ourselves for the exercises," said President Andrew.

"Very well," I said. I took my seat in the college and examined the theses listed on the broadside sheet with great interest. The bachelor exercises began and President Andrew posed questions to the commencers, among them Sir Daniel Newell.

"Sir Daniel Newell, you have taken detailed notes of important scholastic distinctions and definitions in preparation for this commencement day. Please tell the audience about thesis 20 and the meaning of 'contingency,'" said President Andrew.

"There are two questions to address. The first question is," said Newell, "'What is contingency?' My response is that 'contingency is the essential disposition according to which reality can be otherwise than it is.' The second question is, 'In which respect is reality said to be otherwise than it is?' My response is that 'the course of reality could have run otherwise in the divided sense, with respect to the attendant circumstances.'[3] Let me unfold, hopefully to everyone's satisfaction, the meaning of important terms that one must understand in order to interpret this proposition about contingency. The proposition in thesis 20 asserts that it is possible that reality be otherwise than it is. This means that a state of affairs at one moment of time *can* be otherwise than it is, not only at a subsequent moment, but also at the same moment. One might think that the latter proposes an obvious contradiction. But it does not. Let me give you an example from the Presbyterian divine Stephen Charnock. He said, 'When a man writes or speaks, whilst he writes or speaks, those actions are necessary, because to speak and be silent, to write and not to write, at the same time, are impossible.'[4] So here Charnock admits to the obvious objection anyone would have to the proposition, if so interpreted in a compound sense of grammar. The writer cannot both be writing and not writing at the same moment."

"This reminds me of Francis Turretin (1623-87)," said President Andrew, "who affirmed that our faculties possess simultaneous potency or power (*simultas potentiae*) to do otherwise than we choose to do, 'in

---

3. Newell, "Student Notebook, 1700-1731." "Q. 24. *Quid est contingentia? Reply: Contingentia est natura affectio secundum quam natura potest aliter se habere qua habet.* Q. 25 *Quibus respectibus natura dicitur se aliter habere quam habet? Reply: Natura potuit se aliter habere sensu divisos respectu circumstantiarum et adjunctorum separibilium.*"

4. Charnock, *Existence and Attributes of God*, 1: 446.

the divided sense.' But he denied as contradictory the notion that we possess the potency or power of simultaneously (*potentia simultatis*) willing opposite objects of the will, 'in the composite sense.'"[5]

"Indeed, he did," said Newell. "But then Charnock continued. He said, 'Yet our writing or speaking doth not take away the power not to write or to be silent at that time if a man would be so; for he might have chosen whether he would have spoken or write.'[6] Notice that Charnock stipulated that the speaker or writer had *the power* to do otherwise *at that time*. Not a subsequent time, but at that same moment of time that the man is writing, it is possible that he not be writing. The power to do otherwise *at that time* correlates to the contingent features of the proposition. That is, there was nothing necessary about the writer such that he had to write. The point is that there is a particular kind of necessity that comes into play when these two parts of speech are taken together; 'when a writer writes' and 'whilst the writer writes,' necessarily, he or she is writing. The action while it happens is obviously and necessarily happening. Charnock called this type of necessity, 'a necessity of infallibility.' There is no magical illusion going on. When God foresees a writer writing at a moment in time, necessarily, he or she is writing at that moment. 'God cannot be deceived.' But neither is the writer coerced. Charnock made this clear. The necessity of infallibility is not 'a coactive necessity.' The writer is in no way compelled 'intrinsically' by his or her 'own nature.' Why not? It is because the writer, at that moment, retains the power not to write. 'When any of us have done anything according to our wills, can we say we could not have done the contrary to it? Were we determined to it in our own intrinsic nature?' asked Charnock. No. We 'determine ourselves.' Did Adam, Peter, or Judas blame God for stirring them up to their sinful actions? No, they did not."[7]

"Please explain to the audience," said President Andrew, "the distinction between the power to do otherwise *at the same time* and the power to do otherwise at a subsequent moment of time. And what does this have to do with contingency? After all, the proposition under discussion is about contingency, is it not?"

---

5. Asselt et al., *Reformed Thought*, 182–85. For an older translation, see Francis Turretin, *First through Tenth Topics*, 1:659–83. S.v. "simultas potentiae" in Muller, *Dictionary*, 336.

6. Charnock, *Existence and Attributes of God*, 1:446–47.

7. Charnock, *Existence and Attributes of God*, 1:447.

"Indeed, it is," said Newell. "It is one thing to say that things can be otherwise at a subsequent moment, and quite another to say that things can be otherwise *at the same moment of time*. When we speak of a subsequent moment of time we are speaking about diachronic contingency. For instance, to take up Charnock's example, let us say that today I am writing this book at 10:00 a.m., but I have the power to do otherwise at 10:01 a.m. If that were all that Charnock was saying, then he was not claiming anything out of the ordinary, was he? That is what is meant by diachronic contingency. Whether the writer is writing at 10:00 a.m. and continues writing at each subsequent moment is clearly contingent upon many factors. But suppose the writer is intrinsically determined by her own nature to write at whatever time she writes, whether today, tomorrow, or any other day, but without the power to do otherwise, whenever she does write. Would Charnock, would we, consider that she was free to write? No. And why not? The reason is that although she was free to write or not to write at a subsequent moment, she was not free to do otherwise *at the moment* of writing. Her faculty of a simultaneous power to do otherwise was denied her, due to her intrinsic nature. Thus, when we speak of a power to do otherwise *at the same* moment of writing we are speaking of synchronic contingency."

"In the beginning of your explanation today, you mentioned the importance of interpreting the proposition about contingency in the *divided sense*. Would you please elaborate?" asked President Andrew.

"Naturally," said Newell. "Let us address the question of whether a proposition about the past can be contingent. If I say, 'Yesterday, I was blind, but today I see,' my gaining sight was contingent upon something. Furthermore, this represents what I called *diachronic* contingency. The change from blindness to sight occurred over time. The past condition changed, but at a subsequent moment. But does that not imply that the past can be changed? Or that the past could be otherwise than it was? But suppose I read the proposition in the divided sense, taking note of the placement of the comma: *A proposition about the past, can be contingent.* The comma indicates the possibility of a change in the status of the entire proposition. The reality that someone was blind in the past *can* be otherwise. Contingency can point not only to change over time, but to change at the same instant of time. For instance, in the divided sense, we can read the proposition, *The blind, see*, as follows: *It is possible that he who is blind, sees*. Not merely at a subsequent moment, but *at that moment of time*. When read in the compound sense, it is a contradiction to say that

The blind see. But not in the divided sense. Therefore, *A proposition about a past blindness, can be contingent.*"

Shortly after the commencers finished speaking, President Andrew drew the ceremony to a close. I was eager to sit down with Newell and President Andrew to continue our discussion about contingency.

"Sir Daniel Newell, your presentation for the audience was fairly difficult material, but very illuminating. Could you tell us more about contingency and specifically how God foresees future contingencies?" I asked.

"Naturally," said Newell. "President Andrew, please jump in as you like. Let me begin with Charnock, then perhaps we can briefly turn to the opinion of William Ames, Samuel Rutherford, Gisbertus Voetius, Adriaan Heereboord, and Peter van Mastricht. Charnock said, 'God knows all future contingencies.' There are different senses of contingencies. God knows 'all things that shall accidentally happen, or, as we say, by chance,' such as when a branch falls upon someone's head when he is walking in the woods. God also knows 'all the free motions of men's wills that shall be to the end of the world.' Since Scripture says, 'All things are open to him' (Heb 4:13), then so too are 'all contingencies.' A 'mixed contingent' is part necessity, part accident, such as when the arrow killed Ahab (1 Kgs 22:39). It is necessary that an arrow fly and land when released. But it is an accident when the arrow hits an unintended target. But 'voluntary actions are purely contingents, and have nothing of necessity in them. All free actions that depend upon the will of man, whether to do or not to do, are of this nature.' Why? The reason is that they 'depend not upon a necessary cause, as burning doth upon the fire.' Furthermore, a created human being is unique. In his or her own nature, he is 'able to turn to this or that point, and determine himself as he pleases.'[8] This is called freedom *ad utrumque*."

"But was Ahab's death accidental with regard to God?" I asked.

"No," replied Newell. "Charnock said, 'God foretold his death, foreknew the shot, and directed the arrow.' For God, there was no uncertainty about the outcome. No need to manipulate the action to achieve the desired result. The outcome was necessarily linked to God's foreknowledge. But with regard 'to the natural disposition of the immediate causes,' the outcome was 'contingent in its own nature.'[9] You see, we might conjecture

---

8. Charnock, *Existence and Attributes of God*, 1:439.
9. Charnock, *Existence and Attributes of God*, 1:439.

about outcomes, but not God. 'Conjectural knowledge is by no means to be fastened on God,' said Charnock. We know contingencies 'when they come into act, and pass from futurity to reality.' Charnock made it clear: 'It is certain man hath a liberty to act many things this or that way as he pleases.' In sum, he said, even the way someone will 'determine himself' is sometimes unknown beforehand. But his or her future determination is not unknown to God. God cannot be deceived. Crucially, against middle knowledge, Charnock said, if God does not know the free acts of men and women 'till they are done, he would then depend upon the creature for his information.' In that case, God would increase in knowledge, which is absurd to say."[10]

At this juncture, President Andrew turned the conversation to William Ames and his exchange of treatises with the Arminian Nicolaus Grevinchovius (1578–1632).

"As a reply to Grevinchovius's *Theological Dissertation* (*Dissertatio theologica*), 1615," said President Andrew, "Ames wrote, 'A Scholastic Rejoinder' (*Rescriptio scholastica*) (1615).[11] Grevinchovius questioned Ames's doctrine of God and asked how he could believe that the proposition "Peter will believe" is neither true nor false prior to the decree of God's will. For how then could God know what Peter will do with any kind of certainty? How could Ames believe that 'future contingents cannot in any way be known with certainty and infallibility, unless in the divine will as their cause?'[12] Ames's reply was to deny that God must know the proposition as true or false prior, by way of conceiving it, to the decree of God's will determining it to be true or false. In other words, Ames was saying that the proposition "Peter will believe" was a neutral proposition. God had not yet, by way of conceiving it, assigned the proposition a truth value one way or the other. For there was no necessity imposed upon God. There was no necessary nexus between the parts of the proposition, namely, between "Peter" and "belief." Indeed, the very thing itself, if we can speak of Peter's belief in this way, had not been reckoned as a future existent thing, prior, by way of conceiving it, to the decree of God's will. *Faith*, as such, was not a necessary consequent of the proposition. The

---

10. Charnock, *Existence and Attributes of God*, 1:440.

11. Grevinchovius, *Dissertatio Theologica*; Ames, *Rescriptio Scholastica*. For a fuller treatment, see Fisk, "Divine Knowledge at Harvard and Yale."

12. As quoted in Fisk, "Divine Knowledge at Harvard and Yale," 157.

truth value of the proposition was to be squarely rooted in the decree of God's will."[13]

"Perhaps it would be good to state the basic understanding by the scholastics of the notion of *contingency*," said Newell. "Scholastics, like Samuel Rutherford (1600–1661), made a distinction in the doctrine of God between possible states of affairs and future contingent states of affairs. For God, a possible state of affairs speaks of what could have been but will not be. A future contingent state of affairs speaks of what will be but could not have been.[14] And concerning what will and what will not be, would you agree, President Andrew, that Voetius would add that by the decree of God's will, God freely either actualizes a possible state of affairs or does not? In this way God appoints a time stamp, as it were, for each state of affairs or not. In other words, after the decree of God's will, by way of conceiving it, there is no uncertainty about states of affairs that *will not be*. Nor can there be, given God's knowledge of and relation to all possible states of affairs. To be clear, for Voetius, contingency has to do with that which God appoints to exist in the course of this world by the decree of his will."[15]

"Indeed," said President Andrew. "And I could add the testimony of Heereboord to those above since he also taught that contingency meant that a state of affairs can be otherwise than it is. He gave the example of the proposition 'Peter is learned.' He said it could be false, such that 'Peter is not learned.' Like Charnock, Heereboord taught that you and I act freely and are not intrinsically determined by our own natures.[16] Heereboord also taught that human beings have a power and freedom *ad utrumque* at the moment that they elicit an act of the will. This was how he defined free choice:

> The faculty of doing what one pleases (*facultas faciendi quod lubet*). By "faculty," we understand a real or natural (*facultas physica seu naturalis*), not an ethical or moral faculty. In other words: The faculty of the intellect and the will, related to two alternatives (ad *utrumlibet*).[17]

---

13. Fisk, "Divine Knowledge at Harvard and Yale," 159.
14. Rutherford, *Exercitationes Apologeticae*, 88.
15. On this point, see Beck, *Voetius on God, Freedom, and Contingency*, 378–79.
16. For a fuller account, see Fisk, *Edwards's Turn*, 140–48.
17. As reported in Fisk, *Edwards's Turn*, 129.

"Here, by using the term *ad utrumlibet*, Heereboord made clear that you and I have a power to do otherwise than we do."

"But what did he mean by calling our faculty of the will '*real or natural*?'" I asked.

"Heereboord did not want us to think of our faculty of the will in terms of being essentially morally good or bad. But rather as having effective power as a natural attribute. The power to do otherwise is present at the moment of choice," said President Andrew.

"Would you call that 'synchronic contingency,' as we have talked about before?" I asked.

"Yes, I would," said President Andrew. "Freedom *ad utrumque* implies a simultaneous alternativeness. And this natural or physical attribute is not linked to the moral nature of what we choose to do. That is why Heereboord used the word *facultas physica seu naturalis*."

"I recall that Peter van Mastricht, if I am correct," said Newell, "also used the term 'physical' when he taught about God's predetermining will and effective power at work in the physical reality of this world. Like Heereboord, the term did not speak to the moral dimension of divine and human action. Van Mastricht conducted a disputation on the question 'Whether the influx of divine providence removes contingency from all states of affairs, and urges severe necessity?' The respondent answered, 'No, it does not.'"[18]

"Indeed. You are correct," said President Andrew. "Now concerning the proposition today, 'Whether a proposition about the past can be contingent,' Van Mastricht would concur with his predecessors Voetius and Ames, that there is a non-successive structured order, by way of our conceiving it, of God's simple knowledge of understanding, followed by God's will, followed by God's knowledge of vision. God's will determines the time stamp of future contingents prior to which states of affairs have no determinate truth value. Certainly not in themselves, but in the decree (*in decreto divino*). And since God possesses power to do otherwise than he does, and since he possesses this power simultaneously at the 'moment' of the decree of the will, it is possible that the time stamp, whether past, present, or future, be otherwise than it is, that the proposition thus is by nature contingent."[19]

---

18. Van Mastricht, *Theoretico-Practica Theologia*, 396 (q. 3). "*An influxus ille providentiae divinae, e medio tollat omnem rerum contingentiam, duraque urgeat necessitate?*"

19. Fisk, "Divine Knowledge at Harvard and Yale," 168.

"I once heard that there was a virgin mystery that had to do with whether her past could be changed. I think that the Benedictine monk Peter Damian (1007–72) discussed this mystery in the monastery. Could you remind us of the details and whether it has any bearing on our proposition under discussion today?" I asked.

"Indeed, it is relevant," said President Andrew. "Damian recalled a conversation he had had with Lord Desiderius of the monastery of Monte Cassino. He wrote him a letter about their conversation and a passage from St. Jerome (ca. 347–ca. 419) that they had read. Jerome said, 'While God can do all things, he cannot cause a virgin to be restored after she has fallen.'[20] Damian wrote that Jerome of course knew that God could spiritually restore a virgin by freeing her from guilt. In that sense her past could be changed. But Damian was not content to leave it there. For him it was a question of understanding God's omnipotence. Could God truly restore her virginity? Did it boil down to whether God wished to restore her or not? To which Damian said, 'If God can do none of the things that he does not wish to do, he does nothing but that which he wishes; therefore, he can do none of the things at all that he has not done.'[21] But that implies that God cannot heal someone who is sick because he is unwilling, and therefore is unable to do anything about the situation. For Damian, this did not square with divine omnipotence."

"As I recall," I said, "Damian believed that 'the will of God is truly the cause of the existence of all things ... which were already truly and essentially alive in the will of their Creator.' On this point, Damian quoted Saint John, who wrote, 'You are worthy, our Lord and God, to receive glory and honor and power, for you created all things, and by your will they existed and were created' (Rev 4:11). From this Scripture truth, Damian argued that since God's will was the cause of uncreated things yet to be created, 'so it is no less the efficient cause whereby those things that have been lost might return to the integrity of their state.' He asked therefore, 'What could hinder God from restoring a virgin after she has fallen?' Was God unable to do it because he was unwilling?"[22]

---

20. Peter Damian, "On Divine Omnipotence," 143; on Peter Damian, see Marenbon, *Medieval Philosophy*, 116–18. On Damian and the virgin mystery, see Fisk, *A Book of Faith Seeking Understanding*, 67–68.

21. Damian, "On Divine Omnipotence," 143.

22. Damian, "On Divine Omnipotence," 145.

"Damian proposed two ways of understanding the mystery," said President Andrew.[23] "First, God is omnipotent and therefore 'has the power to restore virginity to any woman.'[24] Recall Saint Paul, who promised the Corinthians in marriage to one husband, to Christ, as 'a chaste virgin' (2 Cor 11:2). Some may argue that to spiritually restore someone is one thing, but surely God cannot destroy Rome and expect us to deny the founding of Rome. 'How can God bring it about that something that has happened will not have happened?'[25] Damian answered,

> As God's ability [*posse*] to do all things is coeternal to God, the Creator of all things, so also is his power to know all things; and that he contains, determines, and forever confirms within the compass of his wisdom all times past, present, and future in such a way that nothing new at all can happen to him, nor can anything pass away through forgetfulness.[26]

"For Damian, there was an 'eternal day' and an 'everlasting present.' This was his second solution to the virgin mystery. God's presence neither passes away nor changes into the past. 'In that immutable and ever uniform eternity of his, God is able to bring about that what had happened relative to our passing of time, did not happen.'[27] So God 'can [*potest*] so cause it to happen that Rome, founded in antiquity, would not have been founded.' The present tense *can* is proper in this case, when speaking of God. But for us, we would say, God could have [*potuit*] done so. Remember, 'God's present never turns into the past. His today does not change into tomorrow.'[28] As for Rome, 'God has that power after Rome was founded that it be not-founded; that is, he *could have* caused it not to have been founded relative to us; he *can*, relative to himself.' There is no *before* or *after* Rome, relative to God and his 'immutable and intransient eternity.' Damian concluded his letter by saying, 'If the potency to do all things is coeternal to God, then it follows that God could have caused things that have happened not to have happened. God then 'can do all

---

23. Damian, "On Divine Omnipotence," 145.
24. Damian, "On Divine Omnipotence," 146.
25. Damian, "On Divine Omnipotence," 147.
26. Damian, "On Divine Omnipotence," 147.
27. Damian, "On Divine Omnipotence," 147–48.
28. Damian, "On Divine Omnipotence," 148.

things, either in respect to events that have happened or in respect to events that have not happened.'"[29]

"Isn't it true," I asked, "that Damian also spoke of a term that scholastics used quite frequently, namely, freedom *ad utrumque*?"[30]

"Indeed, he did," said President Andrew. "It meant 'indifferent alternatives.' It had not so much to do with the logic of speech syntax, but rather with 'the variable nature of things,' such as the weather. It may rain today. It may not. The logic of speech concludes that 'if it is going to rain, it is absolutely necessary that it rain.'[31] Likewise, what is past necessarily is past; what is present, necessarily so; what is future, necessarily so. This is the logical pattern of speech."

"Does this mean that Damian would have denied the proposition under review today?" I asked, "'That a proposition about the past can be contingent?'"

"Not at all," said President Andrew. "Damian attributed this 'blind foolhardiness' to the 'art of rhetoric.' With this kind of speech logic, rhetoricians wrongly attributed impotence to God, 'not only regarding things past, but also relative to things present and to come.' Damian spoke harshly about these ignorant schoolchildren who heap abuse on 'the mystery of divine power.' He found much fault with the state of the 'liberal arts,' with 'dialecticians and rhetoricians,' and the application of syllogisms to explain the doctrine of God. The humanities should assume an 'ancillary role as a maidservant,' he thought. None should doubt the power of God, who, if he so acted, could reverse the past, undo what is present, make happen what was not to happen, all relative to our way of speaking, of course. The problem is that liberal arts teachers disputed the mysteries of God as if they were 'problems of dialectical necessity or impossibility in such a way as to keep them solely within the framework of this art, without ever mentioning God in the course of their arguments.'"[32]

"So, what is the place of the liberal arts, of dialectics and rhetoric, in our curricula, and especially in answering the problem of today's proposition and the virgin mystery?" I asked.

"Damian's answer may surprise you," said President Andrew. "There is none, at least not at the bachelor level. I think he speaks words of

29. Damian, "On Divine Omnipotence," 149.
30. Damian, "On Divine Omnipotence," 150.
31. Damian, "On Divine Omnipotence," 150.
32. Damian, "On Divine Omnipotence," 150–51.

wisdom for us today in how we train our students in doing theology. He said these dialecticians did not fear to offend 'the Author of light.' He spurned this kind of liberal arts 'investigation of the power of divine majesty.'[33] For this reason our schools in New England follow the long tradition of reserving the discussion of theological propositions in divinity to the master's students."

I left our discussion, and Yale College, with a renewed reverence for the mysteries of God. I had a better understanding of the place of the dialectical and rhetorical tools in the curricula and the ancillary role of the humanities in attaining to a right understanding of the doctrines of the church. It would be two years before I returned to Yale. I was intent on learning more about the liberal arts curriculum. In fact, there was a bachelor thesis on the Yale 1720 broadside sheet that intrigued me. It had to do with the universal rules that govern the principles of all the liberal arts.

---

33. Damian, "On Divine Omnipotence," 151–52.

6. Universal Rules

UNIVERSAL RULES ARE THE CONSTITUENT PRINCIPLES OF ALL THE ARTS[1]

RECTOR TIMOTHY CUTLER   1720 YALE TECHNOLOGY THESIS 4

IT WAS COMMENCEMENT DAY at Yale College, New Haven, Connecticut, September 1720. I went down to the green and entered the *aula academica* to attend the morning bachelor's exercises. There I met Rector Timothy Cutler (1684–1765).

"I presume that you will preside over the commencement exercises today," I said.

"Yes, indeed," he said. "I am the third rector of Yale College. I succeeded Rector *pro tem* Samuel Andrew last year."

"Who is graduating today?" He handed me the bachelor's commencement broadside sheet so that I could see the names of the graduating students—"the New England scholars," as they were called. There were ten in all.

"I am looking forward to the opening *oratio valedictoria*. Who's giving it this year?" Rector Cutler pointed to a student sitting in a chair, alone, off to the side, nervously looking over his speech. I looked over the names of the students on the broadside and asked, "What is his name?"

"Jonathan Edwards," he said. "He is from East Windsor, one of the students who was studying in Wethersfield. Elisha Williams was his tutor. Jonathan moved here for a brief time in October, two years ago, when they finished the magnificent building of what we call Yale College. But then he and others returned to Wethersfield the following month. They were not so happy with tutor Samuel Johnson. The college made some

---

1. Saltonstall, "Yale College Commencement Broadside 1720." Technology thesis 4 "*Regulae catholicae sunt omnium artium principia constituentia.*"

changes and Johnson left last year. Jonathan returned to Yale last year and finished his degree in May of this year."

I watched the procession enter the *aula* from the yard. After a prayer in Latin—everything was conducted in Latin—Rector Cutler recognized Governor Gordon Saltonstall, the generosity of Elihu Yale, and the piety and prudence of the deputy governor, Nathan Gold. Their names were printed boldly on the top of the commencement broadside sheet. The broadside also made clear that "the young scholars would defend the theses printed on the broadside under the auspices of Rector Timothy Cutler."

Then Mr. Edwards rose to give the opening oration. He began addressing the "most senior gentlemen of the audience," at a gathering where "the greatest teaching abounds and the pinnacle of knowledge resides." He wondered "what orator could there be who would be worthy to stand before you?" In the beginning he displayed his own terror, saying how his "spirit shudders greatly at his own words." But he determined that he must have been chosen to speak because, as he said, "I am a man possessed solely of a mind endowed with a fortunate productiveness, furnished with eloquence and greatly equipped with expert knowledge."[2]

As I listened to Mr. Edwards, and as he got deeper into his oration, I became impressed with his display of virtuosity. He eloquently praised Rector Cutler as a man of "outstanding scholarship." He honored Warham Mather, "justice of the peace," welcomed Joseph Noyes, "the most eminent Minister of the word of God of *Novi Porti*," and Daniel Brown, "the outstanding tutor of this College."[3]

Still, questions arose in my mind, as he ended his oration, praising the inspiration of the goddess Minerva, her father Pallas, and the college as home to Apollo. I was determined to meet with him over lunch if at all possible. But first I had some questions for Rector Cutler about the theses on the commencement broadside sheet.

At this point in the exercises, Rector Cutler rose and began to examine a commencer, Samuel Mix, about three of the physics theses.[4] I

2. Minkema and Levesque, *Jonathan Edwards Tercentennial*, 39–41.

3. Minkema and Levesque, *Jonathan Edwards Tercentennial*, 39–41.

4. There were ten respondents, according to the broadside sheet: Ebenezer Wakeman, Thomas White, Gulielmus Billings, Daniel Edwards, Jonathan Edwards, Daniel Kirkland, Samuel Mix, Ezechias Kilborn, Abrahamus Nott, and Johannes Walton. See Saltonstall, *Yale College Commencement Broadside 1720*; For a presentation of the 1720 Yale commencement broadside, see Minkema and Levesque, *Jonathan Edwards*

noticed on the broadside that there was a finger pointing to theses 4a, 4b, and 4c. They were clearly designated for debate. But Rector Cutler began with physics thesis 2, "'Action and reaction are always equal.' Please explain this for the audience."

The commencer said, "Sir Isaac Newton's Third Law says that for any action there is always an equal and opposite reaction. Take any two bodies, the actions of two bodies upon each other are always equal and always opposite in direction."[5]

Rector Cutler then stated broadside physics thesis 4, "'The same force that has generated motion destroys it.' Who made this proposition and where is it published?"

"Sir Isaac Newton stated these new principles of action and motion in Proposition 70, Theorem 30, in the *Principia mathematica*," he replied. "Newton explained that if two bodies or spheres attract each other equally, but in opposite directions, they then annul each other."[6]

Then Rector Cutler read physics thesis 4a and 4b, "'All matter is the same. All motion is local.' Please explain."

"Descartes argued," said the commencer, "that if space is empty, then there is no diversity of matter in space. But space is not empty, therefore the universe is made up of homogenous matter."

Rector Cutler interjected and said, "Thomas Aquinas said that not all motion is local. But Descartes wrote in a letter to Buitendijk in 1643 that he does not admit various kinds of motion, but only local motion. No other motion is to be feigned in *rerum natura*. Only local."[7]

Mr. Mix then sat down and, after having examined a few other students, Rector Cutler announced the midday break for lunch.

During lunch, after the morning exercises were over, I approached Rector Cutler and asked him some questions about the broadside. I noticed that the broadside divided the bachelor theses into six categories of study: technology, logic, grammar, rhetoric, mathematics, and physics.

"Why are there no theological theses?" I asked.

"We call the theological theses *quaestiones*," replied Rector Cutler. "But the neophyte underclassmen are not allowed to spend much time

---

Tercentennial, 33. Whether Rector Cutler addressed Mr. Samuel Mix or one of the other respondents is pure conjecture.

5. Newton, *Principia*, 417.

6. Newton, *Principia*, 590.

7. On these theses, see Koyré, *Newtonian Studies*, 80, 110, 113; Cottingham et al., *The Philosophical Writings of Descartes*, 3:229–30; Fisk, *Edwards's Turn*, 104–05.

on questions of theology. First, they must apply themselves to the arts and sciences, and first and foremost to the *trivium* of logic, grammar, and rhetoric."

"What is the main point of the first category, the so-called 'technology' theses," I asked, "and why is the category called 'technology?' I thought that Ames had had much influence on the design of both the Harvard and Yale curriculum, and that he himself produced a Ramist-type schematic of what he called 'technometry.'"

"Let me answer your last question first. Yes, indeed, Ames did use the term 'technometry.' Ames drew from many sources for his reform of the arts curriculum, from Greek and Roman Classical works as well as from medieval curricula and scholasticism, and of course from Renaissance humanist sources, not just Peter Ramus, as some may think. Alexander Richardson's *The Logicians School Master*, for instance, was a recent basic model from which he drew. But Richardson spoke of 'technology' theses."[8]

"Would it be correct to conclude, then," I asked, "that Ames adapted what he learned from others and, more or less, substituted the term 'technometry' for 'technology?'"

"Yes. In fact, Ames attempted to subsume the theory of art, *technê*, under one architectonic system, which he called 'technometry.' At the head of his book of theses, he wrote, 'Technometry adequately circumscribes the boundaries and ends of all the arts and of every individual art.'[9] Despite what the term 'technometry' may otherwise suggest, Ames did have influence upon the curricula of the New England schools. Now, to your first question about the function and main point of the technology theses. Ames believed that universal and necessary premises supported an entire vision of a Christian curriculum. He had studied Peter Ramus's reform of the arts and sciences curriculum and, like Ramus before him, Ames formulated three universal rules (*Regulae Catholicae*).[10] The the-

---

8. Ames, *Technometry*, 18, 42.

9. Ames, *Technometry*, 93.

10. Ames, *Technometry*, 23, 99 (theses §§40, 78, 80), 144. A study by Bruyère on Ramus's concept of method and dialectic notes a high recurrence of the "lexical key" of the three laws, "kata pantos, kath' auto, kath' olon prôton," derived from Aristotle's *An. Post.*, in Bruyère, *Méthode et dialectique*, 267.

"Aristotle teaches three marks of skillful material," writes Ramus, "κατα παντός, καθ αὐτό, καθόλου πρῶτον, from which one understands the theorem of the dignity of the place of universal art and instruction. The first mark is such that the precepts of the art of grammar must be not only true, but altogether necessary and true," in Ramus,

ses under "Technology" on the broadside in your hands reflect Ames's vision. Thesis 1 reads, 'Technology is the comprehension of the idea of the arts and sciences in general.' Thesis 3 addresses the young scholar's inquiring mind. It reads, 'Science (knowledge) is the pure contemplation of the well-ordered universe' of all arts and sciences. And thesis 4 teaches students that there are 'Universal rules that are the constituent principles of all the arts.'"[11]

"What are the three universal rules?" I asked. "They do not appear on the broadside sheet."

"The three universal rules would have been debated by the respondents during the academic year. They appeared in the first commencement broadside sheet of Harvard College, when John Winthrop was governor, presided over by Henry Dunster, back in 1642," replied Rector Cutler. "They are found listed under Logic thesis 12: First, κατα παντὸς or *De omni*; Second, καθ' αὐτό, or *per se*; Third, τὸ καθόλου, or *universale*. The three rules serve as a kind of lexical key: (1) The law of truth (*lex veritatis*), (2) The law of justice (*lex justitiae*), and (3) The law of wisdom (*lex sapientiae*)."[12]

"They sound as if they were abstracted from Aristotle and adapted for the curriculum," I said.

"Indeed," said Rector Cutler, "Ramus, Ames, and Franco Burgersdijk as well, who was younger than Ames, but still his contemporary, derived these three universal rules, based on three necessary premises, from interpreters of Aristotle's *Prior* and *Posterior Analytics*.[13] The sopho-

---

Scholae in Liberales Artes, 5 ("*Tres artificiosae materiae notas Aristotelis tradit, κατα παντὸς, καθ αὐτὸ, καθόλου πρῶτον, unde theorema catholicum artis ac doctrinae loco dignum intelligatur. Prima nota praeceptiones artis Grammaticae, non solum verae, sed omnino necessarioque verae esse debebunt*"). (Translation mine).

11. Saltonstall, *Yale Commencement Broadside 1720*, "1. *Technologia est atrium et scientarum idealis in genere comprehension.*" "3. *Scientia est mera contemplatio rerum bene ordinata.*" "4. *Regulae catholicae sunt omnium atrium principia constituentia.*"

12. On these theses, see Fisk, *Edwards's Turn*, 52–54; Morison, *The Founding of Harvard College*, 439; Ames, "Demonstratio logicae verae," in *Philosophemata*, 143; Burgersdijck, *Institutionum Logicarum*, 131.

13. For the three rules, see Ames, "Demonstratio logicae verae," 143. Burgersdijk, *Institutionum Logicarum*, 131 (pagination from the 1651 London edition). For an introduction to Burgersdijk, his other writings, sources, ethics, and influence at Harvard preceding Heereboord, see Fiering, *Moral Philosophy at Seventeenth-Century Harvard*, 86–96. On Burgersdijk and Ramist method, see Bos and Krop, *Franco Burgersdijk*, 15, 20, 22, 39, 86–90.

For the source of the Yale 1720 logic thesis 21, see Aristotle, *Posterior Analytics*,

more students at Harvard learned an interpretation of Aristotle from Burgersdijk's *Institutio Logicarum*, which set forth the three laws, adapted from Ramus. It is important to remember that although Burgersdijk cited Aristotle's *Posterior Analytics* in his text, the principles he extrapolated and applied to his discussion of propositions reflected Burgersdijk's own purposes. He appropriated many sources, including Ramus's method, as seen in the enumeration of three degrees.[14] But as I said, the Harvard 1642 commencement broadside thesis gave the three laws in Greek, 'First, the precepts of the arts must be universally necessary premises, which are true in every instance of the subject (κατα παντὸς). Second, they are essential *per se* (καθ' αὐτό), and third, they have a universal attribute (καθ ὅλου πρῶτον).'"[15]

"These three rules of technology, or technometry, summed up as truth, justice, and wisdom, remind me of metaphysics and the

---

in *Basic Works*, 110 (71a1). The Latin translation from the Greek original is "*Omnis doctrina & omnis disciplina dianoëtica fit ex antecedente cognitione*," cited from Pacio, *Aristotle's Organon*, 413. The four characteristics of this pre-existent knowledge are in Aristotle's *Posterior Analytics* in *Basic Works*: (1) "unqualified scientific knowledge of a thing," (*unamquamque rem simpliciter*), 111 (71b9), (2) which "cannot be other than it is," (*non potest aliter se habere*), 111 (71b15); 156 (88b30–35), (3) "necessary basic truths" (*ex necessariis principiis*), 119 (74b5), upon which demonstrative knowledge rests. And (4) "principia" (*principia*), 185–86 (100b5, 9), apprehended by "intuition" (*intelligentiam*), 186 (100b7).

14. Cutler would not have said it quite like this since the historical revolution would not come before the early nineteenth century. But the point is neither Burgersdijk nor anyone else in the seventeenth and eighteenth centuries conducted historical studies of Aristotle. It is thus misleading to call the student notebooks and teaching at Harvard and early Yale in any historical sense "Aristotelian," as in Kennedy, *Aristotelian and Cartesian Logic at Harvard*. There were three groups as sources for Burgersdijk's logic textbook: the Aristotelians (Hunnaeus, Crellius, Bertius, and Molinaeus, among others), the Ramists, and those like Keckermann, according to Bos and Krop, *Franco Burgersdijk*, 22–24. On the influence of Ramus on Burgersdijk, see Ames, *Technometry*, 83. On the contrast between Aristotle's Greek pre-historic thought and the medieval revolution in Christian thought, see Vos, *Philosophy of John Duns Scotus*, 529–39; 558–71.

15. Morison, *The Founding of Harvard College*, 439: Logic thesis "12. Praecepta artium debent esse κατα παντὸς, καθ' αὐτό, καθ ὅλου πρῶτον." Also in Burgersdijk, *Institutionum Logicarum*, 131. "*Primus gradus necessitatis est, κατα παντὸς, de omni: alter καθ αὐτὸ, per se: tertius καθόλου πρῶτον, universaliter primúm.*" William Ames, for his purposes of a Christian vision of the one genus of art, transformed these three Ramist rules into 1) lex veritatis, 2) lex justitiae, 3) lex sapientiae, in Ames, "Demonstratio logicae verae," in *Philosophemata*, 143 (§83).

transcendental principles, namely, the most true God, the most just, and the most wise," I said.

"Interestingly enough," recalled Rector Cutler, "Rector Increase Mather presided over a Harvard College 1687 technology thesis, number 11, a thesis which was selected for public defense. The thesis read, 'There is no metaphysics discipline that is distinct from all the other disciplines.'[16] And since then, neither Harvard nor Yale has had metaphysics as a distinct discipline in the curricula and on the broadside sheets.[17] In fact, Ames had a thesis in his *Technometry* that in effect censures metaphysics because, as he said, 'It has put its sickle into a harvest not its own.' Ames made it clear in that thesis that he very much favored what he saw as the more certain method of 'etymological' lexical studies in support of his overall scheme of logic. So now you see why, for Ames, as you said before, technometry serves the role of metaphysics."[18]

"What were the underlying reasons for establishing universal rules and necessary premises?" I asked.

"There are three points to make," said Rector Cutler. "First, necessary premises undergird and establish immutable laws which in turn give irrefutable certainty and infallibility to all instruction and learning in the arts and sciences. One consequence of establishing universal rules, and necessary premises—in the sense that we must assent to their truth—is the stability of language that they provide us when we wish to talk about ontological truths, the transcendental truths, and metaphysics that we just mentioned."

"What exactly do you mean about the stability of language?" I asked.

"Since Plato, the classical Western Christian tradition, with some nominalist exceptions, assumed that the inherent meaning of words in a proposition made a truth claim about the actual world. Language had the capacity to refer to a reality beyond language itself. A mind-independent reality, as it were. An originary presence. This was the worldview of both prophets and poets, Christian and pagan."

"So, the first point establishes the crucial place of truth claims and propositions. What is the second point you wish to make about these necessary premises? Is it connected to the levels of necessity?" I asked.

---

16. Andros, "Harvard 1687, Original." "11. *Non datur metaphysica ab omnibus aliis disciplinis distincta.*"

17. In 1730, Yale's fourth Rector, Elisha Williams, brought metaphysics back as a separate discipline, which appears on the Yale College broadside sheet.

18. Ames, *Technometry*, 101, 149.

"Indeed it is," replied Rector Cutler. "The second point has to do with understanding the different degrees of necessity. And once we understand those different degrees, we will see how contingency enters into our discussion of necessary premises and propositions. For there also are contingent propositions derived from the necessary premises. Burgersdijk said that the first level of necessity approached nearest to contingency. That is why he spoke of grades or levels of necessity. He said, 'The necessity of the first grade is minimal in the sense that it most nearly approaches contingency. For it is not absolutely necessity.'"

"Could you give some examples?" I asked.

"Indeed. The first grade of necessity, κατα παντὸς / *de omni*, speaks of universal predication. Burgersdijk asked if we can say of all human beings that they are always just in their actions. They certainly are capable of being just, but humans are not always just. It does not fit the description of each individual person. Likewise, 'Do living things grow?' Normally, but not always."

"I think I understand why you said that this level approaches nearest to contingency," I said. "In each of the above examples, the answer is contingent upon the circumstances. I can at least conceive the possibility of exceptions to the general rule."

"Indeed," said Rector Cutler. "Burgersdijk then gave an example that belongs to the first grade of necessity, but which also can belong to the second grade of necessity. So let's transition from the first to the second grade with this question: 'Are ravens black?' Normally, yes. The predicate, in this case, 'black,' always convenes with or inheres in the subject.[19] But Burgersdijk asked whether there is any necessary reason why, for instance, a raven is black."

"I suppose it is arbitrary, isn't it? I asked.

"Normally, a raven is black, necessarily," said Rector Cutler. "However, the example of a raven is a case *per accidens*. This is because a raven is not blackness, neither is blackness a raven. In other words, the modifier 'black' in 'A raven is black' is a sign of accidental predication. Substance differs from accident and is exemplified by the fact that blackness differs from black, just as truth differs from true, life from living."

"I understand," I said. "For instance, God is not merely true and good, he *is* truth and goodness."

---

19. Burgersdijk, *Institutionum logicarum*, 131.

"Indeed," said Rector Cutler. "In the second grade of necessity, (καθ αὑτὸ) (per se), the subject and the predicate co-inhere in an essential nexus.[20] Now here it gets complicated because Burgersdijk enumerates several different kinds of the second grade of necessity. Some classic examples are, 'Man is an animal' or 'Man is rational (mind-gifted).' These predicates are necessary *per se* when speaking of human beings."

"Before going further, tell me, what is the broader significance of the second grade of necessity?" I asked.

"The firm nexus between the subject and predicate of a proposition affirms that something is true and speaks of philosophical necessity. In other words, the thing spoken about, or, signified, is affirmed and is necessary, philosophically speaking," said Rector Cutler.

"Another example that Burgersdijk gave is, 'Socrates exists,'" said Rector Cutler. "What's more, this mode can be further distinguished by saying that it is only as long as 'Socrates is,' that he is, and in this sense only does he exist necessarily. To use another example, which Charles Morton used at Harvard, a summer rose exists out of itself, *per se*; whereas a winter rose does not exist out of itself in winter. Its essence remains in its unactuated substance. Therefore, 'accidents do not exist *per se*, but *per accidens*, or through the substance.'"[21]

"In the third grade of necessity, καθόλου πρῶτον, (universaliter primúm), the predicate is commensurate with the subject. Moreover, the predicate is not only commensurate, but also reciprocal with the subject. For example, 'Every human, but only a human, is capable of laughter.' Moreover, not only is the predicate reciprocal with the subject, but it holds true in reduplication. For example, *Homo est risibilis*. This is known universally to be true, in any random case of the subject. The reduplicative locution is: 'Man, as man, is capable of laughter' (*Homo, qua homo, est risibilis*)."[22]

---

20. Burgersdijk, *Institutionem logicarum*, 131. Edwards learned this second degree of necessary predication, that is, the essential nexus between subject and predicate, and would later make use of it in Edwards, *Freedom of the Will*, 152–54. It is therefore significant to understand the source of these grades of necessity, to which Edwards certainly would have been exposed at Yale and by way of his tutors, and reading, to wit, by way of Ramus, Ames, Sanderson, Richardson, Morton, Burgersdijk, and Heereboord.

21. Burgersdijk, *Institutionem logicarum*, 132; Kennedy, *Aristotelian and Cartesian Logic at Harvard*, 211.

22. Burgersdijk, *Institutionem logicarum*, 132.

"In the case of the second and third grades, consider which statement is more necessary: 'Man is an animal' or 'Man is risible.' Now, a man cannot *not* be an animal; an animal, however, *can* not be a man. Furthermore, a man cannot *not* be risible. And that which is risible cannot *not* be a man. Thus, the necessity of the second degree is not reciprocal, but the necessity of the third degree is reciprocal and universal. Burgersdijk concluded, 'the universal proposition, grade three, is more necessary than the *per se* proposition, which is grade two, and is not universal.'"

"I begin to see the importance of this discussion about *universal rules*," I said. "The reason why these rules of predication have differing degrees is because, by definition, the second grade includes the first, the third includes the second, but the reverse order does not hold. So, every level (2) *per se* predication is also a level (1) *de omni* predication. And every level (3) *universaliter prima* predication is also a level (2) *per se predication*, but not vice versa."[23]

"If I may sum up," I said, "the first point derived from our discussion is about understanding how propositions signify and affirm that something is true. It is about truth claims and relates to philosophical necessity. The second point is that one must recognize that there are different degrees of necessity. And crucially, that there is contingency in things. The notion that things can be otherwise than they are is a concept derived from the degrees of necessity. But what is the third point? You said that there were three points that you wanted to make."

"Indeed," replied Rector Cutler. "The third point is the broader issue of how we talk about and understand the world outside us. Based on the first two points, we can conclude that the world outside us is contingent. We have seen that there is contingency in the world. Things can be otherwise than they are. The Reformed faith that is taught at the college is far from being Stoic fate."

What I learned today about necessity and contingency built on what I had learned about contingency at the Yale 1718 commencement day. I was well on my way to gathering the intellectual tools, as it were, and building blocks necessary to understand how to defend God against the charge that all things happen necessarily and that ultimately God is the author of evil.

---

23. Burgersdijk, *Institutionem logicarum*, 133. "Hoc est, omnis enunciato per se, est etiam de omni et omnis enunciato universaliter prima, est etiam per se: sed non vice versa."

I then asked Rector Cutler if he would introduce me to the valedictorian, Jonathan Edwards. I said that I wanted to discuss his *Oratio* with him.

"Sure. Come with me. Mr. Edwards is right over there. Mr. Edwards, there is a fellow scholar who would like to meet you and ask you some questions about your *Oratio*."

"Certainly. Please, have a seat. Will you stay, too, Reverend Cutler?" He asked.

"Yes, I am very curious about what this fine gentleman has to say," said Rector Cutler.

"Excellent. So, what is on your mind?" asked Mr. Edwards.

"Mr. Edwards, with all due respect, I do not mean to disparage your *Oratio*, but you certainly seemed to have hit upon Horace's purple patch in your descriptive passages in praise of the college, and the 'Reverend, Sir Cutler.' You called him 'a perennial fountain of the body, the life and motion of this School, the source of its living spirits.'"[24]

"I wrestled with striking the right tone and achieving the expected style of this much-anticipated speech. And I was nervous in the beginning," he said.

"At the end, you mentioned the college being schooled by Minerva, as if in the palace of her father, Pallas. What did you mean to communicate to everyone present and to the Yale College Trustees?" I asked.[25]

"As you well know, Minerva was considered the patron goddess of wisdom and of the arts and sciences. Very appropriate, I thought. And certainly you have heard of a Palladian Palace. Pallas was a reference to the hope we all have for this college, which recently moved here to New Haven, to flourish and become a great place of learning. A Palladium was associated with Pallas Athene, otherwise known as Minerva. Pallas, as you may recall from Greek and Roman mythology, was the great-grandfather of Evander, who founded Pallanteum at the foot of the Palatine Hill. I thus found it very fitting to tie this all together with the founding of Yale College in this city," said Mr. Edwards.

"And while you are at it," I asked, "remind me of the significance of your saying that the college will become 'a home to Apollo.'"[26]

---

24. Minkema and Levesque, *Jonathan Edwards Tercentennial*, 39.

25. Minkema and Levesque, *Jonathan Edwards Tercentennial*, 41.

26. Minkema and Levesque, *Jonathan Edwards Tercentennial*, 41.

"As you recall, I mentioned the patron goddess of the arts and sciences, but there is also the patron god of poetry and music, Apollo. In my judgment, no curriculum is complete without both," he said.

"Indeed," said Rector Cutler, "too often a school honors Minerva and neglects Apollo."

"If you are at all concerned with the college's use of pagan writers," added Mr. Edwards, "remember the motto of Ames, in his *Technometria*, '*Amicus Plato, amicus Aristoteles, sed magis amica veritas.*'"[27]

"Yes," I said. "'Let Plato be a friend, let Aristotle be a friend, but even more let truth be a friend.'"[28] I wanted to transition to learning more about Mr. Edwards's reading and learning. So I moved on from his valedictory oration and asked about life in the new Yale College.

"Mr. Edwards, how is it living in the new Yale College building?" I asked.

"I enjoy my fellow students who now house there," he said. "But I especially enjoy the books housed there and sorting through the Jeremiah Dummer collection of donated books.[29] Did you know that Sir Isaac Newton himself donated a copy of his *Principia mathematica*, published in Cambridge, 1713, as well as his *Opticks*, edited by Samuel Clarke, published in London, 1706?[30] And Mr. Comes donated Father Malebranche's Treatise, *Search of Truth*, published in London, 1700.[31] Mr. Dummer donated many books, including the *opera philosophica* of Descartes, published in Amsterdam, 1674.[32] The honorable Governor Elihu Yale donated a book on what some are calling the new learning and logic, Mr. Locke's *Essay on Human Understanding*, published in London, 1690.[33] The honorable Yale also donated Henry More's *Philosophical Collection*. I especially appreciate More's *Enchiridion ethicum*, published in London, 1668, donated by Mr. Gershom Rawlins."

"You seem to appreciate the more recent books, and the 'new learning' as they call it," I said.

---

27. Ames, *Technometry*, 107.
28. Ames, *Technometry*, 107.
29. Bryant and Patterson, "List of Books," vii–xix.
30. Bryant and Patterson, "List of Books," 464.
31. Bryant and Patterson, "List of Books," 433.
32. Bryant and Patterson, "List of Book," 482.
33. Bryant and Patterson, "List of Books," 435.

"Indeed, I do. But don't forget, the honorable Yale also contributed standard works, such as Calvin's *Institutes,* Downame's *Sum of Divinity,* Rutherford's *Exercitationes Apologetica pro divina gratia,* Burgersdijk's *Institutes of Metaphysical Disputations,* and many more books.[34] And Dummer also donated Jerome Zanchi's *Opera omnia,* published in Geneva, 1619, and William Twisse's *Scientia media,* published in Arnhem, 1639.[35] And mind you, we not only read and even benefit from Greek and Roman classics, but in preparation for the Sabbath, we are obliged to recite William Ames's *Medulla theologiae* and *Cases of Conscience,* Johann Wollebius's *Compendium Theologiae Christianae,* and the Westminster Assembly's *Shorter Catechism,*" he said.[36]

"There were, I believe, over eight hundred volumes that Dummer had collected while in England, acting as our agent," added Rector Cutler. "It has been reported that back in 1714, our college's library did not have any books published in the last one hundred years."

"Naturally," added Mr. Edwards, "we also treasure the classical works, such as Plato's *opera omnia,* Graece and Latine, in folio, donated by Mr. Jeremiah Dummer, Homer's *opera omnia,* donated by Sir Charles Cox, the *opera omnia* of Tully, donated by Governor Yale, and the *opera omnia,* in seven volumes, of St. Augustine, donated by Mr. Jonathan Belcher, Esq. I would also note the donation of the *opera omnia* of Bernard of Clairvaux, by Mr. Brown, published in Antwerp, 1609, and *The Works of Geoffrey Chaucer,* London, 1602, by an unknown donor.[37]

"Mr. Edwards, if I may detain you a little bit longer, I wanted to ask you about your time studying under tutor Elisha Williams, in Wethersfield. Were there any books in particular that he treasured?" I asked.

"Mr. Elisha Williams was a remarkable tutor," replied Mr. Edwards. "He took his bachelor's degree from Harvard in 1711 and his master's in 1714. He was my tutor in Wethersfield from 1716–19. I do recall an interesting story behind a student-copied textbook. It was a commonplace, as you know, for students to transcribe books that were used by their tutors, which in turn were transcribed from a well-known professor's textbook. Now a certain Ebenezer Williams transcribed Reverend Charles Morton's 'A System of Ethicks, and of Moral Philosophy.'"

34. Yale, "A Catalogue of Books Sent by the Honorable Elihu Yale."
35. Bryant and Patterson, "List of Book," 491.
36. Kelley, *Yale a History,* 42; Minkema and Levesque, *Jonathan Edwards Tercentennial,* 33.
37. Bryant and Patterson, "List of Books," 469, 475, 480, 482, 490.

"Were Ebenezer and Elisha related?" I asked.

"No, at least not directly. Ebenezer was two years ahead of Elisha. He took his bachelor's from Harvard in 1709 and his master's in 1712. Ebenezer wrote in the textbook that he had finished copying Morton's 'Ethicks and Pneumatics' on February 7, 1707–08. The transcribed notebook came into Mr. Elisha Williams's possession while he was a student. Now what is interesting about this textbook is that Reverend Morton abstracted large portions of the *Pneumatics* sections directly from none other than Adriaan Heereboord, professor of philosophy at Leiden University. Both Morton's texts and Heereboord's *Meletemata philosophica* or *Philosophical Exercises* are widely transmitted and used at Harvard and Yale."[38]

"Was the student notebook in Latin or English?" I asked. "I understand that Reverend Morton was a great educator and translated Latin texts into English as much as possible."

"That is correct. The English text of William's notebook is most certainly a translation. You can tell from the halted and wooden English and awkward sentence constructions," said Mr. Edwards.

Rector Cutler added, "What is important to know is that Morton's text, and especially Heereboord's *Exercises and Disputations* in Latin, are an important source of philosophical and theological *quaestiones*, that is, questions that master's degree students have to recite and learn to debate."

"Those are the *quaestiones* that are published on commencement broadside sheets for the master's students," I said. "I have seen them. But unlike the bachelor's theses on today's broadside, the master's *quaestiones* are written out as questions, with the name of a student who will either affirm or deny the question posed."

"I am looking forward to preparing for the master's degree," said Mr. Edwards. "I have decided to stay in New Haven. I will have to prepare a synopsis either of logic, natural philosophy, or metaphysics. I also will have to be prepared to discuss philosophical and theological questions such as are discussed in Heereboord's *Meletemata*."[39]

"There is thus no fixed curriculum, is there? You are free to read as widely as you like," I said.

---

38. For the Notebook, see Williams, *Ethicks and Pneumaticks*. For a description of commencement day exercises and reading in the curriculum, see Noble, "An Old Harvard Commencement Programme, 1730," 265–78; On Heereboord's *Meletemata* and the Harvard and Yale connection and curricula, see Fisk, *Edwards's Turn*, 70–72.

39. Fisk, *Jonathan Edwards's Turn*, 70–71n3.

"Indeed, but I will likely take up many duties, such as the resident butler. 'A man's mind plans his way, but the Lord directs his steps.' Who knows but that I will seek pulpit supply, in due course, if the occasion rises," said Mr. Edwards.[40]

As I bade farewell to Rector Cutler and Mr. Edwards and left the *aula academica*, I could not help but think of all the books of learning donated to Yale College. My understanding of necessity and contingency was growing, and I continued to apply my mind to the question of why and how God allows, or, more correctly, how he wills to allow evil in the world. My purpose was to understand the arguments in the philosophical textbooks of the curricula of Harvard and Yale that exonerated God from the allegation that he was the author, if not the actor, of evil. But if things happened by some hard degree of necessity, what degree of formal or material freedom did I retain, after the fall? I determined to investigate, as time would allow, the philosophical disputations of Adriaan Heereboord's *Meletemata*, specifically the ones that concerned necessity, contingency, and freedom. My plan was to attend another commencement day exercise at which the topics of freedom and necessity were debated. As providence would have it, I went to Harvard College.

---

40. Minkema and Levesque, *Jonathan Edwards Tercentennial*, 29–38.

7. The Essence of Free Choice

WHETHER THE ESSENCE OF FREE CHOICE CONSISTS IN
INDIFFERENCE?
DENIED BY EDMUND QUINCY.[1]
PRESIDENT BENJAMIN WADSWORTH
1725 HARVARD QUAESTIONES 2

THERE WERE TWO CONVERSATIONS with two different presidents that I had on two different commencement days. Each conversation had to do with establishing the essence of free choice.[2] The two occasions were with President Benjamin Wadsworth at Harvard in 1725 and President Elisha Williams at Yale in 1735. As was my custom when visiting Harvard, I lodged along the Charles River. President Wadsworth had heard of my earlier visits to Harvard commencements and gave me an enthusiastic welcome. He was an excellent Latinist and knew that my immediate interest was in examining the Latin master's *quaestiones* listed on the commencement day broadside. He agreed to meet with me the day before commencement in order to discuss any of the *quaestiones*. The one that interested me the most was to be disputed by respondent Edmund Quincy. The *quaestio* asked, "Whether the essence of free choice (*liberum arbitrium*) consists in indifference?" Quincy would deny that it did.

"There is an interesting history behind this *quaestio*," said President Wadsworth. "I understand that you met Mr. Jonathan Edwards at Yale

---

1. Wadsworth, "Harvard 1725, Original." "2. *An natura liberi arbitrii consistat in indiffentia? Negat respondens Edmundus Quincy.*"

2. For a fuller treatment of Voetius's teaching on the essence of human freedom, see Beck, *Voetius on God, Freedom, and Contingency*, 440–52. For a fuller treatment of Heereboord's and Morton's teaching on divine and human indifference, see Fisk, *Edwards's Turn*, 149–66, 190–231.

College in 1720. Well, thirty-one years ago Timothy Edwards, Jonathan's father, disputed the same *quaestio* that we have before us at this commencement. In 1694, it was President Increase Mather who presided over the Harvard commencement *quaestiones*. Timothy Edwards denied that indifference was essential to free choice, as Mr. Edmund Quincy will tomorrow."

"Based on what Mr. Edwards told me back in 1720, I would not at all be surprised if some day he wrote a treatise against the indifference of the will," I said. "Tell me, what is the background to the idea of indifference being an essential part of free choice?"

"Let me first provide the framework for the entire question about the essence of free choice," said President Wadsworth. "The scholastics frequently referred to two Scripture passages that have stirred much debate about divine providence: 'In him we live and move and have our being' (Acts 17:28), and 'It is God who is at work in you, enabling you both to will and to work for his good pleasure' (Phil 2:13)."

"These Scripture passages raised questions about how God concurs with human action, both good and bad," said President Wadsworth. "You also see how the ideas of *indifference* and *independence* arose from what these texts claim. For instance, what does it mean that in God we move? That God is at work in us and enables us? The Reformed taught that these passages clearly implied that we are dependent upon God for our lives, our abilities to act, our faculties of intellect and will, and thus that we cannot act independently of God. We cannot act without God, as First Cause, who sovereignly moves in a *first* act upon our faculties and enables us and quickens us thereby to be able to act in what scholastics called a *second* act. Naturally, questions arose whether these texts implicated God in bad human actions and made God the author and actor of sin."[3]

"The Arminian theologians," he continued, "argued that *indifference* played an essential role in preserving human freedom in the concurrence of God's will with ours. Generally speaking, they disagreed with any talk of God sovereignly moving upon our faculties, which is what they understood by the term 'previous' or '*premotion*.' I understand that you learned quite a bit about *concurrence* from President Leverett back in 1715. Arminians claimed that by denying human beings absolute indifference in

---

3. On seventeenth-century sources and quarrels on liberty of indifference, see Schmutz, "Du Péché de l'Ange à la Liberté d'Indifférence. Les Sources Angélologiques de l'Anthropologie Moderne," 169-98; and Boulnois, "Le Refoulement de la Liberté d'Indifférence et les Polémiques Anti-Scotistes de la Métaphysique Moderne," 199-237.

the act of choice toward both sides of competing objects of choice (freedom *ad utrumque*), humans would lose any measure of independence from God. For them, independence from God was necessary if humans were to be free in a genuine manner. The Reformed, however, denied any kind of indifference that would give humans a measure of independence from God and from the divine influx that moved powerfully and effectively upon the human soul."

"I now recall President Willard teaching me about the essence of liberty in his dispute with Mr. Keith. That was at a Harvard commencement in 1702. Indeed, Mr. Keith argued for independence and absolute indifference as essentials to free choice. President Willard mentioned the teaching of the Reverend Charles Morton on this topic. Do students still study the teaching of Reverend Morton?" I asked.

"Indeed they do," said President Wadsworth. "Students regularly make copies of his teaching on the liberty of the will in notebooks, often filling the notebooks with theological commonplaces. The Reverend Morton originally prepared his teaching for students while still in England teaching at the Newington Academy. That was between the years 1679 and 1685. He loved to translate Latin sources into English for students. Many students might not realize it but 'his' teaching was not always original with himself. A former student, Ebenezer Williams, made a very readable copy of Reverend Morton's teaching on the liberty of the will."

"Oh yes. President Cutler and Mr. Edwards told me about Williams's notebook five years ago when I was at Yale College for commencement. But we did not dig into the details of the teaching on the liberty of the will. Could we do that today," I asked.

"By all means," said President Wadsworth. "Let me set up our discussion about different types of indifference and how they relate to the essence of free choice by explaining an old teaching tool for understanding how humans exercise their freedom. The tool is called 'the square of opposition.'[4] Draw a square on a sheet of paper. Now write the term 'willing' (*velle*) on the top left corner. And write 'nilling' (*nolle*) on the top right corner. Then write 'not nilling' (*non nolle*) on the bottom left corner. And 'not willing' (*non velle*) on the bottom right corner."

"I understand that *velle* means 'to will,' but what does *nolle* mean?" I asked.

---

4. I have adapted and expanded this section from Fisk, *A Book of Faith Seeking Understanding*, and from my published research on Charles Morton's teaching transcribed in the Williams' student notebook, in Fisk, *Edwards's Turn*, 220–31.

"*Nolle* means 'to nill' but is still a form of willing in the sense of 'to will that-not,' to will not this or that. 'To nill' means to negate an object, for instance, 'to will-not love,'" said President Wadsworth. "Since *velle* means 'to will,' then *non velle* means 'not to will.' For instance, not to will love. Reverend Morton taught students that *velle* and *non velle* are connected diagonally across the square from the top left corner to the bottom right corner. Likewise, the other diagonal line, from the top right corner to the bottom left corner, connected *nolle* to *non nolle*. Both these diagonal lines were called the freedom of 'exercise,' or, of 'contradictory' acts of the will. Freedom of exercise was considered to be essential and therefore the starting point when discussing freedom. Morton gave a definition commonly held by Jesuits and Arminians of *freedom of exercise*, with which, I note, he disagreed. It ran as follows:

> Of contradiction or as to the exercise of the act (willing or not willing good, nilling, or not nilling evil) is a liberty whereby a power is so indetermined, so that it can act or suspend its act, so say they, (I doubt falsely), the will is free, and herein they place the liberty of the will, namely in indifference to opposites privitive, acting or not acting, but not opposites contrary acting in two contrary species of action; for according to them though the will can't nill an apprehended good yet it may not will or suspend its act of willing, provided it be a subordinate good and not the last end (as felicity) that the will cannot will.[5]

"First," said President Wadsworth, "take note that both *freedom of exercise* (of contradiction) diagonals of the square are represented, namely, from top left to bottom right, willing the good (*velle*) and not willing the good (*non velle*), and from top right to bottom left, nilling evil (*nolle*) and not nilling evil (*non nolle*)."

"What did he not like about this definition?" I asked.

"Morton disagreed with the Jesuit and Arminian notion of indetermination and indifference that was baked into this definition of *freedom of exercise*. Note that they expressly located the essence of freedom in 'indifference to opposites privitive.' The 'opposites' are the opposite acts that I just sketched out with the diagonal lines of the square of opposition, namely, the freedom to exercise those opposite acts, as they said, 'to

---

5. Williams, *Ethicks and Pneumaticks*, seq. 8. For commentary, see Fisk, *Edwards's Turn*, 225. By "privitive" Morton means "not willing," which is a "negative." Furthermore, the notion of "privitive belongs not to God because he is all pure act." Morton does hold to divine "positive" volitions, "willing" (*velle*) and "willing that-not" (*nolle*).

act' or 'to suspend its act.' And the 'privitives' refer to the *non* before *velle* and *nolle*. Thus, the term refers to the privation of a positive act of will (*non velle*) and the privation of a negative act of will (*non nolle*)."

"I notice that they explicitly denied that freedom of the will was located in 'opposites contrary acting in two contrary species of action,'" I said. "If I am not mistaken, that would refer to the *freedom of specification*, correct? That is, the top line from left to right, from *velle* to *nolle*. If correct, what then did they not like about *freedom of specification*?" I asked.

"They denied the *willing* and *nilling* line because, as the definition said, 'the will cannot nill an apprehended good.' In other words, if the last dictate of the intellect presents an apparent good to the will, a person cannot nill the last and greatest apparent good. However, the will can 'not will or suspend its act of willing, provided the good is a subordinate good,'" said President Wadsworth. "The example Morton gave can be summed up like this. Suppose there are two apparent goods, both alike, 'proposed to us.' We 'take one then say one is willed, but the other is not willed.' Then Morton addressed the case of evil proposed to the will. He said, 'So of apprehended evil, though it cannot will it yet it may not will it, or suspend its willing act.' Then Morton said, 'The instance is suffering for a good cause. That is the ancient doctrine of the schools in the dark time of popery.'"

"That reminds me of the 'necessity of indifference' spoken of by Aristotle and popularized by the dilemma posed by Buridan's ass," I said. "Buridan's apocryphal account said that there were two bales of hay placed equidistant before an ass. Each was equally attractive. But the ass died of hunger because it could not choose between the equally good objects. Aristotle had supposed 'a man who was exceedingly hungry and thirsty.' Since he was positioned 'equidistant from food and drink, he was bound to stay where he was,' and as a result, he died from hunger and thirst."[6]

"Tell me, what did the student notebook record about the opponents' definition of *freedom of specification*," I asked, "a freedom which they themselves opposed?"

"Morton agreed with his opponents," said President Wadsworth, "that the will is not free according to the following formulation of *freedom of specification*:

---

6. Aristotle, *On the Heavens*, in *Basic Works*, 433 (295b30–35).

Contrariety or the specification of act (willing and nilling). This is a liberty whereby a power is so indetermined as that it can will or nill (which are contrary species of action) any object proposed whether it be good or evil, and they say rightly the will is not free.[7]

"Morton explained that the problem with this definition was that it assumed that a person had the power to will evil as evil, rather than will evil under the guise of an apparent good. This differed dramatically with the definition of *freedom of exercise*. There they said that a person could will the good and nill evil. But here a person can *will* an evil object that is proposed to the mind. Moreover, they said that a person's power was 'indetermined,' that is, that a person was indifferent toward good and evil. On this, Morton said, 'They say rightly the will is not free' in this sense."

"I now see that one needs to distinguish between 'real and apparent good and evil,'" I said, "since it is 'not the reality but the appearance that moves the will.' In other words, 'a real good, appearing evil, may be nilled, and vice versa.'"[8]

"Precisely," said President Wadsworth. "This is how Morton taught his students to remember the square:

{Of contrariety is willing nilling} or {Of specifying acts is willing nilling} {Of contradiction is willing not willing} or {Of exercise is willing not willing}[9]

"Could you now tell me what Morton's own definition of the essence of free choice is?" I asked.

"Morton defined free choice as follows," said President Wadsworth:

But indeed Reformed Philosophy places the liberty of the will not in indifference to opposites (willing or not willing, nilling, or not nilling) but in a rational spontaneity that is the will uninforced following the practical understanding, or [the thing] spontaneously (that is of one's own accord) for a reason (the word for a Reason) differing the spontaneity from that of brutes, which act not deliberately at all but according to present appetite excited by present sensitive objects; they therefore deny the will of man liberty of contradiction as of contrariety for say they it is impossible they should not incline to a good proposed by

---

7. Williams, *Ethicks and Pneumaticks*, seq. 8. Also Fisk, *Edwards's Turn*, 225.
8. Williams, *Ethicks and Pneumaticks*, seqs. 8–9; see too Fisk, *Edwards's Turn*, 226.
9. Williams, *Ethicks and Pneumaticks*, seq. 9; see too Fisk, *Edwards's Turn*, 227.

the understanding as not only good in itself but at present good for us because the will must always follow the last dictate of the practical understanding.[10]

"Instead of locating free choice in the two types of freedom sketched in the square of opposition, Morton located free choice in 'rational spontaneity,'" said President Wadsworth.

"What does the term mean, precisely?" I asked.

"By 'rational,' he meant that the will does not act blindly, but follows the understanding. By 'spontaneity,' he meant the will acts 'of one's own accord.' Crucially, he took aim at the notion of 'indifference' inherent in these two types of freedom. Whereas the Jesuits and Arminians emphasized indifference to good and evil, and independence from God's sovereign impulses in our soul, he emphasized an 'uninforced will' that followed the last dictate of the practical understanding. That is, the will was not compelled intrinsically by its own nature. Finally, the reason Morton stated for the rejection of these two freedoms by Reformed philosophy was that they held that the will always positively inclines itself to the greatest apparent good 'proposed by the understanding as not only good in itself, but at present good for us,'" said President Wadsworth.[11]

"Which other Reformed theologians located free choice in rational spontaneity?" I asked.

"Francis Turretin (1623–87) located free choice in 'rational willingness,' a term more or less the same as 'rational spontaneity' (*lubentia rationalis*)," said President Wadsworth.[12]

"I recall that President Willard used the similar term, *lubentia rationis*, by which he meant the readiness of the will to act," I said. "Willard also talked about the important distinction between a first act and a second act. Did Turretin?"

"Indeed he did" said President Wadsworth. "Unlike Morton, Turretin made it clear that the discussion about indifference as it related to free choice really had to do with how God concurs with the physical reality of human action in what were called two acts, a first and a second. The first act was reserved for God's initial movement upon 'passive' human faculties whose state Turretin called an 'objective indifference.' In the

---

10. Williams, *Ethicks and Pneumaticks*, seq. 9. See too Fisk, *Edwards's Turn*, 227–29.

11. Williams, *Ethicks and Pneumaticks*, seq. 9.

12. Turretin, *First through Tenth Topics*, 665 (Topic 10, Q. 3.2). Translated in Asselt, *Reformed Thought*, 182. For a fuller account of Turretin's teaching on free choice, see Asselt, *Reformed Thought*, 171–200.

first act, the will could be isolated from the intellect in an absolute sense, which would place the focus on the 'natural constitution' of the will of a created human being. In this sense, Turretin agreed that 'the will of itself' was indifferent to opposite acts and therefore enjoyed freedom of exercise and freedom of specification in 'the divided sense.' You will recall that in *the divided sense* of speaking, there was no logical contradiction to claim that humans possessed an indifferent 'simultaneity of potency' (*simultas potentiae*) or power of the will, such that it can will or not will.[13] But there would be a contradiction to claim that the will had the power of simultaneity (*potentia simultatis*) in the second act, as if humans possessed a power simultaneously to will or not will, to will or to nill, in the compound sense.[14] You should understand that in the first act, it is God alone who works on the physical level of reality, enabling the human will, as Saint Paul said, to act in the second act, and to complete what God began in the first act."

"As I understand it, Turretin said that the real question was what happened in the second act. That is where he differed from the Jesuits and Arminians, correct?" I asked.

"Indeed. In the second act of God's concurrence with human free choice, there is no indifferent power and freedom of exercise and freedom of specification in the compound sense. Humans do not have 'active and subjective indifference.' Furthermore, Turretin denied that 'the will is always so indifferent and undetermined that it can act or not act.'[15] This language and conclusion resembles what Morton said about the essence of Reformed free choice," said President Wadsworth.

"At Utrecht University, what did Gisbertus Voetius teach about the essence of human freedom?" I asked.

"Voetius taught that as created human beings, you and I possess an active, self-determined, faculty of the will," said President Wadsworth. "That was his starting point. In principle, he taught a freedom of exercise, namely, freedom or power to do and to refrain from doing. To be human was to be free. This held regardless of whether one was in a state of original creation, a fallen state, or a regenerated state. Furthermore, this description applied to the created human will prior, by way of conceiving it, to the second act of God's concurrence with the human will in

---

13. Turretin, *First through Tenth Topics*, in Asselt, *Reformed Thought*, 182.
14. Turretin, *First through Tenth Topics*, in Asselt, *Reformed Thought*, 183.
15. Turretin, *First through Tenth Topics*, in Asselt, *Reformed Thought*, 183.

eliciting acts of the will in the reality of this fallen world. The movement of the human will is bound up with God's movement upon the soul. We move because God moves. Perhaps, in this way, Voetius grappled with and made sense of the Scripture passages, 'In him we live and move and have our being' (Acts 17:28) and 'We love because he first loved us' (1 John 4:19). Here is a *quaestio* about freedom *ad utrumque* with a lengthy response by the defendant Godefrido Deys, taken from a disputation at Utrecht University in 1661:

> *Is [the will] freely related to both sides of the opposition? We respond with a distinction.* If the will is considered in itself and without any respect to a particular state, *and if* with 'freedom' the same thing is understood as 'voluntariness,' that is, (as people commonly call it) 'natural freedom' or 'indifference,' or the 'flexibility (*vertibilitas*) of the will,' or 'rational complacence'; or else, if 'freedom' is understood as what they call 'freedom of exercise or contradiction'—if that is the case, then *we affirm.* For that [freedom] can no more be separated from the human will than the will can be separated from a rational human being.[16]

"As would be expected, there are some commonalities between Voetius, Morton, and Turretin, all contemporaries of one another, although Voetius was the senior of the three," said President Wadsworth.

"I notice terms that I have encountered before. Terms such as freedom *ad utrumque*, which appears in the question, 'freely related to both sides,' and of course the terms, 'freedom of exercise' and 'voluntariness,'" I said. "But what did Voetius mean when he spoke about 'natural freedom' and 'indifference?'"

"Indeed. By 'indifference,' Voetius meant that there were contingent eligible propositions proposed to the created will of human beings. Whether to love or to refrain from loving, for instance. There was a sense in which the will, apart from the dictates of the understanding, was indifferent to the propositions. But this definition of natural or formal freedom, as it were, has to do with the nature of human beings who are created in God's image, a freedom which always remains intact, both before and after the fall in Eden. Along this line of argument, Voetius affirmed that freedom of exercise belonged to humans as humans. The power to elicit an act of the will or not was indeed a feature of indifference," said President Wadsworth.

---

16. As quoted in Beck, *Voetius on God, Freedom, and Contingency*, 449.

"But if Voetius presided over this disputation and affirmed freedom of exercise, does that mean that he disagreed with Morton on the essence of free choice?" I asked.

"Excellent question," replied President Wadsworth. "But not at all. We have to take into account the so-called noetic effects of the fall in Eden. In a fallen state, Voetius would agree with Morton's conclusion that Reformed philosophy did not locate the essence of free choice in fallen creatures 'in indifference to opposites (willing or not willing good, nilling, or not nilling evil),' as if it mattered not whether good or evil was proposed to the mind and the will."[17]

"So then, what did Voetius say about the essence of free choice in the sense of what you and I can actually achieve with the power of our wills, in the state in which we now find ourselves?" I asked. "In other words, when not isolating the will in an absolute state?"

"In view of the fall in Eden," said President Wadsworth, "Voetius denied freedom of exercise as an indifferent power of freedom *ad utrumque,* as if you and I could achieve the good without any qualification. Remember, whether Voetius, Turretin, or Morton, they would agree to this qualification, that the mind and will of regenerated persons must be renovated and renewed by the sovereign work of the Holy Spirit moving upon their faculties day by day in order for them to actually achieve any good thing in this life. As Saint Paul said, 'Our inner nature is being renewed day by day' (2 Cor 4:16) and as our Lord Jesus said, 'Apart from me you can do nothing' (John 15:5)."

The next day I attended the commencement ceremonies. President Wadsworth and respondent Edmund Quincy presented many of the arguments and distinctions that we had discussed the day before. Fifteen years later, in 1740, I attended the Yale commencement day exercises. Rector Thomas Clap presided over a master's *quaestio* that intrigued me very much. It had to do with reconciling the divine decrees with human freedom, the same topic that President Willard had addressed at Harvard when I was there in 1702. But I had learned much more about these issues thanks to attending several commencement days, and I was eager to hear what Rector Clap at Yale had to say about it.

---

17. Williams, *Ethicks and Pneumaticks,* seq. 8. At this juncture, I am following Beck's exposition of Voetius, in Beck, *Voetius on God, Freedom, and Contingency,* 450–52.

8. Necessity and Freedom

WHETHER THE NECESSITY OF THE DECREES DENIES
FREEDOM IN CREATURES? DENIED.[1]
RECTOR THOMAS CLAP 1740
YALE QUAESTIONES 10

THE BACHELOR'S BROADSIDE THESES would not help me in my quest to understand freedom and necessity, since they do not normally pose the more complex philosophical and theological questions. I knew that I had to attend a commencement day with master's *quaestiones*, which were usually debated in the afternoon. The day came. It was the year 1740, New Haven, Connecticut.

The Reverend Jonathan Edwards was in attendance, as was his habit in the 1730s and 1740s.[2] I was determined to greet him after the exercises, but I also wanted to talk with the new rector, Thomas Clap, the fifth rector of Yale College, inducted April 2, 1740. He succeeded Rector Elisha Williams, who served from 1726–39.

I took a seat in the *aula academica* and quickly examined the master's *quaestiones* broadside and noted *quaestio* 5. It asked, "Whether whatever God has willed, he would have willed from eternity?"[3] Eli Colton would affirm this. I pondered whether this answer implied that there are no other possibilities open to God when he wills what he wills, and whether that in turn implied some kind of fatalism. I wondered what Rector Clap would have to say about this. Then my eye was drawn

---

1. Clap, "1740 Yale College Commencement Quaestiones." "10. *An Decretorum necessitas, libertatem in creaturis tollat? Negat Respondens Timotheus Judd.*"

2. Fisk, *Edwards's Turn*, 47.

3. Clap, "1740 Yale College Commencement Quaestiones." "5. *An quicquid Deus voluit voluerit ab aeterno? Affirmat Respondens Eli Colton.*"

to *quaestio* 10. It asked, "Whether the necessity of the decrees removes freedom from creatures?"[4] The respondent was Sir Timothy Judd. The broadside indicated that he would answer in the negative. I wondered what this implied. If human freedom remains intact, then would not divine freedom also remain uncompromised? I was eager to hear what Sir Timothy Judd and Sir Eli Colton had to say. And Rector Clap, as well.

Unlike the morning bachelor's exercises, the valedictory oration would come near the end of the master's exercises. Thus, after the opening prayer, Rector Clap asked Sir Timothy Judd to rise and defend thesis 10.

"Esteemed Rector, Reverend Ministers, learned audience," said Sir Timothy Judd, "first we must distinguish between different kinds of necessity. There are many levels of necessity. In his well-known *Loci Communes* (1535 edition), Philip Melanchthon followed the medieval scholastic method of distinguishing between the necessity of the consequence and the necessity of the consequent (*necessitas consequentiae* and *necessitas consequentis*). The purpose was to use the tools of syntax and grammar to help exonerate God from the proposition that God is the author of sin and to defend against the related proposition that whatever comes to pass, must of necessity come to pass, without regard to divine freedom, without regard to human freedom. Melanchthon gave the following example of the necessity of the consequence: 'Jerusalem must be destroyed.'[5] In a conditional syllogistic form, as taught here at the college from Antoine Arnauld and Pierre Nicole, *Logic or the Art of Thinking*, we would say:

> If God wills that Jerusalem be destroyed, then it will be destroyed.
> He wills that Jerusalem be destroyed.
> Therefore, it will be destroyed.[6]

"The line of reasoning is such that when the conditional is true, then necessarily, the consequent follows. The consequent cannot not follow. We derive this line of reasoning from the 'If this, then that' pattern. However, when we consider each component part of the above proposition separately, there is no necessity imposed upon God such that he must will that Jerusalem be destroyed. That is, there is nothing in the nature of

---

4. Clap, "1740 Yale College Commencement Quaestiones." "10. *An Decretorum necessitas, libertatem in creaturis tollat? Negat Respondens Timotheus Judd.*"

5. Vos, "Philip Melanchthon on Freedom and Will," 55.

6. Arnauld and Nicole, *Logic*, 168.

Jerusalem itself such that it must be destroyed, necessarily. According to the 'If this, then that' propositional pattern, the major premise contains the conclusion. Therefore, there is a necessary conditional relationship between the major premise and the conclusion—what God wills to happen and what happens. Each part of the proposition stands on its own. What God wills, he wills contingently. The destruction of Jerusalem is thus contingent upon the will of God."

Rector Clap then interjected and asked, "Well done, Sir Timothy Judd, but could you now move on and explain to the audience why the necessity of the consequent is a harder necessity?"

"Indeed, I shall, Esteemed Rector," replied Sir Timothy Judd. "Now let me explain the notion of the necessity of the consequent. Melanchthon associated the necessity of the consequent with absolute necessity. One example he gave was, 'It is necessary that God exists, that God is good, that God is righteous, and so on.'[7] In syllogistic form,

> If God necessarily exists, then he is necessarily good and just.
> God necessarily exists.
> Therefore, he is necessarily good and just.

"As I already said, in the syllogistic form, the major premise contains the conclusion, and in this case, necessarily so. For it is not possible that God both exist and that he is not good and just. Thus, in this case, neither proposition can be contingent. It is not possible for God not to be good and just. Therefore, the consequent of the 'If this, then that' proposition is necessarily true. From the propositional variables in the following pattern, 'Not both (God exists and He is not good),' one can infer, 'If this, then that.' In that case, the 'Necessity' operator is placed as follows, 'God exists and God is good, necessarily.'"

"Thus far," continued the respondent, "I have established the consequential relation of an 'If this, then that' conditional statement. But I need to say something more about the syllogism: 'If God necessarily exists, then he is necessarily good and just.' Take note of what happens when I treat the antecedent and the consequent clauses separately. When I isolate the consequent proposition, 'God is necessarily good,' I can place the *Necessity* operator before the consequent 'then', instead of before the antecedent 'if'. This results in the necessity of the consequent proposition.

---

7. Vos, "Philip Melanchthon on Freedom and Will," 54.

That is why I placed *necessarily* at the end, 'God is good and just, necessarily. This is the hard necessity of the consequent.'"[8]

"These are only two kinds of necessity," he continued. "Therefore, when speaking of the necessity of the consequence of the divine decree, there is no necessity imposed upon God, nor is there any kind of inherent necessity in humans such that God could not will otherwise than he does."

At this point, Rector Clap interjected and asked, "Could you please explain to us if Jean Calvin made use of the scholastic distinction between *necessitas consequentiae* and *necessitas consequentis*? We know that Martin Luther knew well the medieval scholastic distinctions, but in his usual manner he berated the 'amusing idea' of the 'Sophists.'[9] Now by Sophists, he did not mean Gorgias and other pre-Socratics. He meant Peter Lombard, Thomas Aquinas, and Duns Scotus. But what of Jean Calvin?"

"Esteemed Rector. As you well know, in the Yale Library that you so well attend to, we have the *Tractatus theologici omnes* of Jean Calvin. In the collection of treatises, there is Calvin's treatise, *Concerning the Eternal Predestination of God* (*De aeterna dei praedestinatione*).[10] Calvin knew well the distinction between *necessitas consequentis et consequentiae*.[11] We know that Calvin made a little more use of the scholastic distinctions than Luther, but not as much as the later Reformed theologians whom we also esteem in the New England colleges. He acknowledged the notion of the contingency of events that occur in the world. On this point, he gave the classic example of the frangibility of the bones of Christ, which he correlated with the necessity of the consequence."[12]

---

8. Vos, "Melanchthon on Freedom and Will," 54–55; also Beck, "Zur Rezeption Melanchthons bei Gisbertus Voetius (1589–1676), Namentlich in Seiner Gotteslehr," 319–44; Beck, "Melanchthon und die reformierte Scholastik," 107–28, on 127.

9. *Luther and Erasmus*, 120.

10. Calvin, *Tractatus theologici omnes*.

11. Calvin, *Eternal Predestination of God*, 170. Calvin also makes these distinctions in the *Institutes*: "Whence again we see that distinctions concerning relative necessity and absolute necessity, likewise of consequent and consequence, were not recklessly invented in schools, when God subjected to fragility the bones of his Son, which he had exempted from being broken, and thus restricted to the necessity of his own plan what could have happened naturally," in Calvin, *Institutes*, 210 (1.16.9).

12. Reid translated *necessitas consequentis et consequentiae* as "absolute and consequential necessity," in Calvin, *Eternal Predestination of God*, 170; Latin text: Baum et al., *Corpus Reformatorum*, 8:354.

"An excellent line of syllogistic reasoning, Sir Timothy Judd," exclaimed Rector Clap. "Indeed, the example of the contingency of the breaking of the bones of Christ being fully compatible with the notion of the necessity of the prophecy that Christ's bones not be broken is standard fare in the cycle of disputations and theses debated by students at universities on the continent of Europe, such as at Leiden University.[13]

At this point, Rector Clap thanked Sir Timothy Judd for his performance, and then called upon Sir Eli Colton. "Please briefly explain *quaestio* 5," he said, "and if you would like to add anything to what Sir Timothy Judd has said, please do so. But be concise."

Sir Eli Colton rose and began to speak. "Esteemed Rector, reverend ministers, dear audience. I would like to add to what Sir Timothy Judd said. I call your attention to the bachelor's broadside sheet from this morning's exercises. Logic thesis 12 reads, 'Between the will and consequent action, there is no necessary connection.'[14] In other words, there is no transmission of some kind of hard necessity from the antecedent to the consequent action. This is because there is only an implicative relation between the terms of the proposition that represent the will and the consequent action. The necessity of the consequence is a mere implicative necessity."[15]

"This afternoon's *quaestio* 5 asks, 'Whether whatever God has willed, he would have willed from eternity?' At first sight, it might appear as if there is some question about the wording of the question whether God has freedom to will what he wills. But the *quaestio* intends to lead us to conclude that whatever God wills, he does not will in time, but apart from time, or outside of time. As the learned Dr. Ames wrote in his *Medulla* on the divine decrees, chapter 7, thesis 7, 'Every decree of God is eternal' (*Omne decretum Dei est aeternum*) (1 Cor 2:7; Acts 15:18). And in Ames's thesis 34, 'This will is truly free, because whatever it wills it wills not by necessity of nature but by counsel.' You have heard it said, '*Que sera, sera.* Whatever will be, will be.' Some think that this is what

---

13. Cf. Polyander, *Theses theologicae de providentia Dei*. Thesis 24; on the cycle of disputations disputed at Leiden University, starting in 1596, and after the Synod of Dort, a new cycle began in 1620, under Johannes Polyander, see Te Velde, *Synopsis Purioris Theologiae*, 1.

14. Talcott, "Yale College Commencement Broadside 1740." Logic thesis 12: "*Inter voluntatem et actionem consequentem, nulla datur connexio necessaria.*"

15. Fisk, *Edwards's Turn*, 82–83; on the necessity of consequence as an implicative necessity, see Vos, "Melanchthon on Freedom and Will," 55.

quaestio 5 implies, that is, that even God has no freedom outside of time to will what he will to take place in the course of time. But I recall commencement day physics thesis 24, which actually belongs to metaphysics, from Rector Samuel Andrew, in 1718, which was chosen for debate. It said, 'The will is not subject to coercion.'[16] This applies not only to your will and my will, but to God's will as well."

I was very intrigued with the explanation of the difference between these two kinds of necessities. I was determined to speak further with Rector Clap, and with the Reverend Edwards, after the exercises were over. I was convinced more than ever that I wanted to continue to attend these commencement days at Harvard and Yale.

At this point, Rector Clap thanked Sir Timothy Judd and Sir Eli Colton for their remarkable display of erudition. The valedictory oration was given, and the Rector proceeded to close the ceremonies for the day. He turned to the trustees and said, "Reverend Ministers, I present to you these young scholars, whom I am convinced are sufficiently learned to receive their second degree. Does it please you, *Placetne vobis*?"

"*Placet, placet*," replied the trustees.[17]

With the audience dismissed, Rector Clap made his way over to greet Reverend Edwards. I joined them and together we sat and discussed the day's commencement exercises.

"I myself have been weighing whether to write something on the question of whether God is the author of sin, and whether there is such a thing as freedom of will," said Reverend Edwards. "On the first question, I think one has to ask if there is a difference between our sovereign God being the author of all things, including evil, or God being the actual actor committing sin and evil acts. Our opponents allege that our Reformed, Calvinistic doctrines make God the author, if not actor, of sin. The latter I find repulsive. And concerning so-called freedom of will, I would not allow it if it implies 'freedom of indifference' in the sense of a 'self-determining power', such as the Arminians teach."

"You will recall five years ago," continued Mr. Edwards, "in 1735, under Rector Elisha Williams at Yale, the first-degree commencement metaphysics theses 6 and 7 touched on similar matters as today. Thesis 6 read, 'Divine foreknowledge does not deny human liberty.' Thesis 7 seemed to uphold the self-determining power of the will. I suppose both

16. Saltonstall, "Yale College Commencement Broadside 1718." Physics thesis 24, "*Voluntas coactiones non subjicitur.*"

17. Kelley, *Yale: A History*, 21.

divine and human. If I remember correctly, it said, 'The will is the power of the mind to determine itself.'[18] Aaron Burr was a commencer, as was Joseph Bellamy on that day, both taking their bachelor's degree. But I was not entirely satisfied with what appeared to me to be an Arminian line of reasoning given under my former tutor. For the good of New England, I intend to study and write on these matters in the near future."[19]

I asked Rector Clap if he would elaborate further on the different levels of necessity, as this seemed crucial to understanding the debate about freedom and necessity. Rector Clap seemed delighted with the conversation and began to explain more about necessity.

"Let us consider the case of a decree that is called an 'external necessity.' An external necessity is based on an antecedent supposition, such as a divine decree or prophecy. I think of Calvin's example of the fulfillment of the prophecy that the bones of Christ will not be broken (John 19:36).[20] There is a kind of necessity associated with our foreknowledge of things that will happen. When we know that something will happen, it will happen, by infallible necessity."

"Could you please give us an example?" I asked.

"Certainly. For instance, If I drop a crystal bowl, I know that it will break. But there is nothing necessary about my dropping the bowl. As in *natural necessity*—another kind of necessity which I will explain in a minute—it is in the nature of crystal itself that, if dropped, it will break. Now, in the case of the prophecy about the bones of Christ not being broken, the external necessity is nothing more than a relative necessity. The necessity is called *relative* since it is only the prophecy itself that makes the bones of Christ necessarily unbreakable."

"Indeed," I said. "Otherwise, bones are naturally breakable. So this *necessity* belongs to a unique situation. It is imposed from without. In like manner, I suppose, the prophecy of Jesus that Peter would thrice deny him, and that Judas would betray him, did not remove their guilt. Nor did Peter blame Jesus for his denials, or Judas for his betrayal."

---

18. Talcott, "Yale College Commencement Broadside 1735." Metaphysics theses 6, 7. "*Praescientia divina non tollit libertatem humanam. Voluntas est mentis sese determinandi potestas.*"

19. In January 1746/47 and 1748/49, Edwards would write to Joseph Bellamy that he already had begun to write on these topics in his private papers.

20. Calvin, *Eternal Predestination of God*, 170; also in Calvin, *Institutes*, 210 (1.16.9).

"Indeed," replied Rector Clap. "Now if God through his prophets decrees that the bones of Christ will not be broken, then they will not. The prophecy, indeed, is an externally imposed necessity. Now let me ask you. Was the soldier at the foot of the cross free to wield his spear and break the bones of Christ? I submit to you that he was free. Was his freedom violated or denied by the prophecy? No. It still was possible that the soldier break the bones of Christ. But would he? I submit to you that he would not. The prophecy would be fulfilled, and infallibly so."

I asked if he could return to the notion of *natural necessity* and explain it a bit more.

"Indeed," he said. "Let me tell you what I have learned from Adriaan Heereboord's *Meletemata*. He tells us a lot about these different kinds of necessity, including natural necessity. Fire burns. Bones are breakable or frangible. The earth spins and thus the sun rises and sets. The necessity of nature (*necessitas naturae*) is instituted by God. In principle, this necessity produces its effect. Indeed, this kind of necessity cannot not bring about the naturally derived effect. It comes from itself. It occurs on its own. Nevertheless, the cause-effect relation can be changed by God so that it not produce its effect. *Naturally*, Newton's force of gravitational attraction of two planets is directly dependent upon the mass of each body and inversely proportional to the square of the distance between their centers. What is heavy descends. The earth rotates by itself and by force of its own nature. God, however, can interrupt the action without violating the principle."[21]

At this point I asked if Rector Clap could explain the nuances surrounding the term "infallible." "There seems to be some misunderstanding about the word *infallible*," I said. "Could you please explain what the term means, and continue?"

"I would be glad to," he replied. "When we hear the word *infallible*, it sounds as if it is an absolute kind of necessity. But as I have said, there are several kinds of necessity. This kind of necessity is not as hard as the necessity of the consequent or an absolute necessity. Thus, the meaning of *infallibility* is relative to God's decree. Heereboord, in his *Meletemata*, elaborates on these different kinds of necessity. He says that when we speak of *external* or *infallible* necessity, it points to a kind of hypothetical existence by which an event, when it happens, happens necessarily. But this necessity is totally compatible with contingency. The two are not

21. Heereboord, *Meletemata*, 62.

opposed to one another.[22] For instance, given the supposition that I am married, then, if I am married, I have a spouse. But there is nothing necessary about my being married. It is a hypothetical."

"On the term 'infallible,'" he continued, "I would direct you to Bishop Bramhall's famous debate with Thomas Hobbes on liberty and necessity. It ran from 1645 to 1658. In 1655 Bramhall published *A Defence of True Liberty from antecedent and extrinsical necessity* and in 1658 *The Castigations of Mr. Hobbes, his last animadversions in the case concerning liberty and universal necessity*. By the way, Bramhall's works are catalogued in the Yale Library. Bishop Bramhall makes it clear that Hobbes misunderstands the terms of the debate. When something happens *infallibly*, *inevitably*, or *unfrustrably*, and when it is based on a hypothetical, or a mere supposition, then there is nevertheless the *possibility* of the opposite happening. Thus, for something to happen infallibly means merely that it happens as a necessity of the consequence."[23]

"So, I think we need to temper our understanding of the harshness of this kind of necessity. Why? Because infallibility is a relative term, relative, for instance, to a prophecy decreed by God to be fulfilled in the course of history. Even given such a prophecy, remember that the soldier at the cross was free to swing a club and break the legs of Christ, but he chose not to."

I could tell that Reverend Edwards was either not so happy about Rector Clap's reference to Bishop Bramhall, or that he would like to provide some nuance to the terms of the debate. And so I asked him, "Reverend Edwards, where do you stand on the infallibility of the decrees and possibility of things being otherwise than they are?"

"Let me say this. I myself have not read Mr. Hobbes, but I have heard of the Bramhall-Hobbes debate," said Reverend Edwards. "Let Mr. Hobbes and Bishop Bramhall say what they will, but if Bramhall makes a distinction between the power to act, just prior to the act, and the act itself, it will not stand under scrutiny. I say that there is no freedom in the sense of a self-determining power to act prior to the act, to be distinguished from the act itself. I say that once the mind weighs whether to act or not, the mind already is inclined with a preponderating bias

---

22. "*Necessitas externa ex hypothesi existentiae seu actus est, qua res, cum est, necessario est, cum sit, necessario sit,*" in Heereboord, *Meletemata*, 63.

23. Bramhall, *Works*, 745, 841. For presentation and commentary, see Chappell, *Hobbes and Bramhall on Liberty and Necessity*. On the meaning of "infallible," see Fisk, *Edwards's Turn*, 280–91.

one way or the other. There is therefore no such thing as the Arminians call 'freedom *ad utrumque*,' that is, freedom to choose otherwise than one chooses. Prior to an act of the will the mind or will is in a state of equilibrium. There is, therefore, no praise to be given Bramhall on this point. If my view is closer to that of Mr. Hobbes, the truth itself is not to be rejected on that account," said Reverend Edwards.

I recalled what Sir Timothy Judd said, "*Que sera sera*, whatever will be, will be," and I asked Rector Clap, "What does this kind of thinking imply? Most people think that many things in life just have to happen, by necessity. That things just cannot be otherwise than they are. Whether I matriculate in Harvard or Yale, who I marry, and so forth. But is that so? I wonder myself. That is why I came today. I am beginning to understand these different levels of necessity. But I think that I have much more to learn," I said.

"Indeed, there is much more to unfold," replied Rector Clap. "When the notion of *necessity* is debated at the college, the respondents learn to ask, 'Which kind of necessity are you talking about? There is more than one.' I often explain how yesteryear's theologians, when confronting those who allege that their belief in God's sovereignty amounts to Stoic fate, are quick to point out that there are at least five different kinds of necessity."

At this point, Reverend Edwards took leave of us. I sensed that Rector Clap would soon need to leave, and so I pressed him a little further and I asked him to explain another kind of necessity before leaving.

"Briefly," he said, "there are two more kinds of necessity that you should ponder. Heereboord speaks of an 'independent necessity.' God is said to be a necessary Being. God cannot not exist. This proposition is certain and true. It cannot be false. To God alone belongs this *independent necessity*. This is a supreme necessity. God alone declares and can declare, 'I Am Who I Am' (Exod 3:14). God owes his necessity to nothing, and receives it from nothing."

"If there is *independent necessity*, then there must be *dependent necessity*. I presume that Heereboord says that this necessity belongs to us, as humans, and is derived from God," I said.

"Indeed," said Rector Clap. "God endows humans with the capacity to laugh. To say, 'Humans are risible, necessarily' is to illustrate the kind of necessity that belongs to mind-gifted creatures."

"Why is risibility something necessary?" I asked. "At the moment, I cannot recall the details of the discussion from the Yale 1720 commencement day exercises."

"Think about it," said Rector Clap. "To say the opposite involves a contradiction. By definition, you and I have the capacity to laugh, and necessarily so. Indeed, quite apart from what it means to be a laughing hyena, risibility is necessary in the same sense as to say that a human is rational (mind-gifted)."[24]

"Hold on a minute," I said. "There is no difference in the kind of necessity expressed in the proposition that says, 'Humans are dependent' and that which says, 'God is independent.' In other words, to predicate of God that 'He is' is the same kind of necessity as to say, 'A human is risible.' Isn't it? The sentence has a subject, 'God,' which adheres necessarily in the predicate, 'is.' In this way, the sentence structure itself makes a claim that is necessary, namely, 'God is.' Likewise, the sentence structure about humans makes a necessary claim, 'A human is risible.' Or am I mistaken?" I asked.

"Ah, yes," replied Rector Clap, "but you are confusing talk about God with talk about humans. The subjects of the two different sentences do not cohere with the predicate in the same way. A student would give the following two reasons to overcome the objection. First, self-existence is an essential attribute for God. Thus, *God* coheres with *existence*, and necessarily so. The necessity of human laughter is externally imposed. Human beings are dependent creatures, and therefore differ from God.[25] But there is no necessity imposed upon God from without. The entire proposition 'Humans are capable of laughter' is itself externally imposed. Thus, to claim the opposite about either the proposition about God or about humans is a contradiction. God enjoys an independent kind of necessity, and humans enjoy a dependent kind of necessity. Human beings cannot endow themselves with their own essential attributes. I will close with this. Heereboord said, 'Do not ask if God could have created a human being who is not mind-gifted, or who is not capable of laughter.'"[26]

---

24. "*Ita necessarium est, hominem esse animal, esse rationalem, esse risibilem,*" in Heereboord, *Meletemata*, 61. See, Muller, *Dictionary*, s.v. "Independentia," 170–71.

25. Heereboord, *Meletemata*, 62.

26. "*Si roges, an Deus potuerit creare hominem, qui non esset rationalis, non risibilis, si homo talis est necessario, quia Deus voluit eum talem creare, respondeo, hoc rogandum non esse, nec temere in divinam potentiam,*" in Heereboord, *Meletemata*, 62.

As we ended our post-commencement discussion, I thanked Rector Clap for his generous gift of time. I said that I expected to meet him again in the Yale College *aula academica* for another commencement day exercise. I also could not help sense some tension between Rector Clap and Reverend Edwards, and I wondered if the latter would ever attend a commencement day exercise at Yale again.

I would later learn that Reverend Edwards would attend the Yale commencement for the last time in 1741. I also learned that a new college would open, given Rector Clap's adverse reaction to the New Lights of the Great Awakening, seen in the expelling of David Brainerd from Yale in 1741 and the closing of the college in the Spring of 1742. It would be called the College of New Jersey (*Nova Caeserea*), in Elizabeth-Town, 1747, with Governor Jonathan Belcher as president of the trustees and the Reverend Mr. Aaron Burr as president of the college, according to the Royal Charter. I read this in the New York Gazette, November 21, 1748. Commencement Day was November 9, 1748. The First Charter, sealed October 22, 1746, named the Reverend Mr. Jonathan Dickinson as president.[27] However, Reverend Dickinson died on October 7, 1747.

In the next chapter, I recount two travels to New Haven, two years apart, in 1760 and 1762. Once again Rector Clap presided over both commencement day exercises. There was a bachelor's thesis in 1760 and a master's *quaestio* in 1762 that had the marks of Jonathan Edwards on them. I wondered whether Reverend Edwards had influenced the composition of the theses or *vice versa*.

27. Kelley, *Yale: A History*, 53, 54; Princeton University, "1748 College of New Jersey Commencement Broadside." Also mentioned in New York Gazette, "College of New Jersey Commencement."

9. Moral Necessity and Physical Necessity

Where there is the greatest moral necessity, there is the greatest Freedom.[1]

—RECTOR THOMAS CLAP, 1760 YALE METAPHYSICS THESIS 11

Whether there is any difference between physical and moral necessity? Affirmed by John Phelps.[2]

—RECTOR THOMAS CLAP, 1762 YALE *QUAESTIONES* 24

BY 1760, JONATHAN EDWARDS's treatise *Freedom of the Will* (1754), written in defense of "Calvinistic doctrine" and against the Arminian notion of *Freedom of will, Which is Supposed to be Essential to Moral Agency, Vertue and Vice, Reward and Punishment, Praise and Blame*, had gripped New England for the last six years.[3] After reading the 1760 Yale thesis, "Where there is the greatest moral necessity, there is the greatest freedom," I wondered whether Mr. Edwards's exposition of moral necessity and the essence of freedom had directly impacted the composition of this Yale thesis and *quaestio*. I decided to ask Rector Clap about moral necessity.

The morning of commencement day, Rector Clap and I discussed the day's exercises over a cup of British tea. Present that day were the

1. Fitch, "1760 Yale College Commencement Broadside." "11. *Ubi maxima datur necessitas moralis, ibi maxima libertas.*"

2. Clap, "1762 Yale College Commencement Quaestiones." "24. *An inter necessitatem physicam et moralem ulla detur differentia? Affirmat respondens Johannes Phelps.*"

3. Edwards, *A Careful and Strict Enquiry into the Modern Prevailing Notions of That Freedom of Will.* Here foreward, quotations are from Edwards, *Freedom of the Will*, 432.

most excellent governor of the colony of Connecticut, Thomas Fitch, and the honorable deputy governor, William Pitkin. I asked Rector Clap, "In a nutshell, would you agree that for Mr. Edwards, the greater the moral necessity, the freer one is? In other words, the stronger the previous inclination and bias to one choice over another is, the freer one is? I ask because that is how I would sum up Edwards's doctrine of freedom of the will," I said.[4]

"I would agree, yes," said Rector Clap. "It is a very interesting proposition, indeed. Take a look at the commencement broadside sheet for today. Do you see the finger pointing to metaphysics thesis 11? That finger means that the thesis you are interested in is up for debate today. Indeed, it was Mr. Edwards who taught that only in this way could you and I praise people for virtue, and hold people accountable for vice. Think of it. If people were indifferent prior to a virtuous act, such as rushing into a burning house to save a child, why would they deserve praise? Or if they were indifferent immediately prior to committing a violent act, how could they be held accountable for something they did not intend to do, with malice in their heart? Mr. Edwards repeatedly said in *Freedom of the Will* such things as that there is 'greater virtue and vice in stronger and more established inclination.' I will show you many places where he states this doctrine."[5]

"But first, could you explain what is meant by the term 'moral necessity?'" I asked.

"Yes, certainly," said Rector Clap. "You should know that this year is not the first time to introduce a thesis or *quaestio* about moral necessity. You were asking me earlier if I thought that Edwards's treatise and teaching on moral necessity had influenced the composing of the *quaestio* on moral necessity. But I think it may be the other way around. Teaching on *moral necessity* has been around at the New England colleges for decades. I was drawing up theses about moral necessity and how it was to be reconciled with natural liberty long ago. And so too was President Wadsworth at Harvard. Let me demonstrate."

"Please do," I said.

"President Wadsworth," he said, "presided over a *quaestio* at Harvard in 1729 which asked, 'Whether moral necessity is incompatible with

---

4. For more accounts of Jonathan Edwards's view on this topic, see Fisk, *Edwards's Turn*, 351–85; also Fisk, "Jonathan Edwards and Samuel Clarke on Moral Necessity," 167–79.

5. Edwards, *Freedom of the Will*, 429.

freedom? The respondent John Emerson denies it."⁶ As a matter of fact, on that same broadside was a *quaestio* that asked, 'Whether physical and moral necessity are essentially to be distinguished? The respondent William Willoughby affirms it."⁷ We shall talk about *physical necessity* later. President Elisha Williams presided over a metaphysics thesis at Yale in 1738 which read, 'Moral necessity does not destroy natural liberty.'⁸ Guess who was present at the commencement?" asked Rector Clap.

"Jonathan Edwards?" I guessed.

"Correct," said Rector Clap. "So Mr. Edwards learned about moral necessity from President Williams, me, and others. I presided over the Yale 1749 metaphysics theses 6 and 7, which read, 'Moral necessity is the foundation of natural liberty. Hence, God is by nature an infinitely free agent.'⁹ So you see, Mr. Edwards's idea of 'the moral necessity of God's acts of will,'—a section in Edwards's *Freedom of the Will*—together with the idea that God is infinitely the freest being in the universe, was not original to Edwards."[10]

"It is indeed fascinating to learn how the idea of moral necessity has been taught in the New England colleges," I said. "What about the College of New Jersey?" I asked.

"Aaron Burr Sr. presided over the College of New Jersey's 1755 metaphysics thesis 7, which read, "Physical necessity is not to be inferred from moral necessity."[11] In other words, as we already have seen, they are two different types of necessity. On that same broadside, with a finger pointing at it, was metaphysics thesis 6, which is relevant to our discussion. It read, 'The power of the will is not competent of determining itself.'[12] I think that President Burr was following the opinion of none other than

---

6. Wadsworth, "Harvard 1729, Original." "*An necessitas moralis libertati repugnet? Negat respondens, Johannes Emerson.*"

7. Wadsworth, "Harvard 1729, Original." "*An necessitas physica et moralis essentialiter distinguuntur? Affirmat respondens Guilielmus Willoughby.*"

8. Talcott, "1738 Yale College Commencement Broadside." Metaphysics thesis 5. "*Moralis necessitas non destruit libertatem naturalem.*"

9. Jonathan Law, "1749 Yale College Commencement Broadside." Metaphysics theses "6. *Necessitas moralis est libertatis naturalis fundamentum. Unde.* 7. *Deus est agens naturaliter infinite liber.*"

10. Edwards, *The Freedom of the Will*, 384–96.

11. Burr, "1755 College of New Jersey Commencement Broadside." Metaphysics "7. *Necessitate morali, physica necessitas inferri nequit.*"

12. Burr, "1755 College of New Jersey Commencement Broadside." Metaphysics "6. *Voluntati, sese determinandi, potestas non competit.*"

his friend Mr. Edwards. For Mr. Edwards clearly denied the power of the will to determine itself, whether God's will or man's," said Rector Clap. "I will more fully demonstrate that from Edwards's treatise in a little bit. But for now, consider what he said against the Arminians, 'It has been shewn, that there is not, and never can be, either in existence, or so much as in idea, any such freedom of will, consisting in indifference and self-determination.' Edwards added that contrary to the Arminian's opinion, in order to achieve true virtue, 'It has been demonstrated, that the liberty of moral agents does not consist in self-determining power.'"[13]

"You promised to tell me more about Mr. Edwards's doctrine that *the stronger one's inclination is, the freer one is*, and how that is connected to moral necessity," I said.

"Indeed, I did. Let us look at what Edwards wrote in *Freedom of the Will*. In the conclusion to his treatise, he wrote, 'It has been proved, that nothing in the state or acts of the will of man is contingent; but on the contrary, every event of this kind is necessary, by a moral necessity.'[14] I start with his concluding chapter so that you know how he himself summed up the essential place of moral necessity in explaining his doctrine of freedom of the will. In that same place, Mr. Edwards said that he had 'demonstrated, that the doctrine of an universal determining providence, follows from that doctrine of necessity.' He said that 'God does decisively, in his providence, order all volitions of moral agents, either by positive influence or permission.'"[15]

"I see that Mr. Edwards had a robust view of moral necessity," I said.

"Indeed," said Rector Clap. "Mr. Edwards argued from the notion that *the greater perfection is, the greater the freedom* is. He believed that it was consistent to argue that the greater the moral necessity is, the greater the liberty of the will is. Remember, for Edwards, the greater the moral necessity of what you and I do, the greater the responsibility. Mr. Edwards reversed what the Arminians were claiming and turned their doctrine on its head. They held that 'the greater indifference men act with, the more freedom they act with; whereas the reverse is true,' said Mr. Edwards. He usually stated his own doctrine on the foil of his opponents' view. He said, 'He that in acting, proceeds with the fullest inclination, does what he does with the greatest freedom, according to common sense.' Liberty

---

13. Edwards, *Freedom of the Will*, 433.
14. Edwards, *Freedom of the Will*, 433.
15. Edwards, *Freedom of the Will*, 433.

did not consist 'in indifference.' Rather, 'on the contrary,' the natural light of reason taught that 'the further [a man] is from being indifferent in his acting good or evil, and the more he does either with full and strong inclination, the more esteemed or abhorred, commended or condemned.'[16] Let me give you one of Mr. Edwards's clearest statements about virtuous actions. 'They proceed from a heart well disposed and inclined; and the stronger, and more fixed and determined the good disposition of the heart, the greater the sincerity of virtue.'"[17]

"If I understand Mr. Edwards correctly," I said, "he argues in terms of degrees of strength and proportionality. But he usually argues the inconsistency of his opponent's position. And therefore we have to carefully understand what he deems to be inconsistent in their argumentation."

"Precisely," said Rector Clap. "Reading Mr. Edwards's exposition requires patience and sound logic. Often he argued in the 'If this, then that,' style in order to expose his opponents' inconsistencies. For instance, Mr. Edwards argued, if he were to take his opponents' position on the matter of moral necessity, then he would have to go against common sense, and conclude that

> the nearer the case approaches to such a moral necessity or impossibility, either through a strong antecedent moral propensity on the one hand, or a great antecedent opposition and difficulty on the other, the nearer does it approach to a being neither blamable nor commendable; so that acts exerted with such preceding propensity would be worthy of proportionably less praise; and when omitted, the act being attended with such difficulty, the omission would be worthy of the less blame.[18]

"To be clear, Mr. Edwards immediately clarified that 'the reverse of these things is true.'[19] We might wish that he would just plainly tell us what he himself believed, but he did not write in that way," said Rector Clap.

"Could you explain the quote you just made from Mr. Edwards?" I asked.

"Certainly. Let me break it down for you. His starting point is to argue that common sense dictates that there is no inconsistency in saying

---

16. Edwards, *Freedom of the Will*, 359.
17. Edwards, *Freedom of the Will*, 321.
18. Edwards, *Freedom of the Will*, 359.
19. Edwards, *Freedom of the Will*, 360.

that you and I freely love our children with a strong moral necessity. Moral necessity is not inconsistent with praise and blame. In other words, the stronger the moral necessity to love is, the more commendable our love is. Likewise, the stronger the impossibility of hating our parents is, the more commendable our love is. The more virtuous it is. Praise and blame are proportionally less or more according to the strength of our inclination. So too the greater the difficulty for an alcoholic to put down the bottle is, the greater the vice and condemnation is deserved. But they argue that the greater the propensity to honor our parents is, so much proportionally less is the act deserving of praise," said Rector Clap.

"If I remember correctly, " I said, "Mr. Edwards went on to argue that 'the stronger the inclination is, and the nearer it approaches to necessity in that respect, or to impossibility of neglecting the virtuous act, or of doing a vicious one; still the more virtuous, and worthy of higher commendation.' Likewise, he said that the acts of a vile person, rooted in a 'strong habit or principle of haughtiness and maliciousness, and a violent propensity of heart, is worthy to be detested.'[20] I recall that he succinctly stated that his common sense approach made clear that an 'antecedent bias or motive' rhymed perfectly with an act of the will that is worthy of praise and blame. And therefore, his opponents' doctrine of 'the sovereign power of the will itself' ran against common sense. But as you stated so well, Mr. Edwards inferred this conclusion from demonstrating the absurdity of his opponents' view. For this reason, he said that 'the reverse is true.'[21] I say, one must be very alert when reading Mr. Edwards."

"Indeed. The part of *Freedom of the Will* that we are referring to also included some of his most illuminating examples on this topic," said Rector Clap. "Mr. Edwards said that even if we supposed that 'good or evil dispositions are implanted in the hearts of men by nature itself,' they were no less deserving of praise or blame. It was commonly heard, said Mr. Edwards, "tis his very nature,' or 'he can't help serving the devil.'[22] But Mr. Edwards made a distinction between 'habits and dispositions of the heart,' the moral necessity about which we are talking at present, on the one hand, and 'natural necessity,' on the other.[23] The latter was impossible to avoid and was no one's fault. For instance, quite naturally, when injured,

20. Edwards, *Freedom of Will*, 360.
21. Edwards, *Freedom of the Will*, 360.
22. Edwards, *Freedom of the Will*, 361.
23. Edwards, *Freedom of the Will*, 362.

one feels pain. And 'we assent to the truth of certain propositions,' as Mr. Edwards said. 'That parallel lines can never cross one another.'[24] So he found it impertinent for Arminians to conflate the two distinctly different types of necessity. For instance, would anyone reasonably command 'a man to walk who has lost his legs' and then punish him for disobedience? Or summon 'a man shut up in prison to come forth?'"[25]

"Was it not at that point in his treatise," I asked, "that Mr. Edwards gave the example of two prisoners who received visits from the king, whom they had insulted, but who offered the prisoners forgiveness and honor, if only they would get up, leave prison, fall down before the king, and beg his pardon? In his heart, the disposition of the first prisoner was ready to abase himself. But there was one problem. The prisoner was 'confined by strong walls, with gates of brass.' In the second case, the prisoner had 'a haughty disposition.' His heart was not upright. The prince visited him in prison, freed him from his chains, the doors were wide open, but he was stout and unwilling to accept the offer. His own malice controlled him."[26]

"Yes, indeed," said Rector Clap. "Mr. Edwards wished to make the point that the light of reason taught that the second prisoner was unwilling in his stout heart to obey the command to leave prison, even though he had the power within him to do so. The 'moral necessity' of the prisoner's disposition was perfectly consistent with the condemnation he deserved. Observe too how relative the notion of 'power' is in this case. Any talk of 'power' was relative since the prisoner's will was bound by *moral necessity*. This was Mr. Edwards's great argument against the Arminian doctrine of a so-called 'self-determining power' of the will.[27] In this case, the stout opposition to the prisoner's will could not be overcome, due to

---

24. Edwards, *Freedom of the Will*, 156–57.
25. Edwards, *Freedom of the Will*, 362.
26. Edwards, *Freedom of the Will*, 362.
27. Surprisingly, Yale Rector Elisha Williams (acting 1722–39), Jonathan Edwards's tutor while at Wethersfield (1716–19), presided over a bachelor's thesis in support of the self-determining power of the mind. Edwards was likely in attendance at the 1735 Yale commencement, along with two of the twenty-three bachelor students who would later become famous, namely, Aaron Burr and Joseph Bellamy. See Talcott, "Yale College Commencement Broadside 1735." Metaphysics theses "6. *Praescientia divina non tollit libertatem humanam*" and 7. "*Voluntas est mentis sese determinandi potestas*." (6. "Divine foreknowledge does not deny human liberty," 7. "The will is the power of the mind determining itself").

moral necessity. As Mr. Edwards said, 'it was impossible that it should please him' to will to leave prison.[28]

"Could you tell me more about Mr. Edwards's opposition to the term 'self-determining power' of the will, from *Freedom of the Will*?" I asked.

"Certainly," said Rector Clap. "But I must be brief, since soon I need to leave and prepare to open the day's commencement exercises. I suspect that you will visit us again in the near future. Now to your question about the self-determining power of the will. In addition to what I already told you, Edwards denied a self-determining power not only in human beings, but also in God. He said, 'It will not follow, that there is an infinite number of numerically different possible bodies, perfectly alike, among which God chooses, by a self-determining power, when he goes about to create bodies.'[29] His illustration of the 'peculiar fitness' of God's end purpose and design in the creation of the universe was very interesting. It ran as follows. Suppose 'two spheres perfectly alike,' one to the left, one to the right. Edwards denied God the possibility of the transposition of two perfectly alike spheres, as to "place, time, rest, motion, and circumstance."[30] In other words, Mr. Edwards reasoned, when God created the heavenly bodies, even if the only difference between two identical spheres was numerical, if you were to reposition the left sphere to the right, it would imply the 'nonexistence' of the left sphere. For there was a reason why it was there, and not elsewhere. Furthermore, Mr. Edwards argued that it would be a mistake to assume that God could have transposed two equally alike spheres, even if each appeared to be equally suited to either position. If one asked, 'Why God in their creation placed them so? Why not vice versa?' He would say that it was absurd to ask, since if God were to do otherwise than he did, by a so-called self-determining power, there would be innumerable dangerous consequences throughout the heavens. In other words, there was nothing arbitrary about God's design."[31]

"I understand that Mr. Edwards wrote a letter on July 25, 1757, to John Erskine in Scotland to explain that he rejected the meaning of 'arbitrary decision' if it meant 'self-determining power of the will' and 'liberty *ad utrumvis*,' power of choosing differently," I said.[32]

28. Edwards, *Freedom of the Will*, 363.
29. Edwards, *Freedom of the Will*, 391.
30. Edwards, *Freedom of the Will*, 388.
31. Edwards, *Freedom of the Will*, 388–91.
32. Edwards, *Freedom of the Will*, 454–55 (The letter concerned Lord Kames's *Essays on the Principles of Morality and Natural Religion*, 2nd ed. [1758], published in the

"Indeed, he did," said Rector Clap. "I have enjoyed our time together and hope to see you again on another commencement day. But now I must go."

After the ceremonies, I told Rector Clap that I would visit again. Two years later, in 1762, I found myself once again in New Haven on commencement day. Thomas Fitch, the most distinguished governor (*gubernator insignissimo*) of the colony of Connecticut, was there, along with William Pitkin, the honorable deputy governor, bearer of arms (*armigero*). Rector Clap would preside over the *quaestiones*. It was early morning, and over a cup of British tea we picked up where we had left off two years ago. On today's commencement broadside was a *quaestio* that asked: "Whether there was any difference between physical and moral necessity?" The respondent, John Phelps, affirmed that there was a difference.

Since we had talked about Mr. Edwards's view of moral necessity two years ago, I began by asking Rector Clap what other theologians had said about moral necessity."

"Of the many kinds of necessity," said Rector Clap, "Francis Turretin, who as you know was acknowledged by Mr. Edwards as one of his favorite theologians, said that there was 'moral necessity or of slavery arising from good or bad habits and the presentation of objects to their faculties.' The disposition of the will acquired good or bad habits over time, as we saw in the examples of the prisoners, and 'cannot but act either well or badly.' Crucially for Mr. Edwards, Turretin had said that 'moral necessity' or 'servitude' did not 'overthrow the true and essential nature of liberty.'[33] Since 'moral necessity' is juxtaposed with 'physical necessity' on our broadside *quaestio*, I will briefly tell you how Turretin defined *physical necessity*. He compared it to 'brutes who act from blind impulse of nature or a brute instinct and innate appetite.'[34] Unlike moral necessity, Turretin said that 'physical necessity and brute necessity takes away' a crucial part of free choice, namely, 'choice, which follows the previous light of reason.'"[35]

"As I recall, Isaac Watts (1674–1748) also published a treatise entitled *An Essay on the Freedom of Will in God and in Creatures* (1732),

---

appendix to the 1957 Yale edition of *Freedom of the Will*).

33. Turretin, *First through Tenth Topics*, 662–63.
34. Turretin, *First through Tenth Topics*, 662.
35. Turretin, *First through Tenth Topics*, 662.

wherein he wrote about 'moral necessity' and 'physical or natural necessity,'" I said. "In fact, many of the themes in his *Essay* showed up in Mr. Edwards's *Freedom of the Will* (1754). Mr. Edwards made explicit reference in his own title to his opponents' supposed *Freedom of Will*, just as Watts had entitled his *Essay*."

"Indeed. Mr. Edwards's referred to and quoted Watts's *Essay*, though in a subtle fashion," said Rector Clap. "He profoundly disagreed with Mr. Watts on the issues of 'self-determining power,' 'supreme fitness,' and 'moral necessity.' The *quaestio* today concerns 'moral necessity,' so let us stick to that subject and see what Watts himself said. In his *Essay*, Mr. Watts acknowledged that there were 'great writers' who wished to distinguish between 'a natural and a moral necessity.' They wished to restrict the term 'natural' to 'matter' or 'the mere passive powers of the spirit.' But when speaking of God's nature, he would agree to apply the term 'natural necessity' to 'the very nature of God to act justly and faithfully, so that he cannot will or act otherwise, since it springs from his nature; as well as it may be called a moral one, because it is the action of an intelligent and free agent.'[36] Furthermore, he considered whether one ought to distinguish a *moral necessity* from a *metaphysical necessity*. The latter, he said, was defined by some as 'a necessity arising from the essence or necessity of things, and takes place only where the opposite implies a contradiction.' For instance, he said, 'all the semi-diameters of a circle are necessarily equal.'"

"Mr. Edwards sounds like Mr. Watts on this point," I said.

"Indeed," said Rector Clap. "Mr. Watts appeared to be drawing definitions from Leibniz and his famous correspondence with Samuel Clarke.[37] But do not jump to any conclusions yet about Mr. Watts and Mr. Edwards. Let me continue. Mr. Watts said, 'A moral necessity is that whereby a most wise being is necessarily led to chuse that which is best, or to act that which is fittest.'[38] It is precisely here where Mr. Edwards strongly disagreed with Mr. Watts. Mr. Watts continued his *Essay* by pointing to differences of opinions between 'things necessary and possible.' He explained that things that are 'metaphysically possible' are things that are not by nature contradictory. As such, there are 'ten thousand essences which yet shall never exist.' That seems to be quite a different

---

36. Watts, *On the Freedom of Will*, 458.

37. Leibniz and Clarke, *Leibniz-Clarke Correspondence*, 57, 81; Originally, Clarke, *A Collection of Papers*.

38. Watts, *On the Freedom of Will*, 497.

thing from what is 'morally necessary.'[39] He supposed that God who is an 'all-wise Being wills and chuses out of ten thousand supposed possibles, because of its superior fitness, even though divine wisdom cannot chuse otherwise.' However, he has his own thoughts about this supposed truth. He finds these two necessities, moral and metaphysical, to be 'very near akin.' Both have a 'physical or natural necessity,' both 'equally strong,' since 'the original cause and reason why both of them are necessary, lies in the very nature of things.'[40] In other words, quite naturally, God's nature is such that he cannot bring into existence whatever is inconsistent with his very nature. Nor, then, could God bring about what was unfit to exist. So, Mr. Watts made this conclusion about the notion 'All things are determined by superior fitness,' saying, quite naturally, whatever does not have superior fitness in its very nature is an impossibility and not to be counted among the ten thousand supposed possibilities."

"You said not to jump to any conclusions about whether Watts and Edwards agreed with one another on this very point. So tell me, in what way would Watt' have disagreed with Mr. Edwards, if he had lived to read Edwards's *Freedom of the Will*?" I asked.

"With regard to the necessary nature of God and his attributes, Mr. Watts warned against tying the necessity of God's nature to the hypothesis of the *superior fitness* and *moral necessity* of the acts of God in creation. He questioned, for instance, whether there was a superior fitness of all the positive laws of the Old Testament, such that it was morally necessary that God decree them? The great difficulty, said Mr. Watts, with 'the hypothesis of *all things being determined by superior fitness*,' was that those laws would be as necessary as God himself![41] Was it not possible for God to act otherwise than he did? If there were some kind of 'antecedent fitness' and superiority in those Old Testament positive laws, such as those about 'every pin and tack in the tabernacle of Moses,' about 'every colour and thread in the curtains,' then there really weren't any other commands possible.[42] There would be no *metaphysically possible* states of affairs. Mr. Watts wished, therefore, to distinguish between 'moral commands' that were 'necessary at all times and occasions,' on the one hand, and 'positive laws' that were necessary 'only on some occasions.' Mr. Watts's concern

---

39. Watts, *On the Freedom of Will*, 497–98.
40. Watts, *On the Freedom of Will*, 498.
41. Watts, *On the Freedom of Will*, 498.
42. Watts, *On the Freedom of Will*, 499.

about the hypothesis of *superior fitness* was not to confuse the necessity of God's nature with the necessity of the nature of things commanded by God. One must not make 'both equally necessary.' The result of the hypothesis was that 'God could not appoint any of them [the positive laws] otherwise than he has done,' which was unacceptable for Mr. Watts," said Rector Clap.[43]

"What exactly was the point of difference between Mr. Watts and Mr. Edwards?" I asked.

"The point is, 'There would be no such thing as any liberty of choice and indifference in the world,' said Mr. Watts. To state his position clearly, he said, 'A very wise man who sees the fitnesses of things, would have scarce anything of this freedom, for he would be always necessarily determined in his choice by this superior fitness,'" said Rector Clap.[44]

"I would very much like to learn more about what Mr. Edwards believed about the *superior fitness* hypothesis and what he wrote about Mr. Watts's view. By the way, who were those 'great writers' to whom Mr. Watts referred?" I asked.

"I am afraid that any further discussion about Mr. Watts and Mr. Edwards will have to wait until another day. I must leave and prepare for today's ceremonies. But I can tell you that it is very likely that some of the *great writers* were none other the ones Mr. Edwards also named in his treatise, namely, John Locke, *Essay Concerning Human Understanding* (1690), Samuel Clarke, *Demonstration of the Being and Attributes of God* (1725), and Andrew Baxter, *Enquiry into the Nature of the Human Soul* (1733). Mr. Edwards quoted all three in support of his view of 'superior fitness' and the moral necessity of God's will," said Rector Clap.[45]

An historical note worth making concerns the prisoner illustration made by Mr. Edwards. His distinction between *natural* and *moral* inability, his teaching on the unwilling disposition of the heart due to moral necessity, and his attack on the Arminian teaching of the self-determining power of the will, had a great impact upon English Baptists such as Caleb Evans, John Ryland, and Andrew Fuller. Indeed, *Freedom of the Will* impacted the establishment of the Baptist Missionary Society (1792), the

---

43. Watts, *On the Freedom of Will*, 499.
44. Watts, *On the Freedom of Will*, 499.
45. Edwards, *On the Freedom of Will*, 378–79. For analysis, see Fisk, *Edwards's Turn*, 386–408.

London Missionary Society (1795), and the Scottish Missionary Society (1796).[46]

The next stop on my journey was the newly founded College of Rhode Island and Providence Plantations, the first Baptist college in New England. I met with President James Manning and Professor David Howell on two commencement days, one in the year 1770, and the other in the year 1773. There was a bachelor's thesis on the 1770 broadside about the divine will and providence, and a thesis on the 1773 broadside about human freedom, both of which I was very eager to discuss with the Baptists.

46. Bebbington, "Remembered around the World," and Piggin, "The Expanding Knowledge of God," in Kling and Sweeney, *Jonathan Edwards at Home and Abroad*, 177–200; 266–96.

10. Providence

Theology examines the attributes of God,
will and providence, and human responsibilities.[1]

—PRESIDENT JAMES MANNING, 1770 COLLEGE OF RHODE ISLAND
AND PROVIDENCE PLANTATIONS THEOLOGY THESIS 1

PROVIDENCE, RHODE ISLAND, PROVED to be a very fitting location to discuss the topics of God's foreknowledge, will, and providence. In September of 1770 and 1773, I attended the commencement day exercises of the newly founded and first Baptist college in New England. President James Manning (BA Princeton, 1762), along with professor of philosophy David Howell, presided over the commencement exercises.[2] The highly decorated and honorable Stephan Hopkins (1707–85), the college's first chancellor and chief justice of the supreme court of Rhode Island, was in attendance. Three years later, Stephan Hopkins would sign the unanimous Declaration of the thirteen United States of America. The year of this account is 1773. As was my custom, I sat down with the president in the morning over a cup of tea. Professor David Howell joined us. There were many theses relevant to my interest in the doctrine of providence that I wished to discuss, both from the 1770 commencement and today's commencement broadside. To my surprise, President Manning had invited the well-known Baptist minister Isaac Backus (1724–1806) of the Separate Baptist congregation in Middleborough since 1756 to join

---

1. Hopkins, "1770 College of Rhode Island Commencement Broadside." Theology thesis 1 *"Theologia Dei attributa, voluntatem et providentiam, et hominum officia, perpendit."*

2. As indicated on the broadside sheet. See Hardy, "1762 College of New Jersey Commencement Broadside."

us.³ With everyone present, I spread out the 1770 and the 1773 broadside sheets on the American black walnut, maple, and eastern white pine table before us.

"Welcome, Pastor Backus," said President Manning.

"Thank you, President Manning," said Pastor Backus. "I was eager to accept your invitation to attend this discussion of theology before the commencement exercises begin."

"Why don't you point out the specific theses that you want to discuss?" said Professor Howell, as he looked to me to begin the discussion.

"Very well," I said. "Let's start with the commencement broadside from 1770. I see two *theses theologicae* that are of interest to me and that are related to one another, if I am not mistaken. The first one is listed as *theses theologicae* 4:

> Theology examines the attributes of God, will and providence, and human responsibilities.⁴

"It is a very general thesis and doesn't tell me enough about the college's view on providence. So let's also take a look at *theses theologicae* 4, which reads:

> God can foreknow human actions that are dependent upon free choice.⁵

"Thesis 4 sounds as if the college desires to stress that the certainty of God's foreknowledge in no way violates the liberty of human choice. And, likewise, that the robustness of human free choice in no way imperils, weakens, or in any way compromises the absolute foreknowledge of God. In other words, the two can be reconciled with one another. One does not have to sacrifice the one for the other. I also note that you use the verb 'can' (*posse*) in the formulation of the thesis. To my mind, the formulation implicitly dismisses the need for a Jesuit and Arminian kind of middle knowledge," I said.

---

3. On Backus, the New England Baptists, and traces of Edwardsean influence, see Holifield, *Theology in America*, 282–86; also on Isaac Backus, see Nettles, *By His Grace and for His Glory*, 134–39.

4. Hopkins, "1770 College of Rhode Island Commencement Broadside." Theology thesis 1. "*Theologia Dei attributa, voluntatem et providentiam, et hominum officia, perpendit.*"

5. Hopkins, "1770 College of Rhode Island Commencement Broadside." Theology thesis 4. "*Deus, actiones hominum ex libero arbitrio pendentes, praescire potest.*"

"Pastor Backus," said Professor Howell, "tell us your opinion of thesis 4. Note too today's *theses metaphysicae* number 7. It reads,

> Liberty belongs to the will.⁶

"Notice that it has been chosen for debate today. See the finger pointing to the thesis?"

"Indeed, I see that," said Pastor Backus. "I agree with our guest's assessment of the 1770 theses. There is no inconsistency in holding to God's sovereign will and fixed foreknowledge, on the one hand, and human liberty, on the other. As a matter of fact, I recently published a letter on the subject of God's sovereignty in our election and the liberty of the will. Let me tell you why I wrote the letter. I was replying to a letter that was circulating among our people claiming that a so-called 'reprobation doctrine' was ruining men in pastoral ministry. That writer claimed that 'Some good Christian pastors will not scruple to tell you, that they could find no joy' in ministry 'because they are assured, from St. Paul, that God never had, nor ever will have, mercy upon all men.'"⁷

"The opening lines of my letter suggest how I replied. I wrote, 'A vindication of the sovereign decrees of God.' I took my banner headline from Job 40:2, 'Shall he that contendeth with the Almighty, instruct him? He that reproveth God, let him answer it.' In my letter, I gave the same opinion as expressed in today's *theses theologicae* numbers 5 and 6. I could have composed them. They read:

> 5. The efficacity of grace in the conversion of man in no way depends upon the power of our free choice.⁸ 6. Nor is God by his nature bound to offer this grace to all.⁹

"I addressed my letter," said Pastor Backus, "to my opponent who spoke 'against the doctrine of particular election, and efficacious grace in our salvation, and against those who preach it.'"¹⁰

---

6. Hopkins, "1773 College of Rhode Island Commencement Broadside." Metaphysics thesis 7. "*Voluntati competit libertas.*"

7. Backus, "The Sovereign Decrees of God," 3.

8. Hopkins, "1773 College of Rhode Island Commencement Broadside." Theology thesis 5. "*Efficacia gratiae in conversione hominis minime a viribus liberi arbitrii nostri pendet.*"

9. Hopkins, "1773 College of Rhode Island Commencement Broadside." Theology thesis 6. "*Deus hanc gratiam omnibus praebere ulla obligatione, sua natura tenetur.*"

10. Backus, "Sovereign Decrees of God," 4.

"But how did you address the writer's accusation that what these college's theses are teaching is very alarming to many people who fear the doctrine of election?" I asked.

"Indeed," said Pastor Backus, "in my letter I noted how the writer was troubled by the thought of 'an unknown multitude through all ages of the world, who are inevitably decreed to the eternal fire and damnation of hell: and that an unknown number of others are elected to a certain, irresistible salvation.'[11] There is indeed a disturbing report of preachers, whom the writer accuses, who 'rejoice that God never will have mercy upon all men.' They preach, 'O the sweetness of God's election!'[12] But the writer's 'aim is against all that profess a sweetness in sovereign election.'"[13]

"So, how do you respond to their concerns?" asked President Manning.

"First, briefly, I will restate their concern," said Pastor Backus. "'The advocates for their own free-will in opposition to sovereign grace, have determined that the doctrine of fixed decrees in the divine mind concerning the future state of men, is inconsistent with the liberty of their own wills, and with the proper influence of precepts and promises, rewards and punishments.'[14] I 'firmly hold as any free-willer on earth,' as does this college, I'm sure, that we must be able to freely obey biblical 'precepts and promises, exhortations, and warnings' in order for our obedience to mean anything. But the true state of the question is this:

> Whether the whole plan of God's government, and the final issue of every action through the universe, has not been known and fixed in his counsels from the beginning, so that nothing can be put to it, nor any thing taken from it? (Eccl 3:14). Or whether many events are not held in suspense and uncertainty in his infinite mind, till they are decided by the free-will power of men? We hold the first, they the last side of this question.[15]

"So, what do these Arminians propose in regard to God's foreknowledge and human free choice? Must our choice be independent and outside of or prior to God's foreknowledge in order to grant us, as they see it, true freedom?" I asked. "That is why I asked earlier if their system

---

11. Backus, "Sovereign Decrees of God," 3.
12. Backus, "Sovereign Decrees of God," 4.
13. Backus, "Sovereign Decrees of God," 5.
14. Backus, "Sovereign Decrees of God," 7.
15. Backus, "Sovereign Decrees of God," 8.

proposes a third kind of knowledge, called middle knowledge (*scientia media*)."

"From my reading of Mr. Edwards's *Freedom of the Will*," said Pastor Backus, "The Arminians wish

> To assume a dignity to themselves, that they will not allow to the eternal God; for they claim a self-determining power in their own wills, while they deny it to the Most High; and insist upon it, that his choice of some men to salvation rather than others, is from either a foresight, or aftersight, of good dispositions and good doings in them more than others.[16]

"Indeed, they hold to a middle knowledge, which I hear you have learned much about from attendance at previous commencement day disputations. Their system makes human disposition and faith 'to be the cause of his [God's] choice.'[17] Do you hear that? In sum, on their account of providence, human choice informs God's middle knowledge and determines God's will. God's decrees are based on the foresight of human belief. In other words, God declares that his choice is 'the effect of' the foresight of 'good dispositions and doings.' Moreover, 'God is influenced in his works by motives without himself, at the same time that they hold to a power to determine all their own actions within themselves.'"[18] It is indeed a dangerous step these people take 'to claim a sovereignty to their own wills, while they deny it to God.' Now, to answer your question earlier about how I reconcile God's sovereign decrees with human free choice, we know that 'the hearts of kings are in the hand of the Lord, so that as rivers of water he turneth them whithersoever he will. That is, to act voluntarily as he designs to have them.' In sum, I believe,

> It is evident, that there is no inconsistency in holding God's decrees to be immutable, and yet that men act as voluntarily as if it were not so. And the great reasoners on the other side cannot avoid this consequence, if they would once own that the will of man is always determined in its choice by motive, or by what they at present prefer and think to be best.[19]

"You have mentioned Mr. Edwards. I would like to engage you more on his teaching. But tell me, how would you explain his teaching on the

16. Backus, "Sovereign Decrees of God," 8.
17. Backus, "Sovereign Decrees of God," 9.
18. Backus, "Sovereign Decrees of God," 9.
19. Backus, "Sovereign Decrees of God," 9.

place of motive and the greatest apparent good in regard to human freedom?" I asked.

"Let me put it bluntly," said Pastor Backus. "'A person must be stupid indeed who cannot see, that he in whom we live, move, and have our being, can at any time set things in such a view before our minds, as to make us think it best to choose one way of acting rather than another.' In my opinion, 'it is as great a piece of nonsense, in itself, to hold that a rational soul can act voluntarily in any case, without or against motive.' It would be as if a rational person would act 'without any influence of reason in it.'[20] You know how we say that God ordains the means as well as the ends. Well, they 'exclude the usefulness of means; for if the liberty of man lay in acting against motive or with motive, just as they pleased, where could there be any proper use for means?'"[21]

"There is another thesis on today's broadside sheet. Look at *theses metaphysicae* 2 and 3," said President Manning. "They say:

> Foreknowledge is an attribute of God. Therefore, human beings cannot elect one or another contrary objects.[22]

"I think that Mr. Edwards's teaches this same doctrine in *Freedom of the Will*," I said. "Let's take a look at what he said. I have learned a lot about his teaching on 'the will' from attending past commencements. When we read today's thesis that 'human beings cannot elect one or another contrary objects'; that is what Mr. Edwards taught when he spoke against Arminian 'freedom *ad utrumque*,' a freedom of indifference that claims to be able to choose either of two things.[23] Edwards said that the Church of England scholar Dr. Daniel Whitby (1638–1726) 'calls a freedom *ad utrumlibet*' essential to human freedom when someone is faced with 'laws and commands' and 'prohibitions.' In other words, this 'liberty *ad utrumlibet*,' the power to choose one way or another, was absolutely essential to genuine free choice when, for instance, you or I were offered the promise of eternal life, if we believed."

"Indeed. There are many places where Mr. Edwards spoke against freedom *ad utrumque*," said Professor Howell. "The thesis on our

20. Backus,"Sovereign Decrees of God," 10.

21. Backus,"Sovereign Decrees of God," 11.

22. Hopkins, "1773 College of Rhode Island Commencement Broadside." Metaphysics theses 2, 3 "*Praescientia Dei est attributum. Ergo, hominis contrariorum alterutrum eligere non possunt.*"

23. Edwards, *Freedom of the Will*, 289.

broadside today also makes it clear that our college believes, like Mr. Edwards, that foreknowledge is an attribute of God, which means that what he has decreed, those whom he has elected to eternal life, and those whom he has willed to permit to continue in their rebellion rules out the meaning with which the Arminians wish to fill the term 'freedom *ad utrumque*.' They fill the term with the notion that one has the power to choose between one of two contrary objects of choice. As Mr. Edwards argued, 'God's moral excellency is necessary, yet virtuous and worthy of praise.' There is no inconsistency in holding to this truth. Mr. Edwards found it a curious thing that Dr. Whitby attributed freedom *ad utrumque* to human beings and to our Lord Jesus here on earth. But, like Mr. Edwards, Dr. Whitby would not attribute freedom *ad utrumque* to God. Yet at the same time he acknowledged that 'God is necessarily holy, and his will necessarily determined to that which is good.'[24] Mr. Edwards said that his opponents thought that it was inconsistent for anyone to receive praise, or that respect was due someone, if in fact they acted out of necessity. His opponents saw it this way since Mr. Edwards shunned the implications of the terms 'freedom *ad utrumque*' and 'a self-determining power of the will.' Mr. Edwards eloquently phrased the absurdity of the opponents' conclusion:

> Yea, God has no right, by virtue of his necessary holiness, to intermeddle with that grateful respect and praise, due to the virtuous man, who chooses virtue, in the exercise of a freedom *ad utrumque*; any more than a precious stone, which can't avoid being hard and beautiful.[25]

"In other words," continued Professor Howell, "Just as a precious stone can't help but be beautiful, yet deserves praise, so God can't help but be holy, yet deserves praise."

"Indeed," I said. "Mr. Edwards also said, 'How strange it would be to hear any Christian assert, that the holy and excellent temper and behavior of Jesus Christ . . . was not virtuous or praiseworthy; because his will was not free *ad utrumque*, to either holiness or sin, but was unalterably determined to one.'"[26]

"Did you know," said President Manning, "that the English nonconformist Isaac Watts (1674–1748) and Mr. Edwards shared many themes

24. Edwards, *Freedom of the Will*, 277–78.
25. Edwards, *Freedom of the Will*, 279.
26. Edwards, *Freedom of the Will*, 290.

in common in their respective treatises? Mr. Edwards wrote about all of the following themes that I will list, some of which he explicitly cited from Mr. Watts's *Essay on the Freedom of Will in God and Creatures*. But all of which he read in Mr. Watts's *Essay*. Mr. Watts discussed 'liberty of indifference,' '*libertas indifferentiae ad opposita*,' 'natural and moral necessity,' 'superior fitness,' 'the greatest apparent good,' 'the last dictate of the understanding which does not always determine the will,' 'the self-determining power of the will,' 'equal fitness,' 'the will of God determines itself,' the will as a 'self-moving power,' and 'the principle of sufficient reason.' He also used the common illustration of comparing human freedom and agency to 'scales and balances.' He also spoke of God creating 'two bodies perfectly alike,' or, 'atoms perfectly alike.' Mr. Watts, like Leibniz and Clarke—who had previously written about most if not all of the above mentioned themes in their famous *Leibniz-Clarke Correspondence*—also wrote about 'not confounding metaphysical necessity with moral necessity.'[27] Anyone who has read Mr. Edwards will recognize all of these themes in *Freedom of the Will*."

"Indeed. I spoke about Mr. Watt's *Essay* and the *Leibniz-Clarke Correspondence* in 1762 with Rector Thomas Clap at the Yale College commencement," I said. "There is one illustration that Clarke and Leibniz used, and Mr. Watts as well. It had to do with whether there ever could be two things, perfectly alike, presented to the divine or human mind between which one must choose. Leibniz wrote that if there were such a thing as 'absolute indifference,' then there would be no such thing as 'choice, nor will.' For choice is founded upon reason and motive. 'A mere will without any motive, is a fiction,' he said.[28] Now for the illustration. Leibniz said that he was talking with 'an ingenious gentleman' along with 'Princess Sophia,' the Electress of Hanover, about this very issue, 'the identity of indiscernibles.' The gentleman 'thought he could find two leaves perfectly alike. The Princess defied him to do it. And he ran all over the garden a long time to look for some.'[29] But he failed to find two

---

27. Watts, *On the Freedom of Will*, 457, 458, 460, 462, 463, 464, 466, 467, 474, 475, 477, 481, 485, 490. For most of these themes, and a few themes that Edwards exclusively had in common with Leibniz-Clarke, see Leibniz and Clarke, *Leibniz-Clarke Correspondence*, 45, 55–59, 95–98. For a fuller discussion and analysis of the themes these authors shared in common, and more, see Fisk, *Edwards's Turn*, 352–63, 386–99.

28. Leibniz and Clarke, *Leibniz-Clarke Correspondence*, 36 (Leibniz's Fourth Paper).

29. Leibniz and Clarke, *Leibniz-Clarke Correspondence*, 37 (Leibniz's Fourth Paper).

identical leaves. Leibniz, and Princess Sophia, concluded that there were no two things with an indiscernible difference. Furthermore, 'To suppose that the universe could have had at first another position of time and place, than that which it actually had; such a supposition is an impossible fiction,' said Mr. Leibniz.[30] Notably, Mr. Edwards used this last illustration where one supposed two perfectly alike globes or spheres. And he, like Leibniz, concluded that such a supposition was impossible. He believed that God had a reason why he placed one globe to the left of another. They could not be transposed without dramatic consequences."[31]

"So, it appears that Mr. Edwards agreed with Mr. Leibniz and Princess Sophia when it came to the principle of indiscernibles," said President Manning. "Mr. Watts also took up the illustration of two leaves, but he agreed with Clarke! Let's first look at Clarke's reply to Leibniz and then we will see that Mr. Watts gave the same answer in his *Essay*. Clarke replied to Leibniz saying, 'It is very true that no two leaves and perhaps no two drops of water are exactly alike.' But that is because leaves or drops of water 'are bodies very much compounded. But the case is very different in parts of simple solid matter.' Nevertheless, 'even in compounds, there is no impossibility for God to make two drops of water exactly alike.' Since 'perfectly solid parts of all matter, if you take them of equal figure and dimensions (which is always possible in supposition,) are exactly alike.' And therefore 'it would be perfectly indifferent' if God were to transpose Mr. Leibniz's or Mr. Edwards's perfectly alike globes. The denial of indifference in this matter 'reduces all things to universal necessity and fate,' said Dr. Clarke."[32]

"Let us suppose," said President Manning, "'two things proposed to the will of God or man which are perfectly equal or indifferent,' like 'two leaves of a tree exactly alike,' as Mr. Watts supposed. In such a case, said Mr. Watts, the will would need 'to incline to one side rather than the other.' But of course, 'microscopes will always shew you some difference.' So was Leibniz correct? Not so fast, said Mr. Watts. 'What if there are no two leaves of trees, no two grains of sand, or drops of water or milk perfectly alike, because they are all compounded bodies?' Not only can two bodies of solid matter be perfectly alike, but 'in the divine idea of possibles there may be many parts of matter perfectly alike and equal.' Like Dr. Clarke,

30. Leibniz and Clarke, *Leibniz-Clarke Correspondence*, 37 (Leibniz's Fourth Paper).

31. Edwards, *Freedom of the Will*, 387–93.

32. Leibniz and Clarke, *Leibniz-Clarke Correspondence*, 46 (Clarke's Fourth Reply).

for Mr. Watts, 'the determination of the will of God to create the world in one of these parts of time and space rather than another, was entirely from his own will.'"[33]

"What an interesting alignment between Mr. Leibniz and Mr. Edwards, on the one hand, and between Dr. Clarke and Mr. Watts, on the other, at least on this issue," I said. "I know that Mr. Edwards was really disturbed by Mr. Watts's argument against the notion of 'superior fitness.' But Mr. Watts was equally disturbed by the implications of such teaching, namely, 'if God cannot do anything without the view of superior fitness, this difficulty will extend to the affairs of human nature also, and to the works of providence, redemption and grace.' In *Freedom of the Will*, Mr. Edwards quoted from the following passage in Mr. Watts's *Essay*. Let me cite a few of those key lines about *superior fitness* directly from Mr. Watts himself:

> What a strange doctrine this is, contrary to all our ideas of the dominion of God? Does it not destroy the glory of his liberty of choice . . . and make him a kind of intelligent instrument of eternal necessity, an almost mechanical medium of fate, and introduce Mr. Hobbes's doctrine of fatality and necessity into all things that God hath to do with? . . . In short, it seems to make the blessed God a sort of almighty minister of fate under its universal and supreme influence.[34]

"Curiously, Mr. Edwards skipped the heathen Stoic Latin quote that Mr. Watts gave:

> *Quae nexa suis currant causis, Non licet ipsum vertisse Jovem.*—Seneca. Thus causes run, a long connected train Not Jove himself can break th'eternal chain.[35]

"Mr. Edwards continued with the next line in Watt's *Essay*, 'And it was the professed sentiment of some ancients, that fate was above the gods.'[36] Curiously, three pages prior to this quote from Mr. Watts, Mr. Edwards professed in his treatise, 'There were many important truths maintained by the ancient Greek and Roman philosophers, and especially the Stoics, that are never the worse for being held by them.' Indeed, he added,

---

33. Watts, *On the Freedom of Will*, 489-90.

34. Watts, *On the Freedom of Will*, 493-94; cited in Edwards, *Freedom of the Will*, 375.

35. Watts, *On the Freedom of Will*, 494.

36. Edwards, *Freedom of the Will*, 372.

'The Stoic philosophers, by the general agreement of Christian divines, and even Arminian divines, were the greatest, wisest and most virtuous of all the heathen philosophers.'[37] Why not then provide the quote from Seneca?" I asked.

"On the notion of *superior fitness* to which Mr. Watts objected, please take note of Mr. Edwards's reply," I continued. "Crucially, for his part, he made reference to the scholastic term indicating a *before* and *after* in the non-temporal 'order of nature,' by way of conceiving order in God's nature. As to the non-temporal order, he conceived, 'the knowledge and holiness of God as prior in the order of nature to his happiness.' Likewise, 'the perfection of his understanding' is also prior since it was 'the foundation of his wise purposes and decrees.' And 'the holiness of his nature' was prior to the decree of God's will, since it was 'the cause and reason of his holy determinations.'[38] Mr. Edwards use of the scholastic term 'order of nature'–which the scholastics wrote either as '*signum rationis*' or '*ordine naturae*'—allowed him to conceive of the 'fittest and best' as prior to God's determinations, without sacrificing the moral necessity of God who cannot do any other than 'always choose what is wisest and best.'"[39]

"But Mr. Watts and Mr. Edwards disagreed on another key issue," said President Manning. "Briefly, when it came 'to the words liberty and freedom,' Mr. Watts preferred to speak of 'freedom of choice, a liberty of indifference, or a power to chuse or refuse.' He therefore opposed as inconsistent any talk of 'necessity of choice.'[40] In answer to the question, 'What determines the will to chuse or act,' he said that philosophers usually propose the answer to be 'the greatest apparent good' proposed to the mind. Likely, with Mr. Watts's *Essay* before him, Mr. Edwards proposed a nuanced version of this concept. He preferred to express himself like this, 'That the will always *is* as the greatest apparent good, or as what appears most agreeable, is, than to say that the will is *determined* by the greatest apparent good.' To his credit, Mr. Edwards distinguished between the last dictate of the understanding taking into consideration the long view of what is best for one's life, on the one hand, and the short view of what

---

37. Watts, *On the Freedom of Will*, 493–94; cited in Edwards, *Freedom of the Will*, 375.

38. Edwards, *Freedom of the Will*, 376.

39. Edwards, *Freedom of the Will*, 377. For a fuller analysis of Edwards's reply to Watts, see Fisk, *Edwards's Turn*, 397–99.

40. Watts, *On the Freedom of Will*, 460.

appears 'now most agreeable.'[41] But Mr. Watts understood *the greatest apparent good* theory as more or less the same as 'the last dictate, or better, assent of the understanding,' which he considered to be 'a passive power.' The problem he saw with this answer was that 'then the will is never free with a liberty of choice or indifference.'[42] Crucially, he saw this view as 'the scheme of the fatalists.'[43] No wonder Mr. Edwards chose to respond to Mr. Watts in his *Freedom of the Will*."

"If I may jump in," said Professor Howell. "Crucially, Mr. Watts held that whatever the greatest apparent good might be, 'the power of the will to chuse and act in this case continues the same after the last dictate of the understanding as it did before.'[44] In other words, the power of the will was to be considered and conceived apart from the act elicited by the will. That power always remained intact. This, I think, was the great point of difference between Mr. Watts and Mr. Edwards."

"Mr. Watts claimed that despite the last assent of the understanding to a proposed action presented to the mind," said Professor Howell, "he thought that often 'passion' or other 'biases inclined the will strongly.' Mr. Watts quoted Ovid, the poet, '*Video meliora proboque, deteriora sequor*,' which translated means, 'I see the right and approve it too, and still the worse pursue.'[45] Suppose vice is presented to the mind, said Mr. Watts. He argued that if someone cannot resist a vice, which was the last dictate of the understanding, then 'it frees the criminal from all blame.' Paradoxically, Mr. Edwards argued the opposite. As the moral 'difficulty' to avoid vice increases, so does the liberty of indifference diminish, which jeopardizes the Arminian principle of liberty of indifference and 'self-determination.'[46] Alternatively, Mr. Watts said, suppose two perfectly alike proposals were presented to the mind. What then? There is no 'superior fitness.'"

"This sounds like the problem of Buridan's ass. I also discussed this problem with President Wadsworth at Harvard in 1725. But here we are talking of human beings, endowed with a will," I said.

---

41. Edwards, *Freedom of the Will*, 144, 148.
42. Watts, *On the Freedom of Will*, 462.
43. Watts, *On the Freedom of Will*, 463.
44. Watts, *On the Freedom of Will*, 463.
45. Watts, *On the Freedom of Will*, 463.
46. Edwards, *Freedom of the Will*, 298.

"If I may continue," said Professor Howell. "Mr. Watts concluded that the best answer to this dilemma was that you and I possess 'a sovereign and self-determining power of the soul.'[47] Now let us return to the question of whether Mr. Edwards agreed with Mr. Watts on 'How the will of God determines itself?' At first look, it may appear that the two agree. After all, Mr. Watts began by saying that 'when we speak of the decrees of God, or what he will do, we are constrained to acknowledge that his will always chuses and determines to act what is fit and good, that is, in our way of conceiving.'[48] You will recall that the 'order of nature' referred to the non-temporal order of God's all-sufficient knowledge as *prior* to God's decree of the will, which in turn precedes God's foreknowledge."

"Indeed. I recall President Clap telling me that in the near future, there would be a commencement broadside thesis, such as, 'The divine decrees precede foreknowledge, in a structural order, by way of conceiving it,'" I said.[49]

"If I may continue," said Professor Howell, "Mr. Watts said, 'the blessed God is perfectly wise and perfectly good in all his works and his decrees, in his creation and providence. Nor is it possible that God should be or act otherwise than according to this fitness.'[50] For these fitnesses are eternal. Thus far, Mr. Edwards approved and even cited Mr. Watts's own lines as evidence against him of what he knew to be true. However, Mr. Watts said, 'But there may be several things supposed to come within the view of the divine mind ... which have no real fitness or goodness in themselves, or at least which have all an equal fitness or equal goodness.' Indeed, there may be 'no real superior fitness or goodness in any of them above the rest.' This would prove to be unacceptable to Mr. Edwards. But Mr. Watts made clear that the sovereign God has a self-determining power. He said, since 'there is no determination from his own ideas,' the will of God therefore 'in and of itself determines itself to chuse one thing and not another; and as it were, makes that thing good, that is, makes it pleasing to himself, by his own determination or choice of it.'"[51]

47. Watts, *On the Freedom of Will*, 466.

48. Watts, *On the Freedom of Will*, 472.

49. Fitch, "1765 Yale College Commencement Broadside." Metaphysics thesis 14 "*Decreta divina, in ordine naturae, praescientiae antecedunt*." As indicated, this thesis appeared two years later, in 1765.

50. Watts, *On the Freedom of Will*, 473.

51. Watts, *On the Freedom of Will*, 474. See, Edwards, *Freedom of the Will*, 375, 381–83.

"This makes me think of the Euthyphro mystery, 'Is what is holy holy because the gods approve it, or do they approve it because it is holy?' Mr. Watts appears to go along with the former," I said.[52]

"Indeed," said Professor Howell. "Like many scholastics, Mr. Watts added that God determines the things that he will pass out of a state of 'mere possibility' into a state of 'actual existence' by his will. 'Antecedent to this determination' two possibilities presented to God's mind 'might be both equally fit or good.' In the *Leibniz-Clarke Correspondence*, Clarke had said something similar, that God's mere will can be the sufficient reason why something is the way it is rather than otherwise. 'In things in their own nature indifferent; mere will, without any thing external to influence it, is alone that sufficient reason.'[53] Not surprisingly, Mr. Watts seems to have had the *Leibniz-Clarke Correspondence* at hand. Mr. Watts wrote, 'It is a plain axiom of truth, that nothing is or comes to pass without a sufficient reason why it is, or why it is in this manner rather than another.'[54] Mr. Edwards also stated this principle."[55]

"But cannot the will be that sufficient reason?" I asked.

"That was the opinion of Dr. Clarke and Mr. Watts," said Professor Howell. "Curiously, all four authors, Mr. Leibniz, Dr. Clarke, Mr. Watts, and Mr. Edwards, discussed the illustration of scales and balances.[56] But unlike Mr. Leibniz and Mr. Edwards, who compared motives of the will to the weights in a scale balance, Mr. Watts and Dr. Clarke said that scales are 'passive beings' and therefore they must have an external reason to tip the scales one way or the other when in equilibrium. But with human beings and with God there must be a spring of action. 'The will of God is an active and self-determining power; the will of man perhaps in this respect is the chief image of God in this lower world,' said Mr. Watts.[57] The will of God is the principle of sufficient reason, said Dr. Clarke, 'As in the instance of God's creating or placing any particle of matter in one

---

52. Plato, "Euthyphro," in Hamilton and Cairns, *The Collected Dialogues of Plato*, 178 (10a).

53. Leibniz and Clarke, *Leibniz-Clarke Correspondence*, 30 (Clarke's Third Reply).

54. Watts, *On the Freedom of Will*, 485.

55. Edwards, *Freedom of the Will*, 181, 183.

56. See Leibniz and Clarke, *Leibniz-Clarke Correspondence*, 45, 58, 97 (Clarke's Fourth Reply, Leibniz's Fifth Paper, Clarke's Fifth Reply).

57. Watts, *On the Freedom of Will*, 485.

place rather than in another, when all places are originally alike."[58] With this, Mr. Edwards would take issue. Dr. Clarke had written:

> But the question is, whether, in some cases, when it may be highly reasonable to act, yet different possible ways of acting may not possibly be equally reasonable; and whether, in such cases, the bare will of God be not itself a sufficient reason for acting in this or the other particular manner.[59]

"Let me close our discussion today with this observation," said President Manning. "It was quite customary to cite passages from authors where they supported your scheme, and to oppose the same authors when they did not. Mr. Edwards was no exception. He called Dr. Clarke one of 'the chief Arminian writers,' but also favorably quoted him on the topic of infinite fitness and goodness.[60] Mr. Watts also was one of the chief Arminian writers that Mr. Edwards opposed. Take note of what Mr. Watts said, which upset Mr. Edwards: 'This doctrine of the self-determining power of the will sets the nature and distinction of virtue and vice in this present state in the truest light, together with the rewardable or punishable properties thereof.'[61] As we have seen, Mr. Edwards offered a different solution to the problem of reconciling human freedom with virtue and vice. Forty-two years after Mr. Watts's *Essay*, the title of Mr. Edwards's indicated the theory at which he took aim: *A Careful and Strict Enquiry into the Modern Prevailing Notions of that Freedom of Will, which is supposed to be essential to Moral Agency, Virtue and Vice, Reward and Punishment, Praise and Blame*."

"It seems to me," I said, "that authors from many different traditions, whether Jesuit and Arminian, Lutheran, Anglican, Reformed, Dissenter, or Baptist, all used the scholastic terminology that we have discussed today, and that I have learned while attending many New England commencement day disputations, to advance and vindicate their own theories."

"Indeed," said President Manning. "Let me illustrate what you have said about the broad scholastic enterprise by turning to a draft essay on liberty and necessity that I hear John Wesley (1703-91) is writing in response to Mr. Edwards. I understand he is writing or is planning on

---

58. Leibniz and Clarke, *Leibniz-Clarke Correspondence*, 30 (Clarke's Third Reply).
59. Leibniz and Clarke, *Leibniz-Clarke Correspondence*, 119 (Clarke's Fifth Reply).
60. Edwards, *Freedom of the Will*, 217, 377–78.
61. Watts, *On the Freedom of Will*, 478.

writing an essay called 'Thoughts on Necessity.'[62] In his essay, Mr. Wesley expresses outrage at the idea encapsulated by the 'Westminster divines' that 'Whatever happened in time, was unchangeably determined from all eternity.'[63] As if human beings were 'bound by an invisible chain.'[64] That your freedom and mine is but an illusion. 'In spite of all the labour we create, we only row; but are steer'd by fate.' Then Wesley turned to Mr. Edwards, 'A late writer, in his celebrated book upon free-will.' Like the Westminster divines, said Wesley, 'Mr. Edwards of New England, by abundance of deep, metaphysical reasoning . . . flatly ascribes the necessity of all our actions' to God. Mr. Edwards 'connects together and confirms all the preceding schemes, particularly those of the ancient Stoics and the modern Calvinists.'"[65]

"What was Mr. Wesley's solution?" I asked.

"Mr. Wesley," said President Manning, "drew upon two scholastic distinctions. (1) *Liberty of contradiction* is 'the power of choosing, either to do or not to do.' (2) *Liberty of contrariety* is 'to do this or the contrary, good or evil.' The first liberty is the necessary basis of the second, he said. 'Without it there can be nothing good or evil, rewardable or punishable.' The 'doctrine of necessity,' as taught by 'ancient heathens, or modern Christians, destroys' both kinds of liberty. It destroys 'all morality' and 'makes men mere machines.'[66] Finally, it destroys the basis of virtue and vice, the very thing Mr. Watts, Mr. Edwards, and Mr. Wesley were seeking to establish. For Wesley, God can break the chain of consequences that even Jove could not. Even the 'poor heathen poet' knew this: 'Muses, begin and end with God supreme.'"[67]

My attendance at the New England commencement day disputations taught me that there was no such thing as a European scholastic theology, nor a New England scholastic theology. Scholasticism, rather, comprised philosophical method, propositional analysis, distinctions in syntax, and definitions. The purpose was to serve the students who studied the Latin texts of the New England curricula and disputed theses

---

62. Outler, *John Wesley*, 474–91. Wesley published the essay "Thoughts on Necessity" in Glasgow in 1774. For an analysis of Wesley's use of scholastic terms, see Vos, "John Wesley on Salvation, Necessity, and Freedom," 203–22.

63. Outler, *John Wesley*, 476.

64. Outler, *John Wesley*, 477.

65. Outler, *John Wesley*, 480.

66. Outler, *John Wesley*, 486.

67. Outler, *John Wesley*, 490.

on commencement day. In fact, without an understanding of medieval and post-Reformation scholastic distinctions, one simply cannot make sense of the Latin bachelor theses and master's *quaestiones* printed on the commencement day broadsides.

My travels demonstrated that whether one speaks of the broadly speaking Reformed curricula of Harvard, Yale, and the College of New Jersey, or the Baptist curriculum of the College of Rhode Island and Providence Plantations, all shared one thing in common: the need to understand and draw upon the scholastic tradition in order to express their doctrinal distinctions. Thus, the many and diverse traditions of the Jesuits and Arminians, Lutherans, Anglicans, Reformed, Dissenters, and Nonconformists had all made use of the scholastic terminology that found its way into the New England curricula as evidenced in the commencement broadside theses and *quaestiones*. The task of the college's presidents, tutors, and students was to dispute the use and interpretations of certain scholastic distinctions in a way that advanced and vindicated their schools' own traditions.

There now only remains for me to report on a final roundtable discussion I had with President Edwards at the College of New Jersey. The narration required that I return to the year 1758. The roundtable attempted to pick up the many loose threads that I had left hanging from one commencement to another. I also wished to make sense out of the diverse traditions that I found making use of the same scholastic distinctions.

Concluding Roundtable
with President Edwards

It was February 16, 1758, Nassau Hall (*in aula Nassovica*), Princeton, New Jersey (*Nova Caesarea*). The trustees of the College of New Jersey installed Mr. Jonathan Edwards as President.[1] I held a roundtable discussion with President Edwards that evening.[2] At the roundtable were the Reverend Samuel Davies, who, after Edwards's death on March 22, 1758, would become president and preside over the college's commencements from 1759 through 1761; the reverend Samuel Hopkins (BA Yale 1741), who would become President Edwards's biographer; two sophomore scholars, one named Benjamin Rush (BA College of New Jersey 1760), who would be a signer of the unanimous Declaration of the thirteen United States of America; the other, Enoch Green (Valedictorian BA College of New Jersey 1760), who would go on to pastor the Presbyterian church in Deerfield, New Jersey[3]; lastly, Daniel Farrand (BA College of New Jersey 1750), who was ordained in 1752 and served a congregational church at South Canaan, Connecticut. He also became a classics scholar.[4]

Before I begin my report of the roundtable, I would note that the bachelor program was four years long. Since Enoch Green and Benjamin

---

1. Marsden, *Jonathan Edwards*, 491.

2. While the roundtable with President Edwards is imagined, the characters, date of installation, and quoted opinions of theologians in the narrative are real. The roundtable serves the purpose of pulling all the many threads in part 2 together.

3. Boone, "Princeton University Commencement Records, 1747–Present." Benjamin Rush is listed as one of the graduates on the broadside sheet, along with ten other students.

4. Belcher, "1750 College of New Jersey Commencement Broadside." Daniel Farrand is listed as one of the graduates on the broadside sheet, along with five other students. For more on the beginnings of Princeton, see Alexander, *Princeton College During the Eighteenth Century*, 9.

Rush are listed as graduates on the college's 1760 commencement broadside, that makes them sophomores at the time of the roundtable. As a senior, Enoch Green wrote *Theological Responses* in a notebook dated November 18, 1759, to July 13, 1760, likely in preparation for the 1760 commencement day disputations. Green's notebook gives a clear indication of what the students were learning under Samuel Davies's presidency. Though President Edwards's time at the college was brief, if one also takes into account his previous publications, it is likely that he influenced the theological direction of the college for the rest of the year 1758, and at least the following year, 1758–59, if not longer. The following excerpt from Enoch Green's theological notebook reflects some of President Edwards's notable teachings from *Freedom of the Will*, 1754:

> No. 12 How is the irresistible influence of the Spirit convivent with moral agency? Special or irresistible grace does not destroy but improve the liberty of man's will: when there is a new nature implanted in him, it discovers its energy, it makes a change in all the powers and faculties of the soul; there is a new light shining in the understanding . . . Now this light in the understanding, being attended with the power in the will, it is hereby induced to comply with its dictates, not barely as being prevailed on by rational arguments, but as there is a divine power accompanying them, it is not indeed prevailed on without arguments, for the Spirit makes use of the Word to persuade, as well as to direct.
>
> Though we do not say, that the will is overcome by arguments, as though the victory was owing to our power of reasoning, yet we freely own that we act with judgment and see the highest reason for what we do . . . But all this would be to no purpose, if there were not a previous power determining the will to a thorough compliance therewith; we do not deny that moral suasion oftentimes has a tendency to incline a man to the performance of moral duties; but it is what we choose to call evangelical persuasion or the Spirit of God . . . that makes it effectual for salvation. (Feb 3, 1760).[5]

The following line from the excerpt, "a previous power determining the will to a thorough compliance," clearly reflected a teaching by President Edwards. Furthermore, President Samuel Davies would preside over a 1760 commencement broadside thesis that called to mind President Clap's 1760 identical thesis and President Edwards's teaching, namely,

---

5. Green, *Theological Responses*.

"The greater the moral necessity, the freer one is."[6] President Davies's *Pneumatologia* thesis 1 read:

> 1. They who act from moral necessity enjoy the greatest liberty.[7]

Pneumatologia thesis 6 gave the minimum requirement that all agree is needed for someone to act freely (This truth was taught at Yale College in 1718, when President Edwards was a young scholar, yet in Wethersfield with tutor Elisha Williams):

> 6. The will cannot be coerced.[8]

That is, if someone were coerced to act against his will, then he was not free. The much disputed question was whether human beings internally retained a vital power to do otherwise than they do, even though God has determined that person to one choice over another, and who in fact infallibly will make that choice. I will attempt to identify the position of different theologians in President Edwards's orbit and Reformed tradition along these lines during the roundtable. This will prove to be an illuminating exercise. Finally, President Davies would formulate an ethics thesis in 1760 that may reflect President Edwards's teaching. It read:

> 17. The liberty of a creature does not require the faculty of doing whatever it pleases.[9]

I now turn to the roundtable with President Edwards in order to discern the interplay between his teachings and the formulation of the theses of the college.

"President Edwards, congratulations on your new presidency, may God bless you and the College of New Jersey. Welcome. Would you like to begin with a brief presentation?" I asked.

"I would be delighted to do that. In *Freedom of the Will*, I argued for a freedom of perfection. In a nutshell, the greater the previous inclination, the greater the freedom. 'The stronger the inclination, and so the further from indifference, the more virtuous the heart, and so much

---

6. For President Thomas Clap's similar 1760 thesis, see chapter 9.

7. Boone, "1760 College of New Jersey Commencement Broadside." *Pneumatologia* thesis "1. Qui necessitate morali aguunt, maximâ fruuntur libertate."

8. Boone, "1760 College of New Jersey Commencement Broadside." 6. "*Voluntas cogi non potest*." Cf. Saltonstall, "Yale College Commencement Broadside 1718." *Theses physicae* 24. "The will is not subjected to coercion" (*Voluntas coactionis non subjicitur*).

9. Boone, "1760 College of New Jersey Commencement Broadside." Ethics 17. "*Libertas creaturae, facultatem quicquid velit agendi, non exigit*."

the more praiseworthy the act which proceeds from it,'" said President Edwards.[10]

"Common sense tells us," he said, "that 'indifference' itself, in principle, is actually 'vicious' to a high degree; it is counter-intuitive to hold it as essential to virtue and vice. For who would be cold and indifferent to a friend or one's own family and not already inclined to want to help 'in extreme distress?' To suppose liberty of indifference to be essential to virtue and vice violates our sense of accountability and punishment that fits the crime. It 'destroys the great difference of degrees of the guilt of different crimes.' I think that even the 'least degree of preponderation (all things considered) is choice.' Think about it. How can one be held accountable for a crime which he or she is just as likely not to commit? This principle defies reason. Let us suppose someone who is habitually in such a state of so-called equilibrium before a criminal act, 'wherein the probability of doing and forbearing are exactly equal.' Then according to the 'nature and laws of contingence,' the 'inevitable consequence of such a disposition of things' is that someone should 'choose them as often as reject them.'[11] How absurd. On Arminian principles, the conclusion would be that 'the man Jesus Christ was very far from being praiseworthy for those acts of holiness and kindness which he performed, these propensities being so strong in his heart.'[12] The 'universal sense of mankind' is that actions which are consistent with virtue and vice 'proceed from a heart well disposed and inclined; and the stronger, and more fixed and determined the good disposition of the heart, the greater the sincerity of virtue.'"[13]

"If what I do is by moral necessity, how is it virtuous?" asked Reverend Farrand.

"Let me say it this way," said President Edwards. "The nearer the approach to 'moral necessity in a man's exertion of good acts of will,' and the stronger the propensity to good, 'so much the better the man he is.' The stronger the inclination, and the nearer it approaches 'necessity in that respect,' the more virtuous he or she is.'"[14]

"Is efficacious grace contingent upon the human will?" asked Reverend Davies.

---

10. Edwards, *Freedom of the Will*, 320.
11. Edwards, *Freedom of the Will*, 322–23.
12. Edwards, *Freedom of the Will*, 326.
13. Edwards, *Freedom of the Will*, 321.
14. Edwards, *Freedom of the Will*, 360.

"No, not at all," said President Edwards. "I think 'that nothing in the state or acts of the will of man is contingent; but that on the contrary, every event of this kind is necessary, by a moral necessity.'"[15]

"I have read your treatise, but would you please sum up your thought of Mr. Watts's teaching on the radical contingency of the self-determining power of the will?" I asked.

"Against Mr. Watts, I find the idea of a 'self-determining power in the will' to be absurd. The will is 'determined in every case by some motive, and by a motive which (as it stands in the view of the understanding) is of superior strength to any appearing on the other side.' I teach that 'not only the will of created minds, but the will of *God himself* is necessary in all its determinations.'[16] Furthermore, there is no 'freedom of will lying in the power of the will to determine itself.' The Arminian concern was that the doctrine of moral necessity makes it impossible for you and me to freely and genuinely obey God's commands. Nor does it allow for you and me to do anything virtuous. But I say, 'there neither is any such thing, nor any need of' a self-determining power of the will."[17]

"How do you respond to those who claim that the implication of your teaching makes God the author if not actor of sin?" asked Reverend Hopkins. "And does your teaching include a doctrine of permission?"

"Excellent question, my dear Hopkins," said President Edwards. "'The doctrine of an universal determining providence, follows from that doctrine of necessity. God does decisively, in his providence, order all the volitions of moral agents, either by positive influence or permission.' Everyone agrees, or should agree, that 'what God does in the affair of man's virtuous volitions, whether it be more or less, is by some positive influence, and not by mere permission, as in the affair of a sinful volition.' In other words, God stands positively behind our virtuous acts. He stands asymmetrically behind our sinful acts. Remember, 'God's assistance or influence, must be determining and decisive.' By that I mean 'moral necessity' effectively assists God's work in us. It is God who 'gives virtue, holiness and conversion to sinners, by an influence which determines the effect, in such a manner, that the effect will infallibly follow by a moral

---

15. Edwards, *Freedom of the Will*, 433.
16. Edwards, *Freedom of the Will*, 375.
17. Edwards, *Freedom of the Will*, 436.

necessity; which is what Calvinists mean by efficacious and irresistible grace.'"[18]

"Back in 1750," said Reverend Farrand, "I was a graduate of the College of New Jersey. The Reverend Aaron Burr presided over some *theses metaphysicae* that I think you may find to be in conflict with your teaching. I would like to ask you your opinion of two theses. The two theses read:

> 5. All things are necessary by the necessity of the consequence.
> 6. But this necessity has no influence whatsoever upon the will of moral agents.[19]

"I well remember the broadside theses of 1750," said President Edwards. "As a matter of fact, I wrote a letter to Joseph Paice, dated February 24, 1752, on the backside of the 1750 College of New Jersey broadside sheet. I also used the backside of the 1750 Yale broadside sheet.[20] Good paper was expensive and hard to come by. But to your question. In *Freedom of the Will*, I often invoked the scholastic term 'necessity of the consequence' in defense of my theory. For instance, if God knows that Peter will believe, then Peter will believe. This follows since God's knowledge of Peter's faith cannot fail."

"But is there something necessary about Peter himself such that he must believe?" Asked Reverend Davies? "The above thesis number 6 clearly says that the necessity of the consequence does not necessitate the will of moral agents."

"Indeed. Consider the proposition, 'God knows that Peter will believe,'" said President Edwards. "I have written that 'The subject and predicate of a proposition which affirms something to be, may have a real and certain connection consequentially; and so the existence of the thing may be consequentially necessary.' Furthermore, 'Things which are perfectly connected with other things that are necessary, are necessary themselves, by a necessity of consequence.'"[21]

---

18. Edwards, *Freedom of the Will*, 433–34.

19. Belcher, "1750 College of New Jersey Commencement Broadside." Metaphysical theses "5. *Omnia, necessitate consequentiae, sunt necessaria.* 6. *Sed haec necessitas, in voluntatem agentium moralium, nullam influentiam habet.*"

20. For the Paice letter, see Edwards, "A141. Letter to Joseph Paice." See an account of Edwards's use of broadside sheets and attendance at various commencements, in Fisk, *Edwards Turn*, 47–48.

21. Edwards, *Freedom of the Will*, 153.

"Yes," said Reverend Davies, "but the connection between *God* and *Peter's belief* is merely a consequence of God's knowledge that Peter will believe, even apart from God's decree to move upon Peter's soul, such that he will believe. But my question is if there is something necessary about Peter's belief in and of itself? Is there something necessary about the consequent of the proposition itself? For instance, you are married to Sarah, therefore you are a husband and she is your wife. That is a mere necessity of the consequence of marriage. But there was nothing necessary about marriage itself, nor about marriage to Sarah, or was there?" asked Reverend Davies.

"I do believe that it was most fitting in God's design that I marry Sarah. There is something about our uncommon union that speaks of a superior fitness such that marriage to someone else was not possible," said President Edwards.

"So, you do not really distinguish between the necessity of consequence and the necessity of the consequent" asked Reverend Davies, "as even some Reformed theologians do?"

"What I know is that 'there are truths that are necessary in themselves,'" said President Edwards. "For instance, 'that two and two are four.' And that 'it is necessary, fit and suitable, that men should do to others, as they would that they should do to them.' That the 'subject and predicate of a proposition' that affirms these truths is fixed and necessarily connected.[22] Now to the point at hand, since 'God has a certain and infallible prescience of the acts of the will of moral agents,' such as Peter believing, 'it follows that these events are necessary, with a necessity of connection or consequence.'[23] I see all these truths as consequentially necessary. To your question, I do not distinguish necessity of the consequence from necessity of the consequent the way some Reformed scholastics do. Some of them liken the necessity of the consequence to a conditional necessity. But I do not say, for instance, that my marriage to Sarah was some kind of conditional necessity, contingent upon such and such circumstances."

"At this point, I think it might be useful to see how theologians, whom we respect and who have influenced the teaching in colleges in both Europe and New England, line up with each other on some of the crucial issues," I said. "I have attended many commencement day disputations these past decades and have been intrigued to learn about the

---

22. Edwards, *Freedom of the Will*, 153.
23. Edwards, *Freedom of the Will*, 257.

scholastic sources and distinctions that play into our colleges' theses and *quaestiones*. Let me try to line up various theologians to show where they stand on some of the issues related to providence and free choice."

"Let me begin," I said, "with those who clearly favor a robust notion of freedom *ad utrumque*, or what others call *libertas indifferentiae ad opposita*. I would place here the Jesuit Luis de Molina, the Anglican Dr. Daniel Whitby, the dissenter Mr. Isaac Watts, and the Reverend John Wesley. Those who favored a much more nuanced version of this teaching, using scholastic distinctions, such as the divided sense versus the compounded sense, to qualify their support, are quite a number of Reformed theologians. Additionally, their teaching and texts figured in one way or the other in the development of the New England colleges, namely, Professor Samuel Rutherford at the University of St. Andrews, Professor William Ames at Franeker University, Gisbertus Voetius at Utrecht University, Adriaan Heereboord at Leiden University, Professor Francis Turretin at Geneva, Vice President Samuel Willard of Harvard College, and, as President Edwards called him, 'the eminent divine of Zurich,' the Swiss pastor Johann Friedrich Stapfer. And those who opposed this teaching would be you yourself, President Edwards, as you have made clear today and in your writings, and to a lesser degree Vice President of Harvard Charles Morton."

"As we come to the close of this roundtable," I added, "I would like to underscore my point about the robust teaching on providence of some of these Reformed theologians I have named. I realize that the opinion of the College of New Jersey may differ on some finer points. Briefly, Professor Rutherford argued for a twofold understanding of freedom *ad utrumque*. He did this to counter Arminian freedom of indifference, otherwise known as freedom of contrariety—as explained when teaching the square of opposition. Professor Rutherford opposed their notion of a freedom *ad utrumque* that believed in an 'objective indifference' to objects proposed to the mind. But he affirmed a subjective freedom *ad utrumque* if it meant that you and I always retain an internal, elective power freely to choose otherwise than we do. Notice that for Professor Rutherford, the emphasis was on the will always maintaining its created power, not on whether the will was passive or indifferent when faced with a choice.[24] Likewise, Professor Voetius followed Professor Rutherford in objecting to an Arminian 'freedom of contrariety' in the sense

---

24. Sturdy, *Freedom from Fatalism*, 280–84.

of objective indifference. And he affirmed a freedom of contradiction or exercise.[25] Once again I call on you to recall the teaching of the twofold freedoms, freedom of exercise and freedom of specification, as explained by Vice President Morton by way of the square of opposition."

"I would not dispute your lineup," said President Edwards. "I recall reading in Stapfer's *Institute*s a thesis where he affirmed freedom *ad utrumque*:

> Rational creatures are free and that to which they determine themselves is contingent so that even the opposite is possible. Nor is their liberty removed by the divine decree, so that, although dependent upon God, they can determine themselves to one of two opposites, insofar as the intellect represents to them something either good or bad. Therefore, the act is the specification, that is, the determination by the freedom of the creature to one of two opposites.[26]

"So, clearly, although I appreciated many things in Stapfer," said President Edwards, "and copied passages from his *Institutiones* into my private *Controversies' Notebook*, passages that clearly opposed Arminian teaching, as is the common practice, it does not mean that I agree with all he taught. Likewise, there are philosophers and theologians who more or less agree with me on 'the grand principle of common sense,' the principle of sufficient reason for why things are the way they are and not otherwise. And I would add the doctrine of *superior fitness*, which also plays an important role in understanding a 'universal determining providence,' which I teach."[27]

"As noted in *Freedom of the Will*," he continued, "I named Mr. John Locke, Mr. Leibniz, and the Scot Mr. Andrew Baxter as affirming the doctrine of fitness. I even included Dr. Samuel Clarke and Mr. Watts, although the latter I thought took back what he at first admitted. And I understand Dr. Clarke qualified his support for the idea of fitness in an

---

25. Beck, *Voetius on God, Freedom, and Contingency*, 447–52.

26. Stapfer, *Institutiones Theologicae Polemicae Universae*, 1:201–02. "Creaturae rationales autem sunt liberae, et illud, ad quod se determinant, est contingens, ut etiam oppositum sit possibile, nec illarum libertas decreto divino tollitur, ad utrumque oppositorum sese determinare possunt, prout intellectus illis aliquid vel et bonum, vel ut malum repraesentat. Ergo, actus specificatio sive determinatio ad alterutrum oppositorum a libertate creaturae est."

27. Edwards, *Freedom of the Will*, 181–83, 433–34.

exchange of letters with a gentleman from Cambridge, England, Mr. John Bulkeley."[28]

"At any rate," said President Edwards, "I quoted Dr. Clarke who said, '[God] must needs do always what is best in the whole.' This was a 'necessity of fitness and wisdom, consistent with the greatest freedom, and most perfect choice.'[29] Mr. Locke said of the determination by the will, 'The certainer such determination is, the greater the freedom.'[30] Mr. Andrew Baxter said, 'This Being having all things always necessarily in view, must always, and eternally will all things that are wisest and best to be done.' He added, 'Here then is the origin of moral necessity; and that is really, of freedom.' And, 'the more strong and necessary this determination is, the more perfect the Deity must be allowed to be . . . whose will and power are immutable determined by what is wisest and best.' Indeed, 'It is the beauty of this necessity that is strong as fate itself, with all the advantage of reason and goodness.'[31] These philosophers support my position on *superior fitness* and *moral necessity*, argued in *Freedom of the Will*. As I said, 'If Mr. Hobbes has made a bad use of this truth, that is to be lamented: but the truth is not to be thought worthy of rejection on that account.'"[32]

After the roundtable with President Edwards had finished, and I had thanked each participant for attending, I could not help but think that fifteen years later, in 1773, President Manning and Professor Howell, at the College of Rhode Island and Providence Plantations, would preside over commencement theses that would reflect some of President Edwards's positions on the doctrine of providence. I also thought that President Edwards was very wise to point out that both theological friend and foe may state truths that ought not to be rejected just because one does not espouse all that they teach, nor ought truths to be rejected out

28. Clarke, *Being and Attributes of God*, 124–31. Clarke added a caveat in the Third Reply to Mr. Bulkeley that was much more in line with the Reformed theologians that I named above. "God always discerns and approves what is just and good *necessarily*, and cannot do otherwise; but he always acts or does what is just and good *freely*, that is, having at the same time a full natural or physical power of acting differently," 130 (italics original). It is arguably the case that Edwards would not have agreed with the last phrase. On this topic, see, Fisk, "Jonathan Edwards and Samuel Clarke on Moral Necessity," 167–79.

29. Edwards, *Freedom of the Will*, 377n2.
30. Edwards, *Freedom of the Will*, 378n2.
31. Edwards, *Freedom of the Will*, 379n2.
32. Edwards, *Freedom of the Will*, 374.

of hand because of their bad use or reputation. President Edwards would not slander Mr. Watts nor the dead. Generally speaking, there was to be a certain reverence shown for yesteryear's doctors of the church. Edwards had made this point in his preface to *Freedom of the Will*, which I urged all to read. Such was the ecumenical enterprise in Reformation and post-Reformation Europe and in New England.

To what end were all these disputations at the New England colleges? And those in Europe? Whether Lutheran, Anglican, Jesuit, Remonstrant, Arminian, Reformed, or Baptist traditions, the great effort and story of the scholastic tradition that I have witnessed, expanded, and reported on at all these commmencement disputations was, when all was said and done, to exonerate God from the charge that he was the author, even actor, of sin and evil.

Bibliography

Abelard, Peter. *Dialectica: First Complete Edition of the Parisian Manuscript.* 2nd rev. ed. Edited and compiled by L. M. de Rijk. Wijserige Teksten en Studies 1. Assen, Netherlands: Van Gorcum, 1970.

Aichele, Alexander, and Matthias Kaufmann, eds. *A Companion to Luis De Molina.* Brill's Companions to the Christian Tradition 50. Leiden: Brill, 2013.

Aichele, Alexander, and Dagmar Mirbach. *Baumgarten, Alexander Gottlieb 1714–1762. Themenschwerpunkt: Alexander Gottlieb Baumgarten: Sinnliche Erkenntnis in der Philosophie Des Rationalismus.* Aufklärung 20. Hamburg: Meiner, 2008.

Alexander, Samuel Davies. *Princeton College During the Eighteenth Century.* New York: Anson D. F. Randolph & Company, 1872.

Alluntis, Felix, and Allan B. Wolter, trans. and eds. *God and Creatures: The Quodlibetal Questions.* Princeton: Princeton University Press, 1975.

Altenstaig, Joannes. *Lexicon Theologicum.* 1619. Reprint, Hildesheim, Germany: Georg Olms Verlag, 1974.

Ames, William. *The Marrow of Theology.* Edited and translated by John D. Eusden. Grand Rapids: Baker, 1968.

———. *Philosophemata.* Amsterdam: Joannem Janssonium, 1651.

———. *Rescriptio Scholastica et Brevis Ad Nicolaus Grevinchovii Responsum Illud Prolixum, Quod Opposuit Dissertationi de Redemptione Generali, et Electione Ex Fide Praevisa.* Harderwijk, Netherlands: Nicolai à Uvieringen, 1645.

———. *Technometry.* Edited and translated by Lee W. Gibbs. Philadelphia: University of Pennsylvania Press, 1979.

———. *Theologiae Medullae.* Edited by James S. Candlish. 1648. Reprint, London: James Nisbet & Co., 1874.

Anderson, Wallace E., ed. *Scientific and Philosophical Writings. Volume 6: The Works of Jonathan Edwards.* Edited by Harry S. Stout. New Haven: Yale University Press, 1980.

Andros, Edmund. "Harvard 1687, Original." In *Theses,* box 1, folder 9. https://nrs.lib.harvard.edu/urn-3:hul.arch:29087116.

Aquinas, Thomas. *Existence and Nature of God. Volume 2: St Thomas Aquinas Summa Theologiae.* Translated by Timothy O. P. McDermott. London: Blackfriars, 1964.

———. *On Evil.* Edited by Brian Davies. Translated by Richard Regan. Oxford: Oxford University Press, 2003.

———. *Opera Omnia.* Rome: Leonine, 1882.

———. *Summa Contra Gentiles, Book One: God*. Translated by Anton C. Pegis. South Bend, IN: University of Notre Dame Press, 1975.

———. *Summa Contra Gentiles, Book Two: Creation*. Translated by James F. Anderson South Bend, IN: University of Notre Dame Press, 1975.

———. *Summa Theologica: Complete English Edition in Five Volumes*. Translated by Fathers of the English Dominican Province. New York: Benziger Brothers, 1948.

Aristotle. *The Basic Works of Aristotle*. Edited by Richard McKeon. New York: Random House, 1941.

———. *Organon: IV Les Seconds Analytiques*. Translated by J. Tricot. Bibliothéque Des Textes Philosophiques. Paris: Librairie philosophiques J. Vrin, 2000.

Arnauld, Antoine, and Pierre Nicole. *Logic or the Art of Thinking, Containing, Besides Common Rules, Several New Observations Appropriate for Forming Judgment*. Edited and translated by Jill Vance Buroker. Cambridge Texts in the History of Philosophy. Cambridge: Cambridge University Press, 1996.

Asselt, Willem Jan van, ed. *Inleiding in de Gereformeerde Scholastiek*. Zoetermeer, Netherlands: Boekencentrum, 1998.

Asselt, Willem Jan van, and Albert Gootjes. *Introduction to Reformed Scholasticism*. Reformed Historical-Theological Studies. Grand Rapids: Reformation Heritage, 2011.

Asselt, Willem Jan van, et al., eds. *Reformed Thought on Freedom: The Concept of Free Choice in Early Modern Reformed Theology*. Texts and Studies in Reformation and Post-Reformation Thought. Grand Rapids: Baker Academic, 2010.

Asselt, Willem Jan van, and Eef Dekker. "Introduction." In *Reformation and Scholasticism: An Ecumenical Enterprise*, edited by Willem Jan van Asselt and Eef Dekker, 11–43. Texts and Studies in Reformation and Post-Reformation Thought. Grand Rapids: Baker Academic, 2001.

Asselt, Willem Jan van, and Eef Dekker, eds. *Reformation and Scholasticism: An Ecumenical Enterprise*. Texts and Studies in Reformation and Post-Reformation Thought. Grand Rapids: Baker Academic, 2001.

Augustine. *Augustine: Later Works. Volume 8: The Library of Christian Classics*. Edited and translated by John Burnaby. Philadelphia: Westminster, 1955.

———. *Concerning the City of God Against the Pagans*. Translated by Henry Bettenson. London: Penguin, 1984.

———. *The Confessions*. Translated by Maria Boulding. The Works of Saint Augustine: A Translation for the 21st Century. New York: New City, 1997.

———. *Contra Gaudentium*. Centre Traditio Litterarum Occidentalium. Brepolis Latin: Library of Latin Texts/Series A. Turnhout, Belgium: Brepols, 2010.

———. *Sancti Aurelii Augustii Episcopi de Civitate Dei Libri XXII*. Edited by Bernhard Dombart and Alfons Kalb. Berlin: B. G. Teubner, 2011.

———. *The Trinity (De Trinitate)*. Edited by John E. Rotelle. Translated by Edmund Hill. The Works of Saint Augustine 5. New York: New City, 1991.

Backus, Isaac, "The Sovereign Decrees of God, Set in a Scriptural Light, and Vindicated Against the Blasphemy Contained in a Late Paper, Entitled, On Traditionary Zeal. In a Letter to a Friend." In *Sovereign Decrees*. Evans Early American Imprints. Boston: J. Kneeland, 1733.

Baudry, Léon, ed. *Concerning the City of God Against the Pagans*. Translated by Henry Bettenson. London: Penguin, 1984.

———. *Lexique Philosophique de Guillaume D'Ockham: Étude Des Notions Fondamentales*. Paris: P. Lethielleux, 1958.

———. *La Querelle Des Futurs Contingents (Louvain 1465-1475)*. Études de Philosophie Médiévale 38. Paris: J. Vrin, 1950.

Baum, Guilielmus, et al. *Corpus Reformatorum*. Volumes 29-87: *Ioannis Calvini Opera Quae Supersunt Omnia*. Brunswick: C. A. Schwetschke et Filium, 1863-1900.

Beck, Andreas J. "Gisbertus Voetius (1589-1676): Basic Features of His Doctrine of God." In *Reformation and Scholasticism: An Ecumenical Enterprise*, edited by Willem Jan van Asselt and Eef Dekker, 209-26. Texts and Studies in Reformation and Post-Reformation Thought. Grand Rapids: Baker Academic, 2001.

———. *Gisbertus Voetius (1589-1676) on God, Freedom, and Contingency*. Brill's Series in Church History and Religious Culture 84. Leiden: Brill, 2022.

———. "Melanchthon und die Reformierte Scholastik." In *Melanchthon und die Reformierte Tradition*, edited by Andreas J. Beck, 107-28. Refo500 Academic Studies 6. Göttingen: Vandenhoeck & Ruprecht, 2016.

———. "The Will as Master of Its Own Act: A Disputation Rediscovered of Gisbertus Voetius (1589-1676) on Freedom of Will." In *Reformed Thought on Freedom: The Concept of Free Choice in the History of Early-Modern Reformed Theology*, 149-78. Texts and Studies in Reformation & Post-Reformation Thought. Grand Rapids: Baker Academic, 2009.

———. "Zur Rezeption Melanchthons bei Gisbertus Voetius (1589-1676), Namentlich in Seiner Gotteslehr." In *Melanchthon und der Calvinismus, volume 9*, edited by Frank Günter, Herman J. Selderhuis, and Sebastian Lalla, 319-44. Melanchthon-Schriften der Stadt Bretten 9. Stuttgart: Frommann-Holzboog, 2005.

Belcher, Jonathan. "1750 College of New Jersey Commencement Broadside." Early American Imprints, Series I: 1639-1800, 1750.

Boer, William den. *God's Twofold Love: The Theology of Jacob Arminius (1559-1609)*. Reformed Historical Theology 14. Göttingen: Vandenhoeck & Ruprecht, 2010.

Boethius. *De Consolatione Philosophiae*. Patrologiae Latinae 63. Edited by J. P. Migne. Paris, 1860.

———. *The Theological Tractates and The Consolation of Philosophy*. Edited and translated by H. F. Stewart and E. K. Rand. 1871. Reprint, Portsmouth, NH: Heinemann, 2014.

Boone, Thomas. "1760 College of New Jersey Commencement Broadside." Early American Imprints, Series I: 1642-1800, 1760.

———. "Princeton University Commencement Records, 1747-Present." In *1760 Princeton Commencement Broadside*. AC 115, 1760.

Bos, Egbert, and Henri Krop, eds. *Franco Burgersdijk (1590-1635). Studies in the History of Ideas in the Low Countries*. Amsterdam: Rodopi, 1993.

Boulnois, Olivier. "Le Refoulement de la Liberté d'Indifférence et les Polémiques Anti-Scotistes de la Métaphysique Moderne." *Les Études Philosophiques* 2 *La cohérence des subtils, Duns Scot au XVIIe siècle* 2 (April-June 2002) 199-237.

Bramhall, John. *The Discourses Against Mr. Hobbes*. Volume 4: *The Works of the Most Reverend Father in God, John Bramhall*. Oxford: John Henry Parker, 1844.

———. *The Works of the Most Reverend Father in God, John Bramhall D. D., Late Lord Bishop of Ardmagh, Primate and Metropolitan of All Ireland, Some of Which Never Before Printed, Collected Into One Volume*. Volume 3: *The Castigations of Mr.*

Hobbes, His Last Animadversions in the Case Concerning Liberty and Universal Necessity. Dublin: Benjamin Tooke, 1677.

Bruyère, Nelly. *Méthode et Dialectique dans l'Oeuvre de La Ramée Renaissance et Age Classique.* De Pétrarque a Descartes 45. Paris: Librairie Philosophique J. Vrin, 1984.

Bryant, L. M., and Patterson, M., comps. "The List of Books Sent by Jeremiah Dummer." In *Papers in Honor of Andrew Keogh, Librarian of Yale University,* edited by M. C. Withington, 423-92. New Haven, CT: Privately printed, 1938.

Bucanus, Guillaume. *Institutiones Theologicae, Seu Locorum Communium Christianae Religionis, Ex Dei Verbo, et Praestantissimorum Theologorum Orthodoxo Consensu Expositorum, Analysis: Ad Leges Methodi Didascalicae, Quaestionibus & Responsionibus Conformata: Atque in Usum Ministerii Sacri Candidatorum, Qui Se Ad Examen Doctrinae Subeundum Parant, Accomodata.* Geneva: Iacobi Stoer, 1625.

Burgersdijck, Franco. *Institutionum Logicarum, Libri Duo. Ad Juventutem Cantabrigiensem.* London: Rogeri Danielis, 1651.

———. *Institutionum Logicarum.* Leiden: Commelinum, 1626.

———. *Institutionum Metaphysicarum Libri Duo. Opus Posthumum. Editio Ultima, Longè Emendatior.* Oxford: Impensis Ric. Davis, 1675.

Burleigh, John H. S., ed. *Augustine: Earlier Writings.* Library of Christian Classics 6. Philadelphia: Westminster, 1953.

Burr, Aaron Sr. "1755 College of New Jersey Commencement Broadside." New York: Blaine in Queen-Street, 1755.

Calvin, John. *The Bondage and Liberation of the Will: A Defence of the Orthodox Doctrine of Human Choice Against Pighius.* Edited by Richard A. Muller and Anthony N. S. Lane. Translated by Graham I. Davies. Texts and Studies in Reformation and Post-Reformation Thought. Grand Rapids: Baker Academic, 1996.

———. *Concerning the Eternal Predestination of God.* Translated by J. K. S. Reid. London: James Clarke & Co. Limited, 1961.

———. *Defensio Sanae et Orthodoxae Doctrinae Servitute et Liberatione Humani Arbitrii, Adversus Calumnias Alberti Pighii Campensis.* Amsterdam: Ioannis Iacobi Schipperi, 1671.

———. *Institutes of the Christian Religion.* Edited by John T. McNeill. Translated by Ford Lewis Battles. The Library of Christian Classics 20, 21. Philadelphia: Westminster, 1960.

———. *Ioannis Calvini Defensio Sanae et Orthodoxae Doctrinae de Servitute et Liberatione Humani Arbitrii.* Edited and translated by Anthony N. S. Lane and Graham I. Davies. Series IV. Scripta Didactica et Polemica 3. Geneva: Droz, 2008.

———. *Ioannis Calvini Opera Quae Supersunt Omnia.* Edited by J. W. Baum et al. 58 vols. Brunswick: C. A. Schwetschke, 1863-1900.

———. *Tractatus theologici omnes.* https://orbis.library.yale.edu/vwebv/search?searchArg=Tractatus+theologici+omnes&searchCode=GKEY%5E*&setLimit=1&recCount=50&searchType=1&page.search.search.button=Search.

Chappell, Vere, ed. *Hobbes and Bramhall on Liberty and Necessity.* Cambridge Texts in the History of Philosophy. Cambridge: Cambridge University Press, 1999.

Charnock, Stephen. *A Discourse of Divine Providence. I. In General, That There is a Providence Exercised by God in the World. II. In Particular, How All Gods*

Providences in the World, Are in Order to the Good of His People. London: John Harris, 1685.

———. *The Existence and Attributes of God*. 1853. Reprint, Grand Rapids: Baker, 1996.

Chaucer, Geoffrey. *The Riverside Chaucer*. Edited by Larry D. Benson. 3rd ed. Oxford: Oxford University Press, 2008.

Chytraeus, David. *Piae et Utilliss, Explicationes Vocabulorum: Necessitatis, Determinationis Divinae, Fati, Contingentiae, Virium Humanarum, Liberi Arbitrii*. Rostock: Jacobus Transylvanus, 1565.

Clairvaux, Bernard de. *L'Amour de Dieu et la Grâce et le Libre Arbitre*. Sources Chrétiennes. Paris: CERF, 1993.

Clap, Thomas. "1740 Yale College Commencement Quaestiones." In Early American Imprints, Series I: Evans 1639–1800, 1740.

———. "1762 Yale College Commencement Quaestiones." In Early American Imprints, Series I: Evans 1639–1800, 1762.

———. *The Annals or History of Yale-College, In New-Haven, In the Colony of Connecticut, from The First Founding Thereof, in the Year 1700, to the Year 1766: With an Appendix Containing the Present State of the College, the Method of Instruction and Government, with the Officers, Benefactors and Graduates*. New Haven: printed for John Hotchkiss and B. Mecom, 1766.

———. *Yale College Theses and Quaestiones*. 1747. RU 146. Yale University Library Manuscripts and Archives, Yale University, New Haven, CT.

Clarke, Samuel. *A Collection of Papers, Which Passed Between the Later Learned Mr. Leibniz, and Dr. Clarke, in the Years 1715 and 1716. Relating to the Principles of Natural Philosophy and Religion. With an Appendix to Which Are Added Letters to Dr. Clarke Concerning Liberty and Necessity; from a Gentleman of the University of Cambridge: With the Doctor's Answers to Them. Also Remarks Upon a Book, Entituled, A Philosophical Enquiry Concerning Human Liberty*. London: James Knapton, 1717.

———. *A Demonstration of the Being and Attributes of God, and Other Writings*. Edited by Ezio Vailati. Cambridge Texts in the History of Philosophy. Cambridge: Cambridge University Press, 1998.

Colish, Marcia L. *Peter Lombard*. Brill's Studies in Intellectual History 41/1–2. Leiden: Brill, 1994.

Collins, Ann. *Teacher in Faith and Virtue: Lanfranc of Bec's Commentary on Saint Paul*. Commentaria: Sacred Texts and Their Commentaries: Jewish, Christian and Islamic 1. Leiden: Brill, 2007.

Coogan, Michael D., ed. *The New Oxford Annotated Bible New Revised Standard Version with the Apocrypha*. 5th ed. Oxford: Oxford University Press, 2018.

Corpus Reformatorum. *Corpus Reformatorum Volume 79*. Brunswick: C. A. Schwetschke et Filium, 1834–1900.

Cottingham, John, et al., trans. *The Philosophical Writings of Descartes*. 3 vols. Cambridge: Cambridge University Press, 1984–91.

Craig, William Lane. *The Problem of Divine Foreknowledge and Future Contingents from Aristotle to Suarez*. Brill's Studies in Intellectual History 7. Leiden: Brill, 1988.

Damian, Peter. "On Divine Omnipotence." In *Medieval Philosophy: From St. Augustine to Nicholas of Cusa*, edited by John F. Wippel and Allan B. Wolter, 143–52. Readings in the History of Philosophy. New York: The Free Press, 1969.

Davis, Arthur P. *Isaac Watts: His Life and Works*. 1943. Reprint, Whitefish, MT: Literary Licensing LLC, 2012.

De Rijk, Lambertus Marie. *La Philosophie Au Moyen Âge*. Leiden: Brill, 1985.

———. *Logica Modernorum: A Contribution to the History of Early Terminist Logic. Volume 1: On The Twelfth Century Theories of Fallacy*. Wijserige Teksten en Studies 6. Assen, Netherlands: Van Gorcum & Comp., 1962.

———. *Logica Modernorum: A Contribution to the History of Early Terminist Logic. Volume 2, Part Two: The Origin and Early Development of the Theory of Supposition*. Wijsgerige Teksten en Studies 16. Assen, Netherlands: Van Gorcum & Comp. N.V., 1967.

———. *Middeleeuwse Wijsbegeerte*. Assen, Netherlands: Van Gorcum, 1981.

De Rivo, Peter. "A Quodlibetal Question on Future Contingents Disputed at Louvain in the Year 1465." In *Readings in Medieval Philosophy*, edited by Andrew B. Schoedinger, 252–59; Oxford: Oxford University Press, 1996.

Dekker, Eef. *Rijker Dan Midas: Vrijheid, Genade en Predestinatie in de Theologie Van Jacobus Arminius (1559–1609)*. Zoetermeer, Netherlands: Boekencentrum, 1993.

Dekker, Eef, and Henri Veldhuis. "Freedom and Sin: Some Systematic Observations." *European Journal of Theology* 3 (1994) 153–61.

Dexter, Franklin Bowditch, ed. *Documentary History of Yale University: Under the Original Charter of the Collegiate School of Connecticut 1701–1745*. New Haven: Yale University Press, 1916.

Dingel, Irene, ed. *Die Bekenntnisschriften der Evangelisch-Lutherischen Kirche*. Vollständige Neueition. Göttingen: Vandenhoeck & Ruprecht, 2014.

Dyken, Seymour van. *Samuel Willard, 1640–1707: Preacher of Orthodoxy in an Era of Change*. Grand Rapids: Eerdmans, 1972.

Edwards, Jonathan. "A141. Letter to Joseph Paice." *Jonathan Edwards Center Online*. https://tinyurl.com/mprrn4u5.

———. *A Careful and Strict Enquiry into the Modern Prevailing Notions of That Freedom of Will Which is Supposed to Essential to Moral Agency, Verte and Vice, Reward and Punishment, Praise and Blame*. Boston: S. Kneeland, 1754.

———. *Controversies Book C*. Notebook. GEN MSS 151. Jonathan Edwards Collection, 1696–1972. Beinecke Rare Book and Manuscript Library, Yale University, New Haven, CT. https://collections.library.yale.edu/catalog/10687815.

———. "Controversies" Notebook. Works of Jonathan Edwards Online, Vol. 27. Jonathan Edwards Center, Yale University, 2008. https://tinyurl.com/576b86sd.

———. *Ethical Writings*. Edited by Paul Ramsey. Works of Jonathan Edwards 8. New Haven: Yale University Press, 1989.

———. *Freedom of the Will*. Edited by Paul Ramsey. Works of Jonathan Edwards 1. New Haven: Yale University Press, 1957.

———. *Letters and Personal Writings*. Edited by George S. Claghorn. Works of Jonathan Edwards 16. New Haven: Yale University Press, 1998.

———. *The "Miscellanies," a–z, Aa–Zz, 1–500*. Edited by Thomas A. Schafer. Works of Jonathan Edwards 13. New Haven: Yale University Press, 1994.

———. *The "Miscellanies," 501–832*. Edited by Ava Chamberlain. Works of Jonathan Edwards 18. New Haven: Yale University Press, 2000.

———. *The "Miscellanies," 833–1152*. Edited by Amy Plantinga Pauw. Works of Jonathan Edwards 20. New Haven: Yale University Press, 2002.

———. *The "Miscellanies," 1153–1360.* Edited by Douglas A. Sweeney. Works of Jonathan Edwards 23. New Haven: Yale University Press, 2004.

———. *Writings on the Trinity, Grace, and Faith.* Edited by Sang Hyun Lee. Works of Jonathan Edwards 21. New Haven: Yale University Press, 2003.

Eire, Carlos N. *Reformations: The Early Modern World, 1450–1650.* New Haven: Yale University Press, 2016.

Fiering, Norman. *Jonathan Edwards's Moral Thought and Its British Context.* The Jonathan Edwards Classic Studies Series. Eugene, OR: Wipf and Stock, 2006.

———. *Moral Philosophy at Seventeenth-Century Harvard: A Discipline in Transition.* Chapel Hill, NC: University of North Carolina Press, 1981.

Fisk, Philip John. *A Book of Faith Seeking Understanding: Fifty-Two Lord's Day Readings.* Eugene, OR: Wipf & Stock, 2021.

———. "Divine Knowledge at Harvard and Yale: From William Ames to Jonathan Edwards." *Jonathan Edwards Studies* 4 (2014) 151–78.

———. "Jonathan Edwards and Samuel Clarke on Moral Necessity: A Matter of Distinction, and Why It Matters." *Jonathan Edwards Studies* 10 (2020) 167–79.

———. *Jonathan Edwards's Turn from the Classic-Reformed Tradition of Freedom of the Will.* New Directions in Jonathan Edwards Studies 2. Göttingen: Vandenhoeck & Ruprecht, 2016.

———. "Petrus Van Mastricht and Freedom of the Will." In *Petrus Van Mastricht (1630–1706): Text, Context, and Interpretation,* edited by Adriaan C. Neele. Reformed Historical Theology 62. Göttingen: Vandenhoeck & Ruprecht, 2020.

———. "Que Sera, Sera. The Controversial 1702 Harvard Commencement *Quaestio* on Whether the Immutability of God's Decree Takes Away Human Freedom of the Will." In *Jonathan Edwards Within the Enlightenment: Controversy, Experience, and Thought,* edited by John T. Lowe and Daniel N. Gullota, 283–98. New Directions in Jonathan Edwards Studies 7. Göttingen: Vandenhoeck & Ruprecht, 2020.

Fitch, Thomas. "1760 Yale College Commencement Broadside." Early American Imprints, Series I: Evans, 1639–1800.

———. "1765 Yale College Commencement Broadside." Early American Imprints, Series I: Evans 1639–1800.

Gerhard, Johann. *Locorum Theologicorum.* Jena: Tobias Steinmann, 1610.

———. *On Creation and Angels, On Providence, On Election and Reprobation, On the Image of God in Man Before the Fall.* Edited by Benjamin T. G. Mayes and Joshua J. Hayes. Translated by Richard J. Dinda. Theological Commonplaces. Saint Louis: Concordia, 2013.

Gomarus, Franciscus. *Conciliatio Doctrinae Orthodoxae de Providentia Dei.* Opera Theologica Omnia, Maximam Partem Posthuma: Suprema Autoris Voluntate à Discipulis Edita. Cum Indicibus Necessariis. Amsterdam: Joannis Janssonii, 1644.

———. *Disputationes Theologicae: Habitae in Variis Academiis.* Edited by Johannes Veree Adolphus Sibelius Martinus Ubbenius. Amsterdam: Joannis Janssonii, 1644.

———. *Disputationes Theologicarum Quarto Repetitarum Decima De Providentia Dei.* Leiden: Johannes Patius, 1605.

———. *Theses Theologicae de Providentia Dei.* Leiden, 1595.

Goodwin, Thomas. *Exposition of Ephesians.* Nichol's Series of Standard Divines 1. 1861. Reprint, Lafayette, IN: Sovereign Grace, 2001.

Graetz, Heinrich. *History of the Jews.* Vols 1–6. Translated by Bella Löwy. Chicago: E-artnow, 2021.

Green, Enoch. *Theological Responses*. C0199. General Manuscripts AM 12800, 1759-60. Princeton University Library, Princeton, NJ.

Grevinchovius, Nicolaus. *Dissertatio Theologica de Duabus Quaestionibus Hoc Tempore Controversis, [1] de Reconciliatione Per Mortem Christi Impetrata Omnibus Ac Singulis Hominibus, [2] de Electione Ex Fide Praevisa*. Rotterdam: Batavorum, 1615.

Halevi, Yehuda. *The Kuzari: Arguments in Defense of Judaism*. Revised by Chanan Morrison. Los Gatos, CA: Smashwords, 2012.

Hamilton, Edith, and Huntington Cairns, eds. *The Collected Dialogues of Plato, Including the Letters*. Bollingen Series 71. Princeton: Princeton University Press, 1980.

Hardy, Josiah. "1762 College of New Jersey Commencement Broadside." Early American Imprints, Series I: 1623–1800.

Harvard University. "Commencement Theses, Quaestiones, and Orders of Exercises, 1642-1818." HUC 6642. Harvard University Archives, Cambridge, MA. https://id.lib.harvard.edu/ead/hua03010/catalog.

Haykin, Michael A. G. "Great Admirers of the Transatlantic Divinity: Some Chapters in the Story of Baptist Edwardsianism." In *After Jonathan Edwards: The Courses of the New England Theology*, edited by Oliver D. Crisp and Douglas A. Sweeney, 197–207. Oxford: Oxford University Press, 2012.

Heereboord, Adriaan. *Meletemata Philosophica*. Amsterdam: Joannem Ravesteinium, 1665.

———. *Pneumatica*. Leiden, 1659.

Heschel, Abraham Joshua. *Maimonides: A Biography*. Translated by Joachim Neugroschel. New York: Farrar, Straus & Giroux, 1982.

Hobbes, Thomas. *Leviathan*. New York: E. P. Dutton and Company, 1950.

Holifield, E. Brooks. *Theology in America: Christian Thought from the Age of the Puritans to the Civil War*. New Haven: Yale University Press, 2003.

Hopkins, Stephan. "1770 College of Rhode Island Commencement Broadside." Early American Imprints, Series I: 1639–1800. Providence: Johannes Carter, 1770.

———. "1773 College of Rhode Island Commencement Broadside." Early American Imprints, Series I: 1639–1800.

Hulme, Edward Maslin. *The Renaissance, the Protestant Revolution and the Catholic Reformation in Continental Europe*. New York: The Century Co., 1915.

Jenson, Robert W. *America's Theologian, A Recommendation of Jonathan Edwards*. New York: Oxford University Press, 1988.

John XXI, Pope. *Syncategoreumata*. Edited by L.M. De Rijk. Translated by Joke Spruyt. Studien und Texte Zur Geistesgeschichte Des Mittelalters 30. Leiden: Brill, 1992.

Johnson, Thomas H. "Jonathan Edwards' Background of Reading." In *Colonial Society Transactions 28*, 1930–33.

———. *The Printed Writings of Jonathan Edwards 1703-1758: A Bibliography*. Princeton: Princeton Theological Seminary, 2003.

Junius, Franciscus. *Opuscula Theologica Selecta*. Bibliotheca Reformata. Amsterdam: Muller & Kruyt, 1882.

Keith, George. *An Answer to Mr Samuell Willard His Reply to My Printed Sheet, Called, A Dangerous and Hurtful Opinion*. New York: William Bradford, 1704.

———. *A Refutation of a Dangerous and Hurtful Opinion Maintained by Mr. Samuel Willard, an Independent Minister at Boston, & President at the Commencement in Cambridge in New-England, July 1, 1702. Viz. That the Fall of Adam, and All* the Sins of Men, Necessarily Come to Pass by Virtue of God's Decree, and His Determination Both of the Will of Adam, and of All Other Men, to Sin. Sent to Him in Latine Soon After the Commencement, and Since Translated Into English. By G. Keith, M. A. New York, 1702.

Kelley, Brooks Mather. *Yale: A History*. The Yale Scene University Series. New Haven: Yale University Press, 1974.

Kennedy, Rick, ed. *Aristotelian and Cartesian Logic at Harvard: Charles Morton's A Logick System & William Brattle's Compendium of Logick*. Publications of the Colonial Society of Massachusetts 67. Boston: Colonial Society of Massachusetts, 1995.

Klima, Gyula, et al., eds. *Medieval Philosophy: Essential Readings with Commentary*. Blackwell Readings in the History of Philosophy. Oxford: Blackwell Publishing, 2007.

Kling, David W., and Douglas A. Sweeney, eds. *Jonathan Edwards at Home and Abroad: Historical Memories, Cultural Movements, Global Horizons*. Columbia, SC: University of South Carolina Press, 2003.

Knoles, Thomas, et al. *Student Notebooks at Colonial Harvard: Manuscripts and Educational Practice 1650-1740*. Worcester, MA: American Antiquarian Society, 2003.

Knuuttila, Simo, ed. "Modal Logic." In *The Cambridge History of Later Medieval Philosophy: From the Rediscovery of Aristotle to the Disintegration of Scholasticism 1100-1600*, edited by Norman Kretzmann, Anthony Kenny, and Jan Pinborg, 42–57. Cambridge: Cambridge University Press, 1996.

———. *Reforging the Great Chain of Being: Studies of the History of Modal Theories*. Synthese Historical Library: Texts and Studies in the History of Logic and Philosophy 20. Dordrecht: D. Reidel Publishing Company, 1981.

Kolb, Robert. *Bound Choice, Election, and Wittenberg Theological Method*. Lutheran Quarterly Books 6. Grand Rapids: Eerdmans, 2005.

Koyré, Alexandre. *Newtonian Studies*. Cambridge, MA: Harvard University Press, 1965.

Kretzman, Norman, et al., eds. *The Cambridge History of Later Medieval Philosophy: From the Rediscovery of Aristotle to the Disintegration of Scholasticism 1100-1600*. Cambridge: Cambridge University Press, 1996.

Kristeller, Paul Oskar. *Renaissance Thought and Its Sources*. Edited by Michael Mooney. New York: Columbia University Press, 1979.

Law, Jonathan. "1749 Yale College Commencement Broadside." Early American Imprints, Series I: Evans, 1639–1800.

Leibniz, Gottfried Wilhelm. *Gottfried Wilhelm Leibniz: Opuscules Philosophiques Choisis*. Edited and translated by Paul Schrecker. Bibliothèque Des Textes Philosophiques. Paris: J. Vrin, 2001.

———. *Theodicy: Essays on the Goodness of God, the Freedom of Man, and the Origin of Evil*. Edited by Austin Farrer. Translated by E. M. Huggard. Rare Masterpieces of Philosophy and Science. New Haven: Yale University Press, 1952.

Leibniz, Gottfried Wilhelm, and Samuel Clarke. *The Leibniz-Clarke Correspondence Together with Extracts from Newton's* Principia *and* Opticks. Edited and compiled by H. G. Alexander. 1956. Reprint, Manchester, UK: Manchester University Press, 1998.

Leverett, John. "Harvard 1715, Original." In *Quaestiones*, box 9, folder 54. https://iiif.lib.harvard.edu/manifests/view/drs:428670843$1i.

———. "Harvard 1717, Original." In *Quaestiones*, box 9, folder 56. https://iiif.lib. harvard.edu/manifests/view/drs:428670851$1i.
Lewis, C. S. *Studies in Words*. 2nd ed. Cambridge: Cambridge University Press, 1967.
Lewis, Charlton T., and Short, Charles. "Natura." *A Latin Dictionary*. http://www. perseus.tufts.edu/hopper/text?doc=Perseus%3Atext%3A1999.04.0059%3Aentry %3Dnatura.
Locke, John. *An Essay Concerning Human Understanding*. London: Ward, Lock & Co., 1689.
Lombard, Peter. *Book 1: The Mystery of the Trinity. Volume 1: The Sentences*. Mediaeval Sources in Translation 42. Translated by Giulio Silano. Toronto: Pontifical Institute of Mediaeval Studies, 2007.
———. *Book 2: On Creation. Volume 2: The Sentences*. Mediaeval Sources in Translation 43. Translated by Giulio Silano. Toronto: Pontifical Institute of Mediaeval Studies, 2008.
———. *Sententiae in IV Libris Distinctae*. 3rd ed. Edited by Ignatius C. Brady. Spicilegium Bonaventurianum 4. Rome: Collegii S. Bonaventurae Ad Claras Aquas, 1971.
Luther, Martin. *Assertio Omnium Articulorum M. Lutheri Per Bullam Leonis X Novisimam Damnatorum*. Wittenberg, 1520.
———. *Die Römerbriefvorlesung*. D. Martin Luthers Werke 56. Böhlau: Weimar, 1938.
———. *Luther: Lectures on Romans*. Edited and translated by Wilhelm Pauck. The Library of Christian Classics 15. Philadelphia: Westminster, 1961.
Luther, Martin, and Desiderius Erasmus. *Luther and Erasmus: Free Will and Salvation*. Edited and translated by E. Gordon Rupp and Philip S. Watson. The Library of Christian Classics 17. Philadelphia: The Westminster Press, 1969.
Maimonides. *Doctor Perplexorum*. Edited by Ibn Tibbon. Translated by Johannes Buxtorf Jr. Basel: Jo. Jacob Genath, 1629.
———. *Le Guide Des Égarés, Traité de Théologie et de Philosophie par Moïse Ben Maimon, Publié Pour la Première Fois dans l'Originale Arabe, et Accompagné d'une Traduction Française et de Notes Critiques, Littéraires et Explicatives*. Translated by S. Munk. 3 vols. Paris: A. Franck, Libraire, 1856–66.
———. *The Guide for the Perplexed*. Translated by Michael Friedländer. New York: Barnes & Noble, 2004.
Manning, James. Letter. Providence, RI, 1783. Brown Archival and Manuscript Collections Online. https://library.brown.edu/cds/repository2/repoman.php?ver b=render&id=1080328481453125.
Marenbon, John. *Medieval Philosophy: An Historical and Philosophical Introduction*. London: Routledge, 2009.
Marsden, George M. *Jonathan Edwards, A Life*. New Haven: Yale University Press, 2003.
Masollini, Serena, et al. "Petrus de Rivo (ca. 1420-1499): Portrait(s) of a Louvain Master." https://limo.libis.be/primo-explore/fulldisplay?docid=LIRIAS1893693& context=L&vid=Lirias&search_scope=Lirias&tab=default_tab&fromSitemap=1.
Mastricht, Petrus van. *Theoretico-Practica Theologia, Qua, Per Singula Capita Theologica, Pars Exegetica, Dogmatica, Elenchtica & Practica, Perpetuâ Successione Coniugantur*. Utrecht: Thomae Appels, 1699.
McDermott, Gerald R. "Nathanael Emmons and the Decline of Edwardsian Theology." In *After Jonathan Edwards: The Courses of the New England Theology*, edited by

Oliver D. Crisp and Douglas A. Sweeney, 118–29. Oxford: Oxford University Press, 2012.

McClymond, Michael J., and Gerald R. McDermott. "Free Will and Original Sin." In *The Theology of Jonathan Edwards*, 339–56. Oxford: Oxford University Press, 2012.

McClymond, Michael J., and Gerald R. McDermott, eds. *The Theology of Jonathan Edwards*. Oxford: Oxford University Press, 2012.

Maccoby, Hyam, ed. and trans. *Judaism on Trial: Jewish-Christian Disputations in the Middle Ages*. The Littman Library of Jewish Civilization. Oxford: The Littman Library of Jewish Civilization, 1993.

McGraw, Ryan M. *Reformed Scholasticism: Recovering the Tools of Reformed Theology*. Edinburgh: T. & T. Clark, 2019.

Melanchthon, Philip. *Loci Communes Theologici*. Basel: NA, 1546. https://digitale.bibliothek.uni-halle.de/vd16/content/titleinfo/997777.

———. *Loci Communes Theologici, Recens Collecti et Recogniti*. Wittenberg, 1535. https://download.digitale-sammlungen.de/BOOKS/download.pl?id=bsb00029773.

———. *Melanchthon and Bucer*. The Library of Christian Classics 19. Philadelphia: Westminster, 1969.

Minkema, Kenneth P., and George G. Levesque. *Jonathan Edwards Tercentennial Exhibition: Selected Objects from the Yale Collections 1703-2003*. New Haven, CT: Jonathan Edwards College, Yale University Press, 2003.

Molina, Luis De. *On Divine Foreknowledge, Part IV of the Concordia*. Translated by Alfred J. Freddoso. Ithaca: Cornell University Press, 1988.

Mooney, James E., ed. *Eighteenth-Century Catalogues of the Yale College Library*. New Haven: Yale University Beinecke Library Press, 2001.

More, Henry. *Divine Dialogues, Containing Sundry Disquisitions & Instructions Concerning the Attributes and Providence of God*. London: James Flesher, 1668.

———. *Opera Philosophica*. London: J. Macock, 1679.

Morison, Samuel E. *The Founding of Harvard College*. Cambridge, MA: Harvard University Press, 1995.

Morison, Samuel Eliot. *Harvard College in the Seventeenth Century, Volume 2*. Cambridge: Harvard University Press, 1936.

Morrison, Theodore, ed. and trans. *The Portable Chaucer*. New York: Penguin, 1977.

Muller, Richard A. *Dictionary of Latin and Greek Theological Terms: Drawn Principally from Protestant Scholastic Theology*. 2nd ed. Grand Rapids: Baker Academic, 2017.

———. *Divine Will and Human Choice: Freedom, Contingency, and Necessity in Early Modern Reformed Thought*. Grand Rapids: Baker Academic, 2017.

———. *Post-Reformation Reformed Dogmatics: The Rise and Development of Reformed Orthodoxy, Ca. 1520–Ca. 1725*. 4 vols. 2nd ed. Grand Rapids: Baker Academic, 2003.

Neele, Adriaan C., ed. *Before Edwards: Sources of New England Theology*. New York: Oxford University Press, 2019.

———. *Petrus Van Mastricht (1630-1706): Text, Context, and Interpretation*. Reformed Historical Theology 62. Göttingen: Vandenhoeck & Ruprecht, 2020.

———. *Petrus Van Mastricht (1630-1706) Reformed Orthodoxy: Method and Piety*. Brill's Series in Church History and Religious Culture 35. Leiden: Brill, 2009.

Nettles, Thomas J. *By His Grace and for His Glory: A Historical, Theological, and Practical Study of the Doctrines of Grace in Baptist Life*. Grand Rapids: Baker, 1986.

New York Gazette. "College of New Jersey Commencement." November 21, 1748. AC 115. Commencement records 1748–1860. Princeton University Library, Princeton, NJ.

Newell, Daniel. "Student Notebook, 1700–1731." Beinecke Library, Yale University, New Haven, CT. https://hdl.handle.net/10079/bibid/3915074.

Newton, Isaac. *Philosophiae Naturalis Principia Mathematica*. London: Jussu Societas Regiae, 1686.

———. *The Principia: Mathematical Principles of Natural Philosophy*. Translated by Bernard I. Cohen and Anne Whitman. Berkeley, CA: University of California Press, 1999.

Noble, John. "An Old Harvard Commencement Programme, 1730." In *Publications of the Colonial Society of Massachusetts, Volume 6*, 265–78. Boston: Colonial Society of Massachusetts, 1904.

Novikoff, Alex J. *The Medieval Culture of Disputation: Pedagogy, Practice, and Performance*. Philadelphia: University of Pennsylvania Press, 2013.

Oberman, Heiko. *The Harvest of Medieval Theology: Gabriel Biel and Late-Medieval Nominalism*. 3rd ed. Grand Rapids: Baker Academic, 2000.

Outler, Albert C., ed. *John Wesley*. A Library of Protestant Thought. New York: Oxford University Press, 1964.

Pacio, Julio, ed. *Aristotle's Organon: Gracè & Latine*. 2nd ed. Frankfurt: Wecheli, Marnium, & Aubrium, 1597.

Paulson, Steven. "Luther's Doctrine of God." In *The Oxford Handbook of Martin Luther's Theology*, edited by Robert Kolb et al., 187–200. Oxford: Oxford University Press, 2014.

Pighius, Albert. *De Libero Hominis Arbitrio et Divina Gratia, Libri Decem*. Cologne: Melchioris Nouê, 1542.

Polyander, Johannes. *Theses Theologicae de Providentia Dei*. Leiden, 1620.

Potok, Chaim. *Wanderings: Chaim Potok's History of the Jews*. New York: Fawcett Crest, 1978.

Preus, Robert D. *The Theology of Post-Reformation Lutheranism: A Study of Theological Prolegomena*. 2 vols. Saint Louis: Concordia, 1970.

Princeton University. "1748 College of New Jersey Commencement Broadside." AC 115. Commencement records 1747–present. Mudd Library, Princeton University, Princeton, NJ.

———. "1750 College of New Jersey Commencement Broadside." AC 115. Commencement records 1747–present. Mudd Library, Princeton University, Princeton, NJ.

———. "1755 College of New Jersey Commencement Broadside." AC 115. Commencement records 1747–present. Mudd Library, Princeton University, Princeton, NJ.

Quenstedt, Johann Andreas. *Theologia Didactico-Polemica*. Wittenberg, 1685.

Ramée, Pierre de la. *Dialectique de Pierre De La Ramée*. Paris: André Wechel, 1555.

Ramus, Peter. *Scholae in Liberales Artes: Quarum Elenchus*. Basel: Eusebius Episcopium, 1569.

Rutherford, Samuel. *Disputatio Scholastica de Divina Providentia, Variis Praelectionibus, Quod Attinet Ad Summa Rerum Capita, Tradita s. Theologiae Adolescentibus Candidatis in Inclytâ Academiâ Andreapolitanâ, in Quâ Adversus Iesuitas, Arminianos, Socinianos, de Dominio Dei, Actione Ipsius Operosâ Circa Peccatum,*

Concursu Primae Causae, Praedeterminatione & Contenditur & Decertatur. Edinburgh: Haeredes Georgii Andersoni pro Roberto Brouno, 1649.

———. *Exercitationes Apologeticae Pro Divina Gratia, in Quibus Vindicatur Doctrina Orthodoxa de Divinis Decretis, & Dei Tum Aeterni Decreti, Tum Gratiae Efficacis Operationis, Cum Homini Libertate Consociatione & Subordinatione Amicâ: Adversus Iacobum Arminium Eiusque Asseclas, & Iesuitas, Inprimis Vero Fran. Suarezium, Gabri. Vasquezium, Lodiv. Molinam, Leonard. Lessium, Pet. Fonsecam & Robertum Bellarminum.* Amsterdam: Henricum Laurentii Bibliopolam, 1636.

Saltonstall, Gordon. "Yale College Commencement Broadside 1718." New London: Timothy Green, 1718.

———. "Yale College Commencement Broadside 1720." New London: Timothy Green, 1720.

Saunders, Jason L., ed. *Greek and Roman Philosophy after Aristotle.* Readings in the History of Philosophy. New York: The Free Press, 1966.

Schaff, Philip. *The Evangelical Protestant Creeds.* The Creeds of Christendom 3. 6th ed. Grand Rapids: Baker, 1996.

Schmutz, Jacob. "Du Péché de l'Ange à la Liberté d'Indifférence. Les Sources Angélologiques de l'Anthropologie Moderne." *Les Études Philosophiques* 2 La cohérence des subtils Duns Scot au XVIIe siècle (Avril Juin 2002): 169–98.

Schoedinger, Andrew B. *Readings in Medieval Philosophy.* Oxford: Oxford University Press, 1996.

Scotus, John Duns. *Duns Scotus on Divine Love: Texts and Commentary on Goodness and Freedom, God and Humans.* Edited and translated by Antonie Vos et al. Aldershot: Ashgate, 2003.

———. *Duns Scotus on the Will and Morality.* Translated by Allan B. Wolter and William A. Frank. Washington, DC: The Catholic University of America Press, 1997.

———. *God and Creatures: The Quodlibetal Questions.* Translated by Felix Alluntis and Allan Wolter. Princeton: Princeton University Press, 1975.

———. *John Duns Scotus: Contingency and Freedom, Lectura I 39. Introduction, Translation, and Commentary.* Translated by Antonie Vos et al. The New Synthese Historical Library 42. Dordrecht: Kluwer Academic, 1994.

———. *Ordinatio. Ionnis Duns Scoti Opera Omnia, vol. 1–7.* Edited by Commisio Scotistica. Vatican City: Typis Polyglottis Vaticanis, 1950–73.

———. *A Treatise on God as First Principle: A Latin Text and English Translation of the de Primo Principio.* Edited and translated by Allan B. Wolter. Chicago: Franciscan Herald, 1966.

Seebohm, Frederic. *The Era of the Protestant Revolution.* New York: Scribner, Armstrong, and Co., 1874.

Sibley, John Langdon. *1659-1677. Biographical Sketches of Graduates of Harvard University, in Cambridge, Massachusetts, 2.* Cambridge, MA: Charles William Sever, 1873–99.

Sprunger, Keith L. *The Auction Catalogue of the Library of William Ames.* Catalogi Redivivi: A Reprint Series of Dutch Auction and Stock Catalogues from the 17th and 18th Centuries. Utrecht: H & S HES, 1988.

Stapfer, Johann Friedrich. *Institutiones Theologicae Polemicae Universae, Ordine Scientifico Dispositae.* 5 vols. Zurich: Heideggerum et socios, 1756.

Sturdy, Robert C. *Freedom from Fatalism: Samuel Rutherford's (1600–1661) Doctrine of Divine Providence*. Reformed Historical Theology 68. Göttingen: Vandenhoeck & Ruprecht, 2021.

Sweeney, Douglas, and Oliver D. Crisp, eds. *After Jonathan Edwards: The Courses of the New England Theology*. New York: Oxford University Press, 2012.

———. *Nathaniel Taylor, New Haven Theology, and the Legacy of Jonathan Edwards*. Oxford: Oxford University Press, 2003.

Talcott, Joseph. "1738 Yale College Commencement Broadside." Early American Imprints, Series I: Evans, 1639–1800.

———. "Yale College Commencement Broadside 1735." New London: Timothy Green, 1735.

———. "Yale College Commencement Broadside 1740." Early American Imprints, Series I: Evans, 1639–1800.

Tappert, Theodore G., ed. and trans. *The Book of Concord: The Confessions of the Evangelical Lutheran Church*. Philadelphia: Fortress, 1959.

Te Velde, Dolf, ed. *Synopsis Purioris Theologiae / Synopsis of a Purer Theology: Latin Text and English Translation: Volume 1, Disputations 1–23*. Edited by. Willem Van Asselt et al. Studies in Medieval and Reformation Traditions 187. Leiden: Brill, 2015.

Tucker, Louis Leonard. *Puritan Protagonist: President Thomas Clap of Yale College*. Chapel Hill, NC: University of North Carolina Press, 1962.

Turretin, Francis. *Eleventh through Seventeenth Topics*. Edited by James T. Dennison Jr. Translated by George Musgrave Giger. Institutes of Elenctic Theology 2. Phillipsburg, NJ: P&R Publishing, 1994.

———. *First through Tenth Topics*. Edited by James T. Dennison Jr. Translated by George Musgrave Giger. Institutes of Elenctic Theology 1. Phillipsburg, NJ: P&R Publishing, 1992.

Turretin, Francis. *Institutio Theologiae Elencticae, in Qua Status Controversiae Perspicuè Exponitur, Praecipua Orthodoxorum Argumenta Proponuntur & Vindicantur, & Fontes Solutionum Aperiuntur*. Geneva: Samuelem De Tournes, 1688.

Voetius, Gisbertus. *Selectarum Disputationum Theologicarum*. Utrecht: Johannis a Waesberge, 1648–69.

Vos, Antonie. "John Wesley on Salvation, Necessity, and Freedom." In *Evangelical Theology in Transition*, edited by Cees van der Kooi, E. van Staalduine-Sulman, and A. W. Zwiep, 203–22. Amsterdam: VU University Press, 2012.

———. "Philip Melanchthon on Freedom and Will." In *Melanchthon und die Reformierte Tradition*, edited by Andreas J. Beck, 47–62. Göttingen: Vandenhoeck & Ruprecht, 2016.

———. *The Philosophy of John Duns Scotus*. Edinburgh: Edinburgh University Press, 2006.

———. "Reformed Orthodoxy in the Netherlands." In *A Companion to Reformed Orthodoxy*, edited by Herman J. Selderhuis, 121–76. Brill's Companions to the Christian Tradition: A Series of Handbooks and Reference Works on the Intellectual and Religious Life of Europe, 500–1800 40. Leiden: Brill, 2013.

———. "Scholasticism and Reformation." In *Reformation and Scholasticism: An Ecumenical Enterprise*, edited by W. J. van Asselt and Eef Dekker. Texts and Studies in Reformation and Post-Reformation Thought. Grand Rapids: Baker Academic, 2001.

———. *The Theology of John Duns Scotus*. Studies in Reformed Theology 34. Leiden: Brill, 2018.

Wadsworth, Benjamin. "Harvard 1725, Original." In *Quaestiones*, box 10, folder 2. https://iiif.lib.harvard.edu/manifests/view/drs:425512065$1i.

———. "Harvard 1729, Original." In *Quaestiones*, box 10, folder 6. https://iiif.lib.harvard.edu/manifests/view/drs:425512081$1i.

Walsh, James J. *Education of the Founding Fathers of the Republic: Scholasticism in the Colonial Colleges, A Neglected Chapter in the History of American Education*. New York: Fordham University Press, 1935.

Warch, Richard. *School of the Prophets: Yale College, 1701–1740*. New Haven: Yale University Press, 1973.

Watts, Isaac. *On the Freedom of Will in God and in Creatures*. Works of the Rev. Isaac Watts, D. D. in Nine Volumes 4. 1732. Reprint, Leeds, UK: Paternoster-Row, 1813.

Weis, Frederick Lewis. *The Colonial Clergy and the Colonial Churches of New England*. Baltimore: Genealogical, 1977.

———. "The Colonial Clergy of the Middle Colonies." In *The Colonial Clergy of the Middle Colonies New York, New Jersey, and Pennsylvania 1628–1776*. Worchester, MA: American Antiquarian Society, 1957.

Whitby, Daniel. *A Discourse Concerning Five Points, Election, Redemption, Grace, Liberty of the Will, Perseverance*. 2nd ed. London: Aaron Ward and Richard Hett, 1735.

Willard, Samuel. *A Brief Reply to Mr George Keith: In Answer to a Script of His, Entitled "A Refutation of a Dangerous and Hurtfull Opinion, Maintained by Mr. Samuel Willard."* Boston, 1703.

———. *Compleat Body of Divinity in Two Hundred and Fifty Expository Lectures on the Assembly's Shorter Catechism*. Boston: Green and Kneeland, 1726.

———. "Harvard 1702, Original." In *Quaestiones*, box 9, folder 42. https://nrs.harvard.edu/urn-3:HUL.ARCH:30876693?n=1.

———. "Harvard 1704, Original." In *Quaestiones*, box 9, folder 44. https://nrs.harvard.edu/urn-3:HUL.ARCH:30876701?n=1.

Williams, Ebenezer. *A System of Ethicks and Pneumaticks. Of Morall Phylosophy in Generall & in Speciall*. Manuscript, 1707–08. Harvard University Archives, Cambridge, MA. https://nrs.harvard.edu/urn-3:HUL.ARCH:10919374?n=2.

Wippel, John F., and Allan B. Wolter, eds. *Medieval Philosophy: From St. Augustine to Nicholas of Cusa*. Readings in the History of Philosophy. New York: The Free Press, 1969.

Withington, Mary C., ed. *Papers in Honor of Andrew Keogh: Librarian of Yale University by Staff of the Library 30 June 1938*. New Haven: Privately Printed, 1938.

Yale, Elihu. "A Catalogue of Books Sent by the Honorable Elihu Yale, Esq. 1718." GEN MS Vault Sect. 17. Early Yale Documents, General Collection. Beinecke Rare Book and Manuscript Library, Yale University, New Haven, CT.

Subject Index

affection for justice, 51–2
affection for what is advantageous, 52
Anglican, 217, 227, 230
Aristotelian, 31, 33, 57, 158
Arminian, 86, 116–17, 146, 169, 171, 174–75, 183–84, 187, 190, 193, 196, 201, 204, 206–09, 213–14, 217, 219, 223–24, 227–28, 230
art
    of disputing, 2
    of rhetoric, 151
Asha'ariyah, 25–27

Babylonian Talmud, 30n127, 32–36
Baptist, 138, 202–03, 217, 219, 230
Belgium, 22, 83, 102n26
biblical scholarship, 4, 8
Book of Concord, 56, 59–60
broadside sheets, ii, xiv, xv, 94, 96, 105, 118, 122, 127, 129, 140–42, 152–55, 157–59, 166, 178–79, 182, 183n16, 184n18, 189n27, 190nn1–2, 191–92, 193n12, 196n27, 198, 202–05, 208–09, 215, 219, 220nn3–4, 221, 222nn7–9, 225

Cairo Genizah, 33n139
cathedral schools, 4
Chaucer
    "The Parson's Tale," 33
    "The Prioress's Tale," 33
commencement
    College of New Jersey, xiii–xv, 189, 192, 219–20, 222, 225, 227

College of Rhode Island and Providence Plantations, xiii–xiv, 202–03, 219, 229
Harvard, xiii–xv, 89, 95, 102, 105–06, 112, 114, 117–18, 122, 127, 140, 156, 157–58, 158n14, 159, 161, 165–70, 177, 183, 187, 192, 214, 219, 227
Yale, ii, xiv–xv, 141, 153, 162, 170, 177–78, 183, 188–90, 196n27, 210, 219, 225
compound sense (or composite sense), 6, 9, 11, 14, 22, 23, 102, 103, 111, 142–44, 175, 227
concurrence, 31, 40, 42–43, 49, 55, 90–93, 100, 103, 116–118, 122–23, 129–31, 134–36, 169, 175
confessionalization, 1
contingency, 12–13, 22, 46, 56, 66, 73–75, 88–89, 90, 105–111, 113, 115, 117, 120, 122–23, 125, 128–30, 132, 141–45, 147–48, 160, 162, 167, 181–82, 185
    ad utrumlibet, 13
    diachronic, 112, 144
    radical, 88, 224
    synchronic, 111–12, 115, 144, 148
contingency in things, 107–09
conversion
    given by God, 224
counterpoint
    art of, 3

Declaration of the thirteen United States of America, 203, 220

dialectic, xv, 1–4, 6, 156n10
disputation, xv, 1, 70, 83, 86, 89, 91, 94, 96, 128, 137, 148, 176–77, 230
    Barcelona, 32
    culture of, 1–3, 32, 36
    Jewish-Christian disputations, 32–34, 36
    Leiden, 83
    Leipzig, 36
    medieval, 1–3, 18
    Paris, 1–3, 32–4, 36
    philosophical, 6, 24, 70, 76, 105, 114–16, 161–62, 166–67, 178, 218
    scholastic art of, 3
    Synopsis of a Purer Theology, 91
    Tortosa, 32
    Utrecht, 86, 137, 176
Dissenters and Nonconformists, 219
divided sense, distinction, 5, 6, 10–12, 14, 22–23, 102–103, 110–11, 113, 142–45, 175, 227
divine decrees, 69, 93, 97, 99, 177–79, 182, 185–86, 205–07, 213, 215
Dominicans, 2
Dummer collection of books, 141, 164–65

Eden, 74, 80–2, 96, 176–77
efficacious concurrence, 134, 136
efficacious grace, 134, 205, 223
emanation, 33
Erasmus's Mediating View, 43
eternity, 11, 14, 25n102, 33, 69, 74, 77, 92, 97, 103, 105, 113, 125, 178, 182, 218
Euthyphro mystery, 216

facultas physica seu naturalis, 147–48
faith seeking understanding, 2
fari (speak), 7
fatalism, 26, 178
Formula of Concord, 56, 59–60
France, 2, 34–36
Freedom
    of will, 82, 183, 190, 193, 199, 210, 217, 224

ad utrumlibet, 13n49, 67, 147–48, 208
ad utrumque, 145, 147–48, 151, 170, 176–77, 187, 208–09, 227–28, 228n26
    of exercise (liberty of contradiction), 171, 173, 175–77, 209, 218, 228
    of specification (liberty of contrariety), 172–73, 175, 218, 228
future contingents, xv, 22–23, 74, 86, 102n26, 146, 148
futurition, 97, 135, 137

Germany, 56
glossa ordinaria, 8
Gnesio-Lutherans, 56, 60
God
    absolute power of, 132–33, 138–39
    all-sufficient knowledge of, 132, 215
    as actor of sin, xiv, 93, 96, 121–22, 167, 169, 183, 224, 230
    as author of sin, 9, 224, 230
    as First Cause, x, 70, 73, 79, 92–3, 96, 100–101, 105, 107–08, 115, 117, 119, 120–24, 169
    assistance of, 43, 224
    commands of, 224
    decrees of, 69, 97, 177–79, 182, 186, 205–07, 213, 215
    determinations by, 40, 56, 69, 70, 99, 128, 130, 132, 146, 212
    fitness of his acts, 197, 199, 200–01, 210, 212–15, 217, 226, 228–29
    foreknowledge of, ix, xi, xv, 6–9, 11, 40–2, 45–6, 68–73, 75–7, 83–4, 89, 101, 123, 127–28, 130, 136, 140, 145, 183, 196, 203–06, 208–09, 215
    glory of, 149
    goodness of, 44, 65, 78, 82, 78, 160, 215, 217, 229
    hidden will of, 41, 81
    holiness of, 213
    honor of, 121, 149
    immanent acts of, 97
    immutability of, 42, 47, 75, 95, 98
    impassibility of, 35

influence of, 27, 29, 49, 124, 135, 193, 212, 221, 224
mere (or bare) will of, 30, 216–17
moral excellency of, 209
moral suasion of, 221
ordained will, 41
power of, 6, 7, 11, 12, 14–15, 26, 40, 65, 72, 77–78, 92, 100, 128, 131–33, 135, 137–39, 148, 150–52, 197, 215–16, 229
practical knowledge of, 108
righteousness of, 65, 81–2
self-determining power of, 197, 210, 215–16, 229,
sovereignty of, x, 16, 41, 48, 90, 115, 120, 122, 124, 138, 187, 205
supremacy of, 54
theoretical knowledge of, 108
whether omnivolent, 15, 46, 86, 98
will of, xiv, 115–18, 121, 123, 126, 128–29, 130–33, 135, 137, 146, 148–49, 183, 193, 201, 207, 210, 212–13
wisdom of, 9, 26–27, 30, 44, 65, 68, 72, 78–79, 88, 139, 150, 200, 229
works *ad extra*, 44, 65–66, 97, 99, 115, 117
works *ad intra*, 97, 99
grace
common, 39
cooperating grace, 39
peculiar, 39

Hobbes
doctrine of fatality, 212
holiness
given by God, 224
human action, 8, 21, 26n104, 27, 40–42, 70, 91–2, 97, 100–01, 118, 123, 133, 135–37, 148, 169, 174, 204
human beings
self-determining power of, 116, 137, 183, 186, 193, 196, 196n27, 197–99, 201, 207, 209, 215, 217, 224
virtue and vice of, xiii, 64, 79, 101, 191, 193–94, 209, 217–218, 223–24

impossibility, 11, 151, 194, 195, 200, 211
influx (divine), 20, 29, 89–92, 101, 131, 137, 148, 170
Italy, 2

Jesuits, 86, 115–17, 127, 171, 174–75, 219
as philosophers of Coimbra, 115
Jesus
foreknowledge of, 139

knowledge of God
definite, 83, 87, 101
indefinite, 83, 84, 87
middle, 86, 89, 127–34, 137–38, 146, 204, 207
practical, 92
of simple understanding, 72, 83–5, 89, 125, 132, 137
of vision, 72, 85, 87–89, 127, 137, 148

Lectures on Romans (Luther), 50, 52–3, 55, 61
Leibniz-Clarke Correspondence, 199, 210, 210n27, 211, 216
lex justitiae, 157–58
lex sapientiae, 157–58
lex veritatis, 157–58
libertas indifferentiae ad opposita, 210, 227
liberty of indifference, 169, 210, 213–14, 223
liberty of the will, 49, 102, 140, 170–71, 173, 193, 205
liberum arbitrium, 7, 37, 168
logica moderna, 4, 76
love, 17–18, 20, 30, 37–9, 48–9, 51–4, 57, 59–60, 82, 109–110, 117, 119, 121, 171, 176, 195
Lutheran, 56, 67, 70, 124–25, 217, 230
Lutheran theologians, 70
medieval, 1–4, 24, 32, 36, 48, 50, 52, 54, 61, 94, 156, 158, 179, 181, 219

Messiah, the, 32, 34–5, 41, 101, 123, 135
Minerva, 2, 154, 163–4
Mishneh Torah, 24
modal logic, 4
Mohammedan, the, 25, 26n104
moral nature, 8, 148
Moreh Nebuchim, 23
motets, 3
Mu'tazilah, 30
Mu'tazilites, the, 26–7
Muslim, 33

natural power, 20, 38–9, 43, 49, 59–60
naturaliter, 39, 51, 53–5, 60, 192
necessary premises, 156–60
necessity
  absolute, 41–2, 46–47, 59, 68, 70, 73–77, 82, 98–9, 104, 180, 181n11, 185
  beauty of, 229
  of the consequence, 22, 42, 45–46, 47, 57– 58, 67, 73–74, 82, 98, 134, 179, 181, 182, 186, 225–26
  of the consequent, 42, 45–46, 58–59, 67, 73, 74, 76, 82, 179–81, 185, 226
  doctrine of, 193, 218, 224
  hypothetical, 46, 74, 82, 97
  infallibility of, 97, 104, 143
  moral, 190–201, 210, 213, 222–24, 229
  natural necessity, x, 86, 99, 184–5, 196, 199–200
  relative necessity, 14, 47, 181n11, 184
Neoplatonic, 33
Netherlands, the, 61, 83n370,
neutral power, 7
New England
  colleges, xiv–xv, 104, 152, 156, 181, 191–92, 202–03, 227, 230
  curricula, 1, 156, 218–19,
New England commencement broadsides
  1750 College of New Jersey broadside, 220, 225
  1755 College of New Jersey broadside, 192–93
  1760 College of New Jersey broadside, 222
  1762 College of New Jersey broadside, 203
  1770 College of Rhode Island and Providence Plantations, 203–04
  1773 College of Rhode Island and Providence Plantations, 205, 208
  1642 Harvard broadside, 157–58
  1683 Harvard broadside, 122
  1687 Harvard broadside, 159
  1702 Harvard broadside, 95
  1704 Harvard broadside, 106
  1715 Harvard broadside, 118
  1717 Harvard broadside, 127
  1725 Harvard broadside, 168
  1729 Harvard broadside, 192
  1718 Yale broadside, 141, 183
  1720 Yale broadside, 153, 157
  1730 Yale broadside, 159
  1735 Yale broadside, 184, 196–97n27
  1738 Yale broadside, 192
  1740 Yale broadside, 178–79, 182
  1749 Yale broadside, 192
  1760 Yale broadside, 190
  1762 Yale broadside, 190
  1765 Yale broadside, 215

nunc aeternitatis, 14

ontology of contingency, 66, 88, 111

permission of the divine will
  doctrine of, 17–18, 21, 40, 79–80, 90, 93, 121, 136, 193, 224
Portugal, 35
possibility, 125, 137, 144, 160, 186
  alternate, 6, 46, 110–11, 132, 186
  God's knowledge of, 10–11, 25, 30, 49, 66, 83–8, 97, 107, 109, 112, 131, 137, 178, 200, 216
possible states of affairs, 83–4, 125, 132–33, 138, 147, 201
potentia simultatis, 11, 143, 175
potentiality, 31
praiseworthiness and blameworthiness, 8

SUBJECT INDEX

predestination, 11–12, 14, 37, 46, 48–9, 56, 67, 69–70, 76, 83–4, 181, 184
predetermination, 77, 91, 134, 136, 139
predicates
 per se, 53, 82, 101, 157–58, 161–62
premotion, 122, 169
Presbyterian, 10, 125–26, 132, 142, 220
propositions
 analysis of, 4, 218
 modal, 4
 neutral, 6, 16, 23, 108–09, 146
 truth claims of, 36, 159, 162
providence, 12, 23–31, 37, 62, 67–8, 70–1, 75–8, 82–3, 88–93, 100, 124, 127, 148, 167, 169, 193, 202–04, 207, 212, 215, 224, 227–29

Reformed
 scholastics, xi, 11, 66–7, 91
 theologians (theology), 49, 72, 82, 88–91, 102, 116–17, 122–23, 128–29, 131–32, 137, 141, 162, 169–70, 173–75, 177, 181, 183, 217, 219, 222, 226–27, 229n28, 230
Remonstrants, 116–17, 230
Renaissance, 48–50, 52, 54–5, 156
rhetoric, 3, 22, 151, 155–56

scholasticism, ix, 3, 22, 49, 67, 91, 156, 218
 distinctions, 4, 22, 31, 35, 42, 94, 101, 142, 181, 218–19, 227
 interdisciplinary approach to, 2
 method, 2, 36, 179
 rise of, 3
 scholastics, ix, x, xiii–xv,11, 29, 31, 41–2, 45, 58, 61n276, 66, 72–3, 81, 100, 121–22, 147, 151, 169, 213, 216, 226
 terminology of, 94, 96, 112, 217
 tradition of, xv, 219, 230
scientia media, *see* knowledge of God: middle knowledge

Scripture, ix, xi, 8, 30, 32, 37, 46, 76, 78, 80–1, 84, 89, 91, 93, 98, 100, 118–20, 122–24, 145, 149, 176
 opinion of, 30
 study of, 2, 8
second-order volition, 18
signum rationis, 213
simultas potentiae, 11, 142, 143, 175
sophisms, 4
Spain, 33n140
square of opposition, 170–71, 227–28
Statenvertaling, 83
Stoics, the, 6, 76, 212, 218
superior fitness, 200–01, 212, 215, 229
Synod of Dort, 83, 182n13

The Thirty-Nine Articles of the Church of England (1571), 35
Torah, 24, 24n95, 124
twelfth century, 2, 4, 8
 rise of universities, 2

universal determining providence
 doctrine of, 224
universe, the, 25, 30, 31
universities, 4, 32, 36, 70
 of Franeker , 85
 of Helmstedt, 56
 of Jena, 56
 of Leiden, 82–3, 91, 104, 114, 166, 182, 227
 of Leipzig, 56
 of Paris, 35
 of Rostock, 56
 of Utrecht, 86, 137, 175, 176, 227

velle (to will), 7, 17–18, 65, 113, 170–2
virtue,
 given by God, 224
virtue and vice, 101, 191, 217, 223–24
voluntas (the will), 7, 46, 53, 57, 62, 106, 135
Westminster Assembly's Shorter Catechism, 165
Westminster Confession of Faith (1647), 35
Wethersfield, 153, 165, 196, 222

Name Index

Aaron Burr, 184, 189, 192, 196n27, 225
Abelard, Peter 2, 4–5, 23
Abraham, 28, 87, 138
Adam, 2, 37, 38, 74, 80, 96, 102, 104, 140, 143
Adam of Balsham, 2
Albertus Magnus, 24
Alluntis, Felix, 51
Altenstaig, Johannes, 51
Ambrose, Saint, 8, 43
Ames, William, 85–8, 91, 102–04, 116, 123–25, 145–46, 148, 156–59, 161, 164–65, 182, 227
Andreae, Jacob, 56
Andrew, Samuel, 140–47, 150–51, 153, 183
Anselm of Canterbury, Saint, 1, 2, 51
Anselm of Laon, 8
Apollo, 154, 163–64
Aquinas, Thomas, Saint, 3, 11–12, 17–24, 72–74, 128, 155, 181
Archbishop of Sens, 35
Aristotle, 2–5, 13, 20, 24–31, 50, 61n276, 66, 156n10, 157–58, 158n14, 164, 172
Augustine, Saint, 1, 6–8, 15n58, 18–19, 23, 39, 48, 64, 72, 75–76, 78–80, 121, 165

Backus, Isaac, 204–08
Basil the Great, Saint, 81
Bathsheba, 58
Baxter, Andrew, 201, 228–29
Belcher, Jonathan, 165, 189

Bellamy, Joseph, 184, 196
Bernard of Clairvaux, 2, 165
Beza, 81–2
Biel, Gabriel, 49, 52, 54–5, 60–1, 72–4, 81
Bildad, 30
Billings, Gulielmus, 154n4
Bishop of Senlis, 35
Boethius, 8, 12n47, 45, 69
Bonaventure, Saint, 51
Boso, 1
Brainerd, David, 189
Brown, Daniel, 154
Bucanus, Guillaume, 75
Buitendijk, Gosuinus van, 155
Bulkeley, John, 229
Burgersdijk, Franco, 114–15, 157–58, 160–62, 165

Calvin, John, ix–x, 36–7, 44, 46–7, 61–7, 75, 81, 165, 181, 181n11, 184
Castalion, Sebastion, 82
Charnock, Stephen, 10, 86, 125–26, 132–35, 137–40, 142–47
Chaucer, Geoffrey 12, 33, 165
Chemnitz, Martin, 56
Chrysostom, John, 8
Chytraeus, David, 56–9, 67–70
Cicero (Tully), 6, 50, 165
Clap, Thomas, 177–85, 187–99, 201, 210, 215
Clarke, Samuel, 164, 199, 201, 210–12, 216–17, 228–29, 229n28
Clement of Alexandria, Saint, 78

Collins, Ann, 1
Corranus, Antonio, 82
Cox, Charles, 165
Cutler, Timothy, 153–55, 157-7, 170
Cyril of Alexandria, Saint, 8, 78

Damascenus, 79–80
Damian, Peter 149–52
David, King, 58, 67, 124, 133, 137–38, 202–03
Davies, Brian, 21
Davies, Samuel, 220–23, 225–26
Descartes, René, 155, 164
Dickinson, Jonathan, 189
Donin, Nicholas, 34–5
Downame, George, 165
Duke George of Saxony, 36
Dunster, Henry, 157

Eck, Johannes, 36
Edwards, Daniel 154n4
Edwards, Jonathan, 13, 44, 83, 96, 125, 141, 146, 153–54, 163, 165–68, 170, 178, 183, 186–87, 189–92, 194–97, 202, 209, 212, 216–30
Edwards, Sarah, 226
Edwards, Timothy, 169
Elihu (Book of Job), 30, 154, 164, 165
Eliphaz (Book of Job), 30
Epicurus, 24
Erasmus of Rotterdam, xi, 37–46, 48
Eve, 37–8, 74, 80

Farrand, Daniel 220, 220n4, 223, 225
Florents, Adrian (Pope Adrian VI), 61
Franciscus Junius Sr., 82
Fulgentius, Saint Bishop of Ruspa, 19

Gerhard, Johann, 70–82, 92, 121, 124–25
Gold, Nathan, 154
Gomarus, Franciscus, 82–5, 87
Graetz, Heinrich, 34–6
Green, Enoch, 220–21
Grevinchovius, Nicholas, 146

Halevi, Judah, 32

Heereboord, Adriaan, 104, 112, 145, 166, 167, 185, 227
Hilary, Saint Bishop of Poitiers, 8
Hobart, Nehemiah, 127
Hobbes, Thomas, 186–87, 212, 229
Homer, 165
Hopkins, Samuel, 203–05, 208, 220, 224
Hopkins, Stephan, 203
Horace, 163
Howell, David, 202–05, 208–09, 214–16, 229

Isaac, 28, 81

Jacob, 28
Jerome, 8, 36, 75, 149, 165
Jesus, 20, 32, 34–7, 41–2, 45–6, 58, 87, 100–01, 123, 125, 133–36, 139, 177, 184, 209, 223
John of Damascus, 8
John of Salisbury, 2, 72
Joseph, 35, 80, 81, 122, 124, 154, 184, 225
Jove, 212, 218
Judas, 20, 40–2, 45–6, 75, 137–38, 143, 184

Karlstadt, Andreas Bodenstein, 36
Keith, Mr. (Missionary from Scotland), 96, 98, 100, 101, 102, 104, 105, 170
Kilborn, Ezechias, 154n4
King Bulan of the Chazars, 32
Kirkland, Daniel, 154n4
Knuuttila, Simo, 5, 6
Kolb, Robert, 56, 68–70
Kristeller, Paul Oskar, 48–9

Lane, Anthony, 61
Lanfranc, Archbishop of Canterbury, 1
Leibniz, Gottfried Wilhelm, 199, 210–12, 216, 228
Leo the Great, Saint Pope, 80
Leverett, John, 118–23, 126–27, 133–34, 136–37, 139–40, 169
Lewis, C. S., 50

NAME INDEX

Locke, John, 164, 201, 228
Lombard, Peter, 6, 8, 8n33, 9–12, 14–19, 23, 40, 48, 51, 79, 181
Lorenzo Valla, 69
Ludovicus Vives, 76
Luther, Martin, ix, xi, 36–7, 44–50, 52–55, 60–2, 66–7, 69, 181

Maccoby, Hyam, 32–6
Maimonides, Moses, xi, 23–31, 78
Malebranche, Nicolas, 164
Manning, James, 202–03
Mariam, 35
Mary (mother of Jesus), 34–5
Mastricht, Peter van, 88–91, 145, 148
Mather, Increase, 159, 169
Mather, Warham, 154
Melanchthon, Philipp, xi, 46–7, 56, 58, 60, 62, 179, 180–82
Mix, Samuel, 154n4
Molina, Luis de, 89, 127–37, 139, 227
More, Henry, 164
Morrison, Chanan, 32
Morton, Charles, 102, 161, 161n20, 166, 170–71, 171n5, 172–77, 227–28
Moses, 24, 27, 34, 70, 123, 200
Musculus, Wolfgang, 82

Nebuchadnezzar, 28
Newell, Daniel, 141–45, 147–48
Newton, Isaac, 155, 164, 185
Nott, Abraham, 154n4
Novikoff, Alex, 1–3, 3n9, 36

Oberman, Heiko, 49
Occam, William of, 74
Origen, 8

Pallas, 154, 163
Pandira, 35
Pappos ben Judah, 35
Pauck, Wilhelm, 55, 60–1
Paul, Saint 1, 41, 43, 50, 120, 137–38, 150, 175, 177, 205
Pelagius, 38
Perkins, William, 82
Peter Martyr, 81, 82

Peter of Spain, 12, 13, 14
Peter, Saint, 12, 22, 23, 51, 101, 102, 123, 124, 125, 135, 136, 138, 139, 143, 146, 184, 225, 226
Pharaoh, 41, 47, 81, 123, 124, 125
Pico della Mirandola, 48
Pighius, Albert, 37, 44, 61, 62, 63, 64, 65, 66, 67
Piscator, Johannes, 75
Plato, 92, 159, 164–5, 216
Polyander, Johannes, 91, 182n13
Pope Adrian VI, 61
Pope Gregory I, 8
Pope Gregory IX, 34
Pope John XXI, 12
Potok, Chaim, 33
Princess Sophia, the Electress of Hanover, 210–11
Prosper of Aquitaine, 69

Quincy, Edmund, 168–69, 177

Ramus, Peter, 156, 156n10, 157–58, 158n14, 161n20
Rawlins, Gershom, 164
Richardson, Alexander, 156
Rijk, Lambertus Marie de, 4, 5
Rivetus, Andreas, 91–3
Rivo, Peter de, 22–3, 102
Rupert of Deutz, 2
Rush, Benjamin, 220–21
Rutherford, Samuel, 145, 147, 227–28

Saltonstall, Gordon, 141n1, 153n1, 154, 154n4, 157n11, 183n16, 222n8,
Sanderson, Robert, 161
Scaliger, Julius, 77–8
Scotus, John Duns, 14, 16–18, 20n80, 23, 39, 48, 50–5, 60, 74, 77, 84, 104, 106–15, 181
Selnecker, Nikolaus, 56
Shimei, 81, 124
Socrates, 4–5, 12–13, 161
Solomon Ibn Gabirol, 33
Stapfer, Johann Friedrich, 227

Thysius, Antonius, 91

Trelcatius, Lucas, Sr, 82
Tully (Cicero), 165
Turretin, Francis, 142–43, 174–77, 198–99, 227
Twisse, William, 165

Voetius, Gisbertus, 6, 86–8, 137–38, 145, 147–48, 168n2, 175–77, 227–28
Vos, Antonie, 55, 83

Wadsworth, Benjamin, 168–77, 192, 214
Wakeman, Ebenezer, 154n4
Walaeus, Antonius, 91
Walton, Johannes, 154n4
Watts, Isaac, 199–201, 209–18, 224, 227–28, 230
Wesley, John, 217–18, 227

Whitby, Daniel, 208–09, 227
White, Thomas, 154n4
Willard, Samuel, 95–108, 110, 112, 114, 117, 122, 125, 170, 174, 177, 227
William of Auxerre, 72
William of St. Thierry, 2
Williams, Ebenezer, 165, 170
Williams, Elisha, 153, 159n17, 165–66, 168, 178, 192, 196n27, 222
Wollebius, Johann, 165
Wolter, Allan, 51

Yechiel ben Joseph, 36

Zanchi, 81
Zofar, 30
Zwingli, 81

Scripture Index

Hebrew Bible

Genesis

1:1	24
2:16, 17	38
19:21–22	15n58

Deuteronomy

25:16	81

1 Samuel

2:9	29
23:14	138

2 Samuel

16:10	124

1 Kings

22:39	145

2 Chronicles

18:22	121

Job

40:2	205

Psalms

104:27	71
5:4	81

Proverbs

16:4	119
16:9	167
28:9	100

Ecclesiastes

3:14	206

Isaiah

45:6–7	18
45:7	24

Jeremiah

14:14	121
18:8	69

Ezekiel

3	75
14:9,11	121
18:2	26

Daniel

3:19–27	70

Habakkuk

1:12, 14–15	28

Zechariah

8:17	138

APOCRYPHA

Wisdom of Solomon

11: 24	19, 81

Sirach (Ecclesiasticus)

15:14–15	37
15:15–16	38

NEW TESTAMENT

Matthew

3:9	87, 138
5:45	70, 78
6:8	8
11	133
18:7	58
23:37	41
26:53–54	87, 139

Luke

10:27	53
22:62	123
24:25	123
24:26	58

John

1:3	17, 19
13:27	20

Acts

15:18	182
17:28	xiv, 20, 78–79, 89, 91, 92, 100, 118, 169, 176

Romans

1:19–20	38
1:24	93
7:18	50
9:20	41

1 Corinthians

2:7	182
2:14	59
4:7	8
5:5	120

2 Corinthians

4:16	177

Ephesians

1:11	77

Philippians

2:13	xiv, 43, 118, 169

Colossians

1:17	78

2 Thessalonians

2:10, 11	121

Hebrews

1:3	78
4:13	145
6:3	93

1 John

1:5	81
4:19	117, 176

Revelation

4:11	149

Rabbinic Writings

Babylonian Talmud

Tractate *Gittin* 56b	34n149
Tractate *Sanhedrin* 43a	34n149
Tractate *Sanhedrin* 67a	35n150
Tractate *Shabbat* 88b	30n127

www.ingramcontent.com/pod-product-compliance
Lightning Source LLC
Chambersburg PA
CBHW050344230426
43663CB00010B/1979